"Surviving a life that's found you endlessly wal[...] simply remarkable. Realizing God's grace and [...] accounting for it all in written word to challeng[...] is a truly meaningful labour of love. With raw transparency, Kevin White walks readers through the dark worlds he's known, ultimately to find the most radiant of lights awaiting at the end of each one."

—Tim Huff, author, speaker, social-justice worker

"I was as moved by Kevin John White's devastating and glorious story as I was by his manner of telling it—sometimes elegant and wise, at other times believably raw and unvarnished. Always leaning into meaning and grace, *Dancing on a Razor* is humbling and beautiful."

—Steve Bell, singer-songwriter, author

"This is a story that God wrote through the pen of a modern-day wandering minstrel. In his faithfulness, God walked with Kevin through the valleys. Then, through the body of a small-town Presbyterian church, God reached into Kevin's life and breathed in new hope—hope that he was afraid to believe in, but hope that proved to be trustworthy. This is a book of hope for the hopeless. Read it and weep. Read it and laugh. Read it and have hope. Real hope."

—Julie Hill, BScN

"Our identity as believers is that we are found 'in Christ,' completely on the basis of his work on our behalf, and it has nothing to do with our performance. I once looked at someone like Kevin and saw a lifestyle that proved to me he wasn't a believer. Kevin's story in fact proves the exact opposite. He was loved and pursued as a child of God's kingdom, even when it seemed he couldn't have been farther from God. This runs absolutely counter to the programmed thinking that we maintain when we see ourselves as righteous compared to someone like Kevin.

"His story speaks powerful words of encouragement and deliverance to the person caught in a vice and having a hard time shaking it. Kevin's story speaks even more to the church and says, '*You are Kevin*, and just like Kevin, there is hope for you too.' This is what distinguishes Kevin's story from all other 'recovery stories.' It is a convicting exposé of how much we *all* need a Saviour and how relentless that Saviour is toward us, in spite of ourselves, no matter what it is that holds us or what we are recovering from (even from our own self-righteousness). It is out of God's love for us, extended to us through his Son, that he pursues us with such deliberate intent. We cannot hide from his love once it has us in its sights."

—Steve Hill, MD, CCFP

"Kevin's father, Dr. John White, once told me that God revealed to him before Kevin was born that Kevin would be a difficult son who would live the 'razor's edge' life of addiction, which Kevin describes in this book. Incredible as these stories are, I know they are true, because I have lived with Kevin during his struggles. The stories point toward the preposterous grace and unfathomable mystery of a God who loves and shows mercy against all normal human understanding. Fasten your seat belt and hang on."

—Helmut Boehm, co-founder of Wagner Hills Ministries, Langley, BC

"*Dancing on a Razor* by Kevin John White is a brutally honest account of one man's battle with addiction while fighting the very solution that ultimately allows him to keep his condition in check. Especially now, when our country is faced daily with the overwhelming tragedy of narcotic abuse and overdose, this very personal story offers important insights into the condition that is addiction. It proves that in life there is always hope no matter how hopeless it appears to be."

—John Rea, MD, CCFP, Huntsville, ON

"This is a remarkable book! It is a testimony that reveals an intimacy in the father-heart of God when his children experience his grace, his forgiveness, his reconciliation, and his restoration in their lives. In a revealing and transparent manner, Kevin describes his journey with such honesty and forthrightness that the reader almost becomes part of the journey. Kevin reveals how he was in the battle zone between Heaven and Hell and what it is really like to enter into the pit of hopelessness. Yet God never forgets about him. *Dancing On A Razor* is a graphic description of the power of God's redemption in our lives—and shows that God really is a heart-reader more than a lip-reader no matter what we are going through. This book is for you!"

—Rev. Dr. Alistair P. Petrie, executive director of Partnership Ministries

"What a book! I know Kevin, and a story that I was part of actually made it into the final draft. As I read the book, I laughed and cried and got angry. Kevin draws out raw emotions from people through his stories and his life. He will not leave you ambivalent. Spending a few moments in the book is like sitting at a campfire listening to him weave his stories into a beautiful tapestry. In the 1930s we might have called him a hobo or a drifter. I call him a friend."

—Randy Emerson, pastor, Cloverdale, BC

"Kevin's account will stretch your understanding of the unfathomable love of Christ, his omnipotence, his omnipresence, and his compassion. Jesus paid the price to rescue the perishing, the hopeless, and the outcast; he is active 24-7 reaching out to those trapped in their circumstances. Kevin's testimony will encourage countless parents with prodigals of their own to keep their confidence, to look to the one with all power and authority, and to keep their eyes on the horizon. Is it your prodigal or someone else's on the way home?"

—James D Lunney, BSc, DC, retired MP, BC

"A minister of the gospel cannot always be recognized by outward appearance, title, position in the community, alma mater, piety, or exemplary lifestyle. Kevin is a very gifted minister of the gospel. He knows '200 proof grace,' and I enjoy the blessing of God through him."

—John Vanden Ende, police officer

"Kevin's past 40 years truly illustrated God's agape love in ways only he can do. One conclusion: GOD IS LOVE; indeed, HE IS PERFECT LOVE! I don't need to doubt or fear anymore!"

—Lucy Cheung, pastor of Church of Zion, Surrey, BC

"Somehow, it seems that there's something like a shadow, or perhaps it's the Hound of Heaven, constantly stalking this journey—sometimes interfering, sometimes even speaking through our trailblazer, but never giving up in spite of Kevin's giving up a thousand times.

"Somehow after 40 years of Kevin stumbling and clawing at hope … God shows up. Well, actually he doesn't show up; it turns out he's been there all along. Here we see a story that can only be appreciated if we acknowledge God's faithful, superabundant, undeserved, relentless love and a mother's tireless prayers for a wandering prodigal. Read it; be overwhelmed. It will activate your hope, but be careful—it might challenge your theology."

—Albert Zehr, author, pastor of Church of Zion, Surrey, BC

DANCING ON A

RAZOR

TALES OF MERCY FROM THE LIPS OF A PRODIGAL

KEVIN JOHN WHITE

DANCING ON A RAZOR
Copyright ©2019 Kevin John White

Published by: Castle Quay Books
Burlington, Ontario
Tel: (416) 573-3249
E-mail: info@castlequaybooks.com | www.castlequaybooks.com

Edited by Marina Hofman Willard and Lori Mackay
Cover design and book interior by Burst Impressions
Printed at Essence Publishing, Belleville, Ontario

Library and Archives Canada Cataloguing in Publication
Title: Dancing on a razor : tales of mercy from the lips of a prodigal / Kevin John White.
Names: White, Kevin John, 1960- author.
Description: "The heart of a desperate rebel?"
Identifiers: Canadiana 20190073810 | ISBN 9781988928104 (softcover)
Subjects: LCSH: White, Kevin John, 1960- | LCSH: Christian biography. | LCSH: Musicians—Biography.
  | LCSH: Addicts—Biography. | LCSH: Homeless persons—Biography. | LCGFT: Autobiographies.
Classification: LCC BR1725.W45 A3 2019 | DDC 277.108/3092—dc23

CASTLE QUAY BOOKS

*For my father and mother, who gave me life and never
once lost hope ...*

and

*for Steve and Julie Hill, who gave that life back
to me—then stood patiently by my side while I figured out
how the silly thing worked.*

*Where can I go from your Spirit? Where can I flee from your
presence? If I go up to the heavens, you are there; if I make my bed
in the depths, you are there. If I rise on the wings of the dawn, if
I settle on the far side of the sea, even there your hand will guide
me, your right hand will hold me fast ... You hem me in behind and
before, and you lay your hand upon me ... You have searched me,
Lord, and you know me ... Such knowledge is too wonderful for
me, too lofty for me to attain.* (Ps. 139:7–10, 5, 1, 6 NIV)

Contents

ACKNOWLEDGEMENTS

My deepest thanks to Larry Willard of Castle Quay Books for taking a chance on a wild-eyed scallywag like myself. To even consider working with such a dark horse was a real demonstration of both faith and courage. Thank you, Larry, for giving me a chance to tell of God's great mercy to me and allowing me the privilege to share this story with others.

My specific thanks to the editors at Castle Quay Books, in particular Marina Hofman. I pray for your speedy recovery after what I'm sure was a deeply disturbing job (and that I NEVER find myself in your shoes!). Rest assured, the English language is once again safe due to your heroic efforts. My blessings and deepest respect. Thank you once again!

My particular thanks to the judges of the Word Guild Contest for both reading and appreciating the stories contained in *Dancing on a Razor* (and I'm dreadfully sorry for any grey hairs you may have accumulated as a result!).

Steve and Julie Hill: There are no thanks I could possibly give that would adequately express my gratitude for all the great patience, love, courage, and wisdom you have so generously lavished on my head. Thank you from every single atom in me, for not only your commitment to the work God began in me but also for your deep and very evident faith in our God, who brought you to the astonishing decision to reach out and help me.

To the rest of the Hill family—Ashley, Laurel, Megan, and Robert—all I can humbly say is *"Yes! Your mother was abducted by an alien from outer space and needs all of you—so she can recover ... from the shock!"* Truthfully, I am astonished at the grace and patience you have shown me, both while I lived with you in your home and while I lived at your home when I had my *own* home to go to. Thank you, each one. I have watched and prayed as you have struggled and grown and overcome what looked to be insurmountable obstacles, as I'm sure you have with me (and likely with far graver misgivings!), and I must say, I find a strange pride welling up inside my heart whenever I think of each one of you. I am proud that you are a part, now, of my heart. You are my family, and I would fight with all my strength for any one of you. Thank you from the bottom of my heart and soul for sharing both your mother and your father with me, a complete stranger. And thank you for the love you showed and the words of encouragement you gave to me along the way.

Now, to my noble-hearted editor/literary agent, Julie Hill. First, I am deeply sorry for the horrific beating you suffered at my ignorant hands. Your patience and courage (as well as endurance!) over these years have been nothing short of biblical in their application! Your commitment to excellence and detail is, to me, astonishing and reflects your character very well. Thank you, also, for acting as my etiquette advisor. (I now know that using such words as "with no clothes on" and "Statue of Liberty" in the same sentence is entirely in bad taste!) And Julie, without your constant encouragement, I would have lost faith in this project long ago. Thank you for all of it.

My deepest love and gratitude as well to John Vanden Ende, who was responsible for almost single-handedly saving my life several times over and whose uncanny "people skills" have earned my undying respect! Thank you for understanding me so well, my friend.

My love and deep gratitude to my *other* very own doctor, Dr. Rea, who has nursed me back from the gates of death, yelled at me, worried for me (SO sorry!), and been a true friend to me while I was being a royal pain in the glutes!

Thank you, George and Audrey Anderson, my oldest of St. Andrew's friends, who, in more than one way, were responsible for this entire extravaganza, and in particular George, for your many prayers, shared

Scriptures, insights, and unfailing commitment to see God's plans and purposes fulfilled in my life. God bless you, George! Thank you from the bottom of my heart.

There is one man in particular I wish to express my deepest and most sincere gratitude to. Someone who knew me while I was nothing but a backpacking gutter tramp—my dear friend Tom Nichols, whom I love with all my heart. Tom, thank you for standing by my side, picking me up time and again, for praying for me, encouraging me to never give up, and for bending so far backwards for me that it went beyond any rational thought or expectation, all at great personal cost. Thank you, my friend. You knew me long before my freedom, and you loved me when I was at my most unlovely. In the words of the great Vulcan, Spock, "You have been, and always shall be, my friend!"

I wish also to express my gratitude to both Steve Bell and Tim Huff, not just for reading and responding to *Dancing on a Razor* but for being a standard and an example for me to aspire to. I can only pray that my life has even a fraction of the impact you and your messages have had on this sorely troubled world.

Special thanks to Cathie Raynor, a teacher, a reader, and a wonderfully positive support. Thank you for reading through *Dancing on a Razor* (three times?) and for valuable insight into certain key areas. Blessings on you, Cathie!

Thanks as well to Susan Wilkinson, for all your wonderful encouragement and kind words. Also, for your valuable input on *Dancing*.

My particular thanks go out to Jeff and Bonnie Harris (a.k.a. my "Rock and Pillow"), whom I love deeply, and to John and Hilda Van Gysell, my two dear friends and elders who not only loved me but I think actually liked me as well! Special thanks to Hilda for publishing various articles of mine in the St. Andrew's newsletter.

My deepest love and gratitude to my entire small group Bible study folk: John and Ivy Rooney, Sylvia and Richard Wakelin, Cathy Maindonald, Paul and Susan Evans, Florence and Sheldon Culham, and Steve and Julie Hill, for your great understanding and your patience with my "spontaneous outbursts of enthusiasm."

My sincerest thanks and deep affection for certain friends of mine: John Bedore (for the many rides to and fro), Joel Harrower (for all your wise words), Bill Paterson (my dear and unflaggingly loyal friend), and George D. (my first 12 Step sponsor ... that I ever actually used!). I also thank God for Doug Hall, whom I know God placed into my life and my heart. All of you played an important and irreplaceable part in my recovery.

Thank you, Doug and Bonita Austin, for your many prayers and all the other ways in which you supported me. Special thanks to Doug, for all your genuine efforts to understand addiction and how to be of help.

And of course, to certain key friends at St. Andrew's Church and elsewhere, my love and thanks: Ryan and Becky Campese, Mike and Christina Degazio, Brian Maxwell, John and Jerilyn Roycroft, Alister and Jan Harrison, Grant Bartlett, Glen Marnoch, Rob Tesky, Kathy Kaye, Cathy Faubert, Les Tihor, and Nancy and Peter Slater.

Now for my own. Mother of mine, there simply are no words I can speak. Perhaps God may know the love and honour I hold in my heart for you. Thank you for the ocean of wisdom from which I have come and the steadfast gentleness of your own heart. Miles and Leith, you are my two pillars—my strength. Liana, you're my stone and pestle—my wisdom. Scott, you are my beauty, my fragrant rose—and I love you all! I thank God for the family we have—*that we are*—and I would have no other!

To my Lord and my God: Even though my words will fail, I thank you, my glorious God, for showing me your beauty. I thank you for showing me your grace and your mercy and for all the faithful love you have had for me throughout my entire life! I bow low before you, Lord, for I am stunned by your grace. You are my King and my God! You are my heart, my life, and my deepest desire! You are everything—*and I am yours!* I belong to you, Jesus, body and soul, for better or worse—for forever and ever, amen! *All of this is your story! All this, everything, is you—your love, your power, your grace, and your mercy.* I thank you for it all! I ask you, Lord Jesus, for your name's sake, only one thing more. Please, my God! Let me see more! *Let me see more of you*—every promise of God, fulfilled and revealed—the Holy One, full of glory. I ask, Father, let this be so ... (to be continued).

Amen!

PREFACE

The vast majority of this book was written over a course of seven months in a drug and alcohol treatment centre. I had absolutely no idea what I was doing. Not only that, but I'd never written anything in my life before. When I first put pencil to paper I was still in withdrawal and shaking so hard that the words I wrote were almost illegible. I was sick, depressed, utterly hopeless, and suicidal. This would be my sixteenth treatment centre over a 40-year period, and I had absolutely no reason to think this one was going to make any more difference than any of the other 15 centres (or all the other times I had done everything I could think of to stop drinking). Even people who were close to me in all sincerity had asked me more than once why I even bothered getting up any more—why I even bothered trying. I had been advised on several occasions to just take a shotgun and blow my head off—that I should put myself and everyone else out of their misery because misery was all I was capable of creating. Many times I had asked myself the same questions—in fact, many, many times. I knew of more than one way to put an end to my life: a quick heroin overdose, or maybe just one step onto the highway and into the path of an oncoming semi-truck. BAM! Done.

But I couldn't help it. I just had to stand up one more time, just once more—because I knew something. Way deep down inside of me I knew something that no one else did. I knew God, and I *knew* what he had promised me. And I *still* knew, even when I was in the pits of hell, that he *had* promised and that he would keep his promise. I would try to quit trying—to stop believing and not care anymore, to just give up completely and *stay* that way. I wanted to forget that hope even existed—because it hurt, because hope was for dreamers and idiots. But it was impossible to forget. You see, I knew too much, and I had seen way too much. For a time, I walked on that razor-thin line between faith and apostasy, life and death, heaven and hell—and for almost two years I begged God not to take my life—not yet. So there I sat, with no hope, full of hope, hoping against hope that just maybe, maybe somehow, maybe something would change—somehow. I had no idea how close I was to discovering a freedom I could never have dreamed possible, that light and life and overwhelming joy were right around the corner, and that I would laugh in tears of wonder at what I would discover.

One of the things they told me to do at the centre was to journal every day. Journal? I could barely keep a coherent thought in my head for more than five minutes. Besides, I didn't like being told to do *anything* every day. Not my style. That, and I was in a state of total and helpless depression. Actually, it was more than just depression. This was a soul-sick weariness born of utter desolation. I honestly thought that going through this centre was nothing more than the pathetic motions of futility—an absolute waste of time. Again. But for some reason I stayed put. I don't know why. I mean, I could probably have taught everything they thought I was learning. You pick up a lot of information in the course of 15 treatment centres. I knew it all, so why in the world was I there? I asked myself that question at least once a day.

I sighed and stared rather glumly at the irritatingly empty page, in a whole journal full of irritatingly empty pages, which made me even *more* irritable—sick, depressed, and miserable—and tried to figure out what in the world I could possibly scratch onto this stupid piece of paper for an exercise I considered a complete waste of time. But then something happened—something wonderful. I thought of King David, the greatest king of all Israel, and that's when everything began to change.

I really liked this character, 'cause when David was down, he was really, really down. He just cracks me up because one minute everything is so terrible and he's so depressed and everybody hates him and all his friends are a bunch of no good low-life back-stabbing scum and his mouth is full of dust and worms and God has forgotten all about him and he's going to lie down in the dirt and eat camel dung and die and no one is even going to come to his funeral 'cause everybody hates him (or something like that!).

But then he does something. One time while he was really depressed, he says, "I will remember the deeds of the Lord; yes, I will remember your wonders of old. I will ponder all your work, and meditate on your mighty deeds" (Ps. 77:11–12), and then David begins to list all the wonderful things God has done for Israel, and by the time he's done listing everything he's all like "Yeah, God! And, you're on my side 'cause I'm a really good guy, and I love you and you love me, and me and you should go and obliterate all those other fools, 'cause they're real bad and I'm real good, so let's go bust their teeth right out of their mouths and break their jaws (and their arms and legs too!), and we should go and grind those dirty evil uncircumcised dogs so far into the dust they'll never see daylight again 'cause you really, really love me, and between you and me, God, the whole world should give us all their money and say you're really great—and that I'm great too, RIGHT?!" *HA!* This guy just kills me! Talk about mood swings!

Anyway, that is exactly what I did. I began to think about all the times God had done this really strange stuff in my life—things that I had almost forgotten about—like, *amazing* things. That's when I became really confused. I couldn't figure out what God was up to with all this crazy stuff he had done. *Why* did he do it? It just didn't make any sense! I had to get organized. I had to be able to look at it all and try to piece it together. I wanted to understand—I *needed* to understand. So I made a list of what I wanted to look at, and I began to write.

As I went over my notes and read the stories of what God had done for me and carefully thought through what was there, ever so slowly I began to see that over and over the same message was being pounded into my thick skull time and again—until I finally actually got it. I suddenly understood! After I put it all down on paper, all together in one place, suddenly everything became clear. How can I possibly explain the beauty and wonder of what was right in front of me? As I thought about all the many miracles he had done in my life, the reality of them, and the great mercy and love he had so consistently shown me year after year, it seemed as if inside me a giant floodgate suddenly burst wide open, and the reality of his love washed over me like a tidal wave. And it didn't subside; it grew more and more powerful day after day, every single time I looked at the hard evidence of his love, right in front of my eyes! You see, it was as I was writing about what God did for me and as I read and reread my notes that he actually broke the chains *that had kept me bound for 40 years!*

That is what God's love is! *It is freedom!* I wept then. I wept and I wept and I wept—for months on end. I still weep. Many times, I have to stop writing, get out of my chair, put my face on the ground, and try so hard to express my heart to him. Gratitude, love, adoration—none of these words come even close to what I felt as God opened my eyes to show me his hand in my life. I worship him now with a depth never before known to me, possible only because *I have seen. I know now! My eyes have been opened to him and to his impossible love.* How so very merciful is our God! So worthy of praise! Nothing in all of heaven or earth can compare to him! He doesn't just love. *He is love!* The kindnesses he has done for me. The grace. The mercy. The protection he has had over my life—it's just simply too big for my words to express, and I am left in tears again trying in vain to explain the great mercies of my God. I know now that I am loved, and no one and nothing can ever take that love away or separate me from it.

So now, I *must* share what I have found. His love brings with it a freedom impossible to deny, and all I want to do is share that freedom. If only I could touch you for a moment—if only somehow I could give to you what it is I have found, I would do it with all my heart! But all I can do now, all I can *ever* do, is try as hard as I can to transmit the tremendous love, power, and freedom I have found in this God who loves me, *no matter what!*

So, read on then, and my fervent prayer is that the Lord, the God of hope, would flood your heart with light, so that you may know and come to experience the love and mercy I have found while writing these pages.

May God bless you and keep you in his love always,
Kevin John White

PROLOGUE: FIRST CONTACT

I remember now how all of this began. For so long, it was as though I'd been dreaming a terrible nightmare, and I've only now just awakened. A lifetime has passed, and I had almost forgotten what happened that night so many years ago.

I was only a child then, perhaps 10 years old, but certainly no more than that. Yet as I wandered back through my heart and quietly walked through my memories, I found it there, still as wondrously beautiful as the day it first appeared and still shining just as brightly.

That night I had slipped silently from my bed and crept very quietly to my window. We always kept it open at that time of year. The sounds and scents of the night seemed somehow mysteriously transformed into an intoxicating mixture of subtle fragrances, a heady concoction exhilarating to my young imagination. I loved to sit secretly by the window, my gateway to other worlds, and breathe deep the fragrant breeze as I let the warm summer night fill and awaken all my senses.

I remember, too, gazing wistfully up at the stars and as I searched them, feeling … alone somehow. Not lonely really, just sort of quietly alone. As I sat there, searching, scenting, listening, the night breeze brought a curious sound to my sharp young ears. It was the sound of people laughing.

I was an unusually inquisitive child (much to my parents' exasperation), and so intrigued, I focused intently, eager to hear more of this mystery.

It was a group of people. They were all talking and laughing together, having fun, like a gathering of good friends. They sounded so happy to me—like they were glad to be together.

It was the sound of friends telling funny stories or sharing secrets known only to them.

I hadn't many friends—any friends at all really, not even a best friend. Our family had travelled far too much for that. Besides my brothers and sister, I don't think I'd ever even had a real friend before.

I'm not sure why, perhaps that night the evening air had mixed with I know not what, but as I listened to those distant voices, something happened to me. That night something broke wide open inside me.

It was as if somewhere in my heart, a great yawning chasm had been torn open, and from within it poured out a deep and terrible longing—a powerful yearning for what I heard in that far-off laughter. I longed for the friendship and companionship of people who recognized me, who knew me, who knew my name, and with whom I had a place, even if they were people I could only hope to know.

I longed for friends that I could laugh and play with, and right then, at that very moment, I knew for the first time in my life how very apart I was, how separate and how lonely I'd actually been, and how very much I wanted to belong.

It all came in a rush—painful, hurting me—and that night, deep in my heart, a fierce determination was born, a determination born of desperate loneliness and longing. I listened even closer, straining, using every sense I had to determine from whence this laughter had come. It seemed closer than I thought at first, yet still distant—a trick of the wind perhaps?

I was very bold as 10-year-olds go, so it was nothing for me to decide I was going to find these voices—that I would find them, and I would very boldly say "Hello" to them, and I would play my guitar for them and sing to them, and they would all like me, and we would all be friends. We would laugh and talk and play together as friends do. All this I determined to do that same night, for I was 10 now, and I was very brave.

As I pulled myself away from the window I quickly formulated a daring plan of escape. I must be silent as an owl feather, for my brother lay fast asleep in his bed, and should I wake him he would tell me I mustn't go outside or I would be in terrible trouble again.

I was often in trouble for going out when I shouldn't, as I had a tendency of not coming back. There were many times I had to be fetched home again (sometimes by helicopter). I meant no harm by it. It just turned out that the places I needed to go were often quite far away, and there always seemed so much to do when I got there.

By the time I finished dressing, I had become a "Green Beret," "Special Forces," "Black Ops," "Military Commando," and so executed my plan with the greatest precision. Just as in the tales I had read (which were many), I quietly knotted together my sheets, blankets, and pillowcases (in that exact order) and tied my makeshift rope to the radiator (whom I was terribly fond of, for even unprovoked, he would suddenly hiss at me quite fearfully and *very* unexpectedly and could spit and growl wonderfully like some terrible ill-tempered beast). Then, with the other end tied around my guitar and already out the window, I slipped over the sill, through the window, and, silent as the shadows, was down the side of the house to crouch in the soft wet grass below.

I quickly untied my guitar and, pausing only long enough to sling it across my back, was swiftly out of the backyard, across the alley, through the neighbour's yard, and onto the moonlit road beyond.

It was glorious! I was mesmerized by the size of the night and, stepping into the middle of the street, felt that familiar thrill of freedom rush and tingle through me. With my heart pounding lightly, I paused and, feeling the night wrap itself around me, remembered once more the wildness in my soul. I was almost feral again, scenting the cool of silver dewfall, sensing the mood of the world that night, listening hard into the dark—and then, suddenly satisfied, l became nothing more than a whisper among the shadowy protection of the great spreading oak trees lining the sides of the road.

I had heard them when I paused—the laughter and the voices. They were still carried to my ears on the cool night breeze, beckoning me forward.

With my guitar tight on my back, I slipped quietly up the street, always in the shadows, my bare feet making no sound on the still warm asphalt. I had now become a "Great Warrior," trained since childhood always to move with grace, speed, and great stealth, as do all creatures of the wild, and truly, that night, I had become a wild thing indeed.

As I moved quietly, unseen by all but the moon, my brother the wind would often bring news of them to me, so I knew to walk with my face towards him, always intent on my goal. It did not occur to me that I might not find them. I simply focused and did, always. That was the way of things for me. I would find them no matter what.

After a time, however, it seemed that among so many streets and houses the wind became confused and began to falter. I could no longer hear clearly the laughter of those voices. Often, I had to pause much longer to wait for snatches of sound, of conversation, and then chase after them. I would cut to another street, and then another, and then back again, climbing over fences and through yards. I would often have to backtrack two or three times and, with a rising fear chasing hard after my heart, head up still yet another street, venturing farther and farther, and hearing less and less.

Up and down I walked, desperately searching, but no matter which road I took or how hard I listened, I could never seem to draw any closer to those now fading voices, until after a time I could hear them no longer, and I found myself alone on the empty road with only the streetlamps for company.

I had to stop then. I couldn't listen—it hurt to listen—anymore. I wanted to call out, to cry to them, but I knew they couldn't hear me any more than I could hear them. I was alone, and all that I had felt before came crashing in like some great black wave. My heart ached. It ached so much for the companionship of I know not what or whom. Inside me was only a dark and frightening hole, empty where there should have been a great bonfire with cheery friends, and laughter, and sparks twirling and dancing, spiralling upward to greet the stars, who would look down upon them so tolerant and kindly, flattered by their brave ambition. There would be laughter and friends and just … somebody.

I walked again, very slowly, my guitar keeping time, thumping my back as if to console me. All of my 10-year-old boldness and bravery had vanished, just as those voices in the wind had vanished. Just like a part of me had vanished, and my heart was cast down inside me. I was alone. Again.

I really don't know exactly how to describe what happened to me as I walked slowly back home that night, but I must try, for what happened changed my life, changed everything … forever.

As I walked, it was as though I heard a voice gently yet very powerfully speak my name and say, "Kevin, I want to talk with you." I was startled by its clarity and impact, and I clearly remember faltering to a halt and listening, questioning … "What?" almost shocked, but in so low a voice I could scarcely hear it myself.

For a long moment there was nothing. The whole world seemed silent. I was just about to start walking on when I heard it speak again, very clearly, still gentle, but somehow even more powerfully than before.

"Kevin, I want to talk with you!"

For another long moment I could hear nothing. Cautiously I whispered, "Who are you?" but deep down inside of me, I already knew. This time the answer came almost immediately.

"I am God, Kevin, and I want to talk with you."

I didn't know it then, but that voice was the one voice I would come to long for, had already yearned for, more than any other voice in the whole world, for my whole life and, I know now, beyond even life's end.

I began to walk again, but this time, it appeared I wasn't alone. Of course, then came the inevitable questions. I feel myself smiling now, almost with tears in my eyes, because so many of those questions I still ask to this very day, 45 years later. (Oh! And also, because talking to him is like talking to an answer, and a question, and a great big magnifying glass with a wonderful sense of humour all at once.)

"How do I know you're really God?"

"Because I have just told you so."

"Well, what I really mean is, how do I know that I'm not just talking to myself?"

"Do you really believe that, Kevin? Besides, I'm the one who started this conversation."

Then came the kind of trying to trick him, and trying to think of something he couldn't possibly know, or trying not to think about anything at all, then, thinking-about-something-totally-different-really-really-fast, and then thinking about something different entirely while asking him to tell me what I had been thinking about when I'd thought about something really fast while trying very hard not to think about what I had just thought—before. Which he quickly pointed out was just plain nonsense and really rather silly as he *was* God and already knew everything about me. I had to concede the point.

Stymied but still quite suspicious, I slowly began my long walk home as we continued our conversation. I also remember feeling a slowly growing acceptance of this odd new inevitability and somehow feeling as if I remembered this voice from before—from another time.

I'm so glad now that I was still young then. Glad I could still be a "Green Beret" and a "Wild Untameable Savage." (And I was, too!) I'm grateful for all of those evenings after supper and a bath when as a child I sat with my brother and sister on the floor, my toes burning on the electric heater in my father's study, as he read to us of Narnia and of Aslan—"The Great Lion," "Son of the Emperor Over the Sea," "The King of All High Kings." I am so pleased now that the cynicism and sophistication of many years had not dulled my ears nor deadened my heart to wonder and mystery.

I found out that night there was another world, but unlike Narnia, this world was not a bedtime fairy tale. This unseen realm was very real and had just invaded my life, and I would never be the same again—I *couldn't* be the same again—ever.

I remember asking many other questions and that we talked about them all. Other than one, I don't remember specifics about particular questions, but I would suppose they were all in the nature of what any lonely ten-year-old would ask God in the middle of the night as he walked down the middle of the road on his way back home. I do remember he always answered me, though, and that many of his answers seemed to be questions I had to answer for myself. This vexed me somewhat, but he always answered nonetheless. We walked together that night, he and I, and slowly we began to speak as friends would speak, of many things, the voices in the distant wind long forgotten.

The one question I do remember asking was "Why? Why are you talking with me?" His answer, try as I may, was something I cannot quite recall.

However, before we got home that night so long ago, he did tell me one thing that I do remember. It was something I have kept in my heart always and will keep there till I am at his side forever.

He said that I could believe in him or not but that he would always talk with me—always—no matter what.

Not very long after, I noticed something. Something wonderful. In that dark and frighteningly empty hole so deep in my heart, there mysteriously appeared a wondrously beautiful sphere of purest crystal, and inside it burned a single flame of fire. No wick, no candle, just a light in that terrible darkness—a flame that nothing in this world or any other could ever possibly extinguish—the very life of God in me. I can see it clearly still to this very second, and I long for it to consume me utterly and completely—the very fire of God in my heart of hearts.

And our conversations? They have continued, unbroken, to this very day. He has kept his promise to talk with me always, no matter what. And we talk as friends would talk, and I still have so very many questions to ask, and he remains as vexing as ever, "The Great Answer and a Question and a Great Big Magnifying Glass with a Wonderful Sense of Humour All at Once," only now … I'm not alone. Now I'm never alone.

1
THE SET-UP

I suppose I should introduce myself. My name is Kevin John René White. Legally my name is John René, but both God and my mother call me Kevin. Now I'm pretty sure the two of them pack a whole lot more wallop than any government on earth (especially my mother—ask God … he'll tell you), so that being said, I shall call myself Kevin.

What I'm going to tell you is rather odd, but that's not surprising seeing as how I'm the one who's doing the telling. What is surprising, however, is that I'm alive with enough brain activity to write anything at all!

That also being said, everything I'm going to write down here is the honest truth about some extremely unusual events. I know they're true because they happened to me, which means I was there when they happened, so I should know better than anybody—right? Except for the parts where I wasn't born yet … and I am a little sketchy on the parts where I was crawling around in diapers (don't remember—very embarrassing time … rather messy actually).

Now before I really get going here I think perhaps I should mention something. I am not the only one in my family that's a little bit … well, odd really. It just seems like I got a double portion of this weirdness, so it's actually quite normal that I turned out the way I did (I mean, being a tad whacked and all).

The parts where I wasn't born yet go like this:

During World War II my father served in the British navy as a dive bomber and a reconnaissance photographer aboard the HMS *Trumpeter*. In civilian terms that meant he and his pilot pal flew around the Atlantic Ocean picking fights and taking pictures of everything that had an enemy flag attached to it. At least everything they could find. My dad would hang out the tail end of a British fighter plane and say "smile" to all the guns and crew on the enemy vessels while his pilot pal made steep dives so Dad could drop his bombs and take good pictures of what type of guns they had. This intel was then sent to headquarters monitoring enemy activity in that area of the Atlantic. While Dad was occupied with that, his buddy was real busy trying not to get them blown right out of the sky.

What was even trickier was taking pictures over land. They'd have to dive straight into the antiaircraft guns and take pictures of them so the bomber crews would know what kind and how many guns they would be facing in any offensives they were planning. They got shot at a lot. Oh yeah, during those missions they were not armed, so they couldn't even shoot back.

Now none of this really has any bearing on what I want to write about other than to say I think Dad secretly loved the adrenalin rush and was definitely a bit mad. That, and I'm really proud of him (which I never told him while he was alive). Oh—and most importantly—I definitely inherited from him on both counts!

After the war, he returned to England and became a surgeon, working mostly in an emergency room. I guess he must have read a few books or something. My dad was a pretty smart guy.

After a while, I think God told him that there were even better things than bodies to save, so he got it into that wonderful head of his that being a missionary and saving poor savage souls was just the thing for him. So, off he went and hooked up with an outfit called New Tribes Missions and for the second time in his life found himself in a war, this one even more important than the last. This was around when the miracles started. At least the ones I heard about. I'm sure there were plenty of others.

See, before my father went to New Tribes boot camp, God told him that was where he would meet his future wife. Well, when he got there, missionary school was a total bust. No single dream girl in sight. But because God says, and Dad's Dad, he decided to stick it out and began teaching. Seems like he taught wherever he was, at least as I recall it. He did this for a while, but as the clock ticked on and time got short, there was still no sign of Mrs. Right. Or should I say—Mrs. White.

One day in camp he was kicking back on his bunk with a prayer chain magazine, and he stumbled across an article about a young Canadian girl who, while serving with New Tribes in the Pacific, had contracted tuberculosis of the spine. At that time this particular type of tuberculosis permanently crippled or killed everybody who got it.

Now, for some reason this pissed my father off something *fierce*, and as he recounted to me, after reading it, in a heartbeat he tumbled out of his bunk, was onto his knees, and started getting real pushy with God—like actually arguing and demanding that God heal this woman—and with fast quickness too!

Dad told me that as he'd been reading he became frustrated and angry at God. Dad felt that this was *all* wrong! He began pointing out in no uncertain terms that God needed to really re-examine himself on this particular issue, reconsider exactly what he was doing here, heal this girl up right quick, and get her back in the saddle again, *pronto!* As in right away! The funny thing about it all is that Dad didn't even believe divine healing existed anymore. But for some reason that didn't slow him up too much that day.

Now there is a point to all this, and I'm getting to it now. The facts are that miracles were running way wild in my family long before I ever showed up. You see, I come by the kind of things I am going to describe to you honestly. Premonitions, visions, and manifestations of God's incredible love and holiness were shared by both me and my father. I didn't ask for them. I didn't go looking for them, and there are many times I wished I'd never experienced them. Also, I'm going to show you, very clearly, that none of this is my fault, that I never stood a chance, and that I was set up from the get-go. Here are two miracles right off the hop, and then I'll get to the "Big Set-Up."

What my father could not have known was that right around the time he was in this big kerfuffle with God, the young lady who was responsible for said row was already back in Canada and headed for a sanatorium. There she was to be put in a body cast, probably for several years. (That's if she lasted that long.)

The thing was, she had stopped at a church in Halifax to speak to some young people about the mission field, and right in the middle of her speech God just stepped in and "Bingo!" she was completely healed! Just like that! No trace of any illness in her body at all. Her spine just went completely straight again, and there was not a single sign of tuberculosis in her body. Done! In her own words, it happened like this:

When I arrived at the church I was led up to the front towards a chair, but as I started toward it God said to me, "Where do you think you're going? I want you to stand at the podium!" So I did. When I began speaking I was leaning heavily on it, bent over, as I could not stand upright. As I continued speaking, all of a sudden the young people of the church started clapping. I had absolutely no idea at all why. I continued to speak but later they started clapping again, only this time they were laughing as well. I thought perhaps I had said or done something foolish, but I kept on talking anyway. What I didn't realize was that as I was speaking I had begun to stand up straight. By the time I finished speaking I was standing erect and completely straight. The young people had seen all of this and that's why they had started clapping in the first place. They knew before I did that God had been healing me as I spoke.[1]

After having x-rays redone and freaking everybody out, she returned to boot camp for reassignment less than a month and a half later with a straight back and no trace of tuberculosis. At 90 years old, she still stands erect and without pain.

Healed in May, back in July, and I bet you have no clue who she runs into at boot camp! Yep! You got 'er!—a certain daring (but very lovesick) young naval intelligence officer. The fireworks were ballistic. (What is it about camps and romance? Sigh.)

Now according to my father, he was just standing around minding his own business one day when he was, and I quote, "struck suddenly by a vision of beauty" who just happened to wander by. (Minding his own business?) Well Dad, not being one to waste any time, does a bit of fancy

---

[1] Lorrie White, interviewed by the author, November 2015.

footwork *and a few hours later* has his "glory" *alone* on a riverbank and is asking if she wants to marry him and have four children (*not* a good example, Dad!).

Now I just love my mother. She says she wouldn't mind the babies, but she's not too sure about the boy. Poor Dad. You can tell she's a fisherman's daughter though, eh? Brilliant technique!

As things turned out they had to decide quickly as they were both going to be headed to different parts of the world very soon, so they shook hands on it (or something) and decided that they were going to tie the knot. Ten days later they were married, and they stayed that way happily for 45 years without one single serious argument, until my father passed away at home in her arms. This was after they had both lived incredibly amazing lives together, travelling all over the world in God's service. Together they raised five children, and in all of my life there was never once that I ever thought ill of my father—ever. He is the reason it is so easy for me to call my God "Father." As for my mother, no words can describe the love I hold in my heart for her.

It's funny though; they didn't put the whole—Mom getting healed and Dad praying for her—thing together until some years later. It must have been special for them—you know, all romantic and stuff. That was miracle #1 by the way. Here comes miracle #2.

You're probably wondering where and when I come into the picture, but you'll just have to wait because my big brother came first, and he's the one who saved all our lives while I was still inside my mother just itching to get out and cause some trouble. (That's not the miracle part—believe me.) For the miracle part, we've got to time warp forward about five years.

Now just to set the stage, Mom and Dad had been doing their missionary job at a leper colony in Bolivia up until my father got re-posted to work with InterVarsity Christian Fellowship, strengthening, encouraging, and organizing the Christian university students in Latin America. This of course means Mother got re-posted to work strengthening, encouraging, and organizing my six-year-old brother Scott and an unborn hell-raising Kevin onto an airplane and, of course, into a completely different country.

We catch up to my mother cruising at altitude over the Andes Mountains as Scott (who's as nervous as an untended whisky bottle in a back alley) is whispering, "I really don't like this plane, Mommy!" like he is just about to pull a 20 dollar bill out of an unsprung mousetrap, and he won't stop whispering, *"I really don't like this plane, Mommy!"* until poor pregnant Mommy makes him a promise that they will get off at the very next stop. They did.

This decision saved our lives. When that plane took off to get to its final destination, it had barely cleared the runway when something went terribly wrong, and it crashed into a huge ball of flame, killing everyone on board except a tiny baby they pulled out of the wreckage. (It was all kind of spooky really.) It was one of the biggest airplane disasters in South American history.[2]

These narrow scrapes with death were to become pretty regular occurrences in my future.

Oh yeah, this gets even stranger. You see, Scott wasn't the only one who knew that plane was going to crash.

The following entry is from one my father's books, *The Cost of Commitment*. I came across it while I was reacquainting myself with him through his writings by rereading all his books. (I'm still trying to find 20 or so I'm still missing.) I felt a need to get closer in my heart to him. I'd hurt him pretty bad while I was growing up. I miss him so much now—his wisdom and gentle ways. You know, he never once raised his voice or said a single cruel or unkind word to me in all my life. Not once. I just wish he could have been here to see me finally get free.

This was such an interesting find, and is so much like him:

A Paradox and a Premonition

Once I had a premonition that my wife and infant son would be killed in a flying accident. We were to travel separately from the U.S. to Bolivia, South America. She would fly via Brazil and Buenos Aires, then north to Bolivia. I was to visit Mexico, several Central American countries, Venezuela, Colombia, and other countries to strengthen Christian work among students, before joining my family in Bolivia.

---

[2] "All 52 on Jet Die in Brazil Crash; Argentine Comet Dives to Earth Just After Taking Off—American Aboard All 52 on Argentine Jet Killed in Crash on Take-Off in Brazil" Associated Press, *New York Times* (November 24, 1961).

The premonition came with sickening certainty just before we parted on the night of a wild snowstorm. I felt I was a cowardly fool as I drove away and saw Lorrie silhouetted in the yellow light of the doorway, surrounded by swirling snowflakes. Why didn't I go back and tell her I would cancel the flights? Why didn't I act on this foreboding?

I didn't believe in premonitions—and had never even heard of "words of knowledge." Lorrie would probably laugh. Besides I was late, I had to get to the place where I would spend the night before my early morning flight. No conversation was possible with the man who was driving me to my hotel. Fear, shame, guilt, and nausea all boiled inside me.

In bed I tossed in misery. Of course I prayed. By faith I was going to have it licked. Faith? In the presence of so powerful a premonition? My mouth was dry. My limbs shook. God was a million miles away. The hours crawled by, each one a year of fear. Why didn't I get dressed, hire a car and go back to them?

"What's the matter? Can't you trust me?"

I was startled. Was God speaking?

"Yes, I'll trust you—if you promise to give them back to me."

Silence.

Then, "And if I don't promise? If I don't give them back to you, will you stop trusting me?"

"Oh, God, what are you saying?" My heart had stopped and I couldn't breathe.

"Can you not entrust them to me in death as well as in life?"

Suddenly a physical warmth flowed through all my body. I think I wept a little. My words came tremblingly and weakly, "Yes, I place them in your hands. I know you will take care of them in life or in death."

And my trembling subsided. Peace—better by far than martinis on an empty stomach—flowed over and over me. And drowsily I drifted off to sleep.

Hate them? How could I ever hate them? Yet by faith I had said in effect, I will do your will whatever it costs to me or them, and I will trust you.

Their plane crashed. Everyone on board was killed. But my wife had also had a premonition and cut their journey short, getting off the plane the stop before the tragedy occurred.

I am grateful for the way it worked out. But I didn't know beforehand that things would go as they did. And had it not worked out that way, I would have grieved (God knows how I would have grieved), but I would not have regretted my decision to trust and to go forward ... This is what it means to follow Christ fully. This is the effect he wants to have on all our personal relationships—family members, spouses, friends—whatever they may be. The fear that may hold you back is a fear of unbelief. But defy your fear and go forward. For to follow Christ fully means to take steps along the perilous pathway of trust, roped to the safest Guide in the universe.[3]

Mom told me he got it *all* mixed up. (Ever hear a married couple tell the same story?)

It is interesting to me how that same event impacted two people so powerfully. You see, there is even more to this tale. Other factors were involved. It was actually impossible for us to have been killed aboard that plane. Here's why:

Besides becoming a real pain in the ass real quick, I was also the answer to a whole lot of prayer—the prayers of my mother and father. (I guarantee you they got a little more careful about what they asked for after having me.)

I knew nothing of any of this until my father told me when I was in my late twenties. I was in Cook County Jail in Chicago for stealing a six-and-a-half-foot Burmese python named Monty. Needless to say, I was stoned and drunk. To put it *very* mildly, it was during a terribly dark time in my life, and I'll leave it at that. There are some things better left alone.

This was the first time I'd heard of what I now call "The Set-Up." Is that a fair name? You be the judge ...

It was in a holding cell in jail for a visit with my father that I first heard of it. That he was even there was in itself a miracle. How he got

[3] John White, *The Cost of Commitment* (Downers Grove: InterVarsity Press, 2006), 72–74, 79–80.

in to see me was so typical of him. Believe me, he was an amazing man. (Contact visits were strictly prohibited.)

Well, after the pleasantries were done he gently took my arm and said, "Kevin, there is something that I can tell you now." Then he told me a story that shed some light onto the insanity of my life.

He said that after my brother Scott was born they couldn't seem to have another child for almost five years. They had prayed often about it, first for a son, then asking why my mother couldn't conceive. There seemed to be no real answers.

Late one night while they were on leave in Paris, taking some much-needed time away from their work at the leper colony, my father went for a walk in a nearby park. He told me he was troubled about them not being able to conceive. At a bench deep in the park he got to his knees and began to pray.

He asked God for a son—a good son, a child he could raise up in the knowledge of God, one who would love him with all his heart, strong and full of the Holy Spirit, who would serve and honour God—a child who would bring glory to his name.

Right at that point God very powerfully interrupted him with a question.

"To my glory or to your glory? What about Adam and me?"

This was immediately followed by a rapid and equally powerful series of visions and emotions that included stone prison walls, shame, bitter struggle, great pain, and all the sin, disgrace, and terrible heartache that may follow. He said it shook him powerfully.

God spoke once again. "I am going to bring this child into the world. I am offering him to you. If you do not want him, if you do not accept him, I will give him to another."

Here is how he put it in his own words. It's something that, once again, I stumbled upon while reading one of his books, *The Pathway of Holiness: A Guide for Sinners*. It was in the chapter on pride and its pitfalls.

> God taught me this lesson during the long delay between our firstborn and subsequent children. My wife and I were older, and in a hurry. Disturbed by the delay, I knelt one day in a park

in Paris, when there were few people around. I asked God for another son with the caveat "if he will live to your glory."

Quite distinctly the Holy Spirit said, "To *my* glory, or to *yours*?"

I was shaken a little. Then came "What about me and Adam?"

At first perplexed, I began to realize that at the time of creation God had known of all the wars, the cruelty, the diseases, the terrible tragedies that would follow the entry of satanic pride into human history. Yet he had still given Adam life. Was he asking me to do something similar?

I asked, "What d'you mean?"

Immediately into my mind came a picture of the walls of a prison not far from the home of my childhood. I felt sick.

"You mean he would go to jail?" The possibility of having a son who would go to jail frightened me. I could feel moisture penetrating my trouser knees. But I did not rise. I knew I was being offered a son who would go to jail. I also knew I could refuse that son. Perhaps someone else would have him. I have no idea how a sovereign God works this sort of thing. But there was no answer to my feeling of panic, only silence.

Finally, rather shaken, I said, "OK. I'll have him!"

Two months later our second son was conceived. By that time, I had forgotten the prayer "conversation." My dialogue with God did not lead to a sort of self-fulfilling prophecy. I gradually forgot about it, and I recalled it only much later when the clear differences between Kevin and our other children became so obvious that they could no longer be ignored.

A nightmare began then. Did God *cause* my second son to sin? Obviously not. But he had known what would happen. And he had given me a choice.

Later came two prophecies, both from men with established reputations for accurate prophecy. A cloud of darkness rested on that particular son. At some date in the future it would be snatched from above his head, and he would change. In the meantime, Kevin never lost his longing for the things of God. In jail he would organize Bible studies. He would lay his hands on other prisoners, and these would occasionally fall to the ground, overwhelmed by the Spirit of God. How does one explain such things?[4]

For some strange reason, my father said yes. That he hadn't the slightest idea what he was doing I have no doubt. If it were me, I would plead temporary insanity.

I've often puzzled on what he told me that day. In one sense, I was relieved that there was some sort of explanation for my insanity. Somehow, I had always known this was all part of a plan—that my life was being carefully guided and guarded for some reason, but I also was tempted at one point to become very angry—furious.

How dare you! Both of you! Who do you think you are?! Why did you even make me? So I could suffer hell over and over again? Here? And then when I'm dead too? WHY?! Why didn't you just say "No"? I just so wished you'd have said "No! No! No!"

But he didn't. He said, "Yes." I understand now. You see, when my father said he trusted God, he really meant it. No matter what it cost. He may not have understood fully what his decision would mean. I think I do now.

Through that choice God revealed himself to both of us in a way that nothing else could have allowed him to. God revealed his incredible love and faithfulness to us both in ways neither of us could have experienced had we not gone through what we did, my father in his way and I in mine.

I would not trade the wonder of knowing him the way I do for *anything*. My father once told me that pain is the shovel God uses to dig us deep—that the hole would never be empty but would become a clear pool of life-giving water, overflowing from the springs of joy far beneath, clean and fresh, and full of the love of God. Those springs of joy bubble up now every single time I think on his great love and the wonders he has shown me, and I long to share what I've found with you.

Sometimes I think about it. God said, *"I am going to bring this child into the world. If you do not want him, if you do not take him, I will give him to another."* (What's he got? Contingency plans?)

---

[4] John White, *The Pathway of Holiness: A Guide for Sinners* (Downers Grove: InterVarsity Press, 1996), 38–39.

What if Dad had said "No"? If God said it, somehow I'd still be here. Sometimes it's cool to think what I'd be like if I wasn't me but somebody else. Would I still be *me?*

I'd like to get into a scrap with him! What a blast! *This world ain't big enough for the two of us, pal!* (Ha! I'd win either way!) But I digress ...

Well, obviously Dad said yes, so "Bada-bing! Bada-boom!"—my mother was pregnant and my life began. (Yahoo!) (Gotta love Paris in the springtime, eh? Sigh ... again.)

There you have it. "The Set-Up."

So, back to the airplane—now you can see why we couldn't die. I hadn't been born yet! I was still alive inside, so I hadn't pulled off any more trouble than a bad craving for tuna-fish ice cream and a mild case of heartburn. (By the way, I fully intend on having a *very* serious conversation with both God *and* my father about all this later on.)

Well, from here on in things get a whole lot noisier because now, I've got to get born! And man! I was hell on wheels right from the start. My mother told me that I hit the ground running and did not let up for one second. She said if I wasn't in sight, I could always be found at a locked door trying to puzzle out how to get my way through it. She told me it seemed like I just had this fascination with going somewhere.

My mother told me that when I was still a toddler I figured out this one door and immediately made a beeline straight to the back of the yard, dug myself a tunnel under the fence, and escaped out to the road. Well, she flipped! (We lived in a small village in rural Argentina.) The whole house was in an uproar, because to them I'd vanished into thin air. (I'd purposely shut the door when I left, to buy myself more time.)

Long and short of it was they caught up to me some three long blocks away lying on my belly with my chin in my hands less than a foot from a busy trucking highway, just watching the traffic and trying to puzzle out how to get across that road too. The funny thing about all this is that I clearly remember formulating this plan of mine before executing it. And just before my great escape, I also remember looking down at my legs and thinking, *I got this! I can walk now! (And if I get tired I can always crawl for a bit too.)* "I" was going exploring, and that was that! This kind of behaviour stuck with me till, well ... today really.

2
DECISION

For many years now, I have sought for some reasonable explanation as to why I made the most ruinous and destructive decision of my life. That I was very afraid, I already know. Why I was afraid and why I chose that catastrophic course of action to deal with my fear is what completely bewilders me now. Perhaps part of it was because I made that decision when I was only seven years old, and I was afraid, and very alone.

I had what I see now as an unusually good childhood—my early one at least. We were all loved and well cared for, and I have fond memories of times with my siblings and both my parents. I know I was treated no differently than any of the other children. The same love and discipline were given to each of us. I was a bit more independent than the other kids, but there is nothing I can think of that could possibly account for such a drastic decision. Life was pretty happy for all of us. Other than when he was preaching, I've only heard my father raise his voice once. We were being quite loud downstairs, and he was trying to study for a very difficult exam which would admit him to practice psychiatry in Canada. It shocked us, and we looked at each other—frightened and a bit bewildered. The exam has long since been banned as being far too difficult. He passed it. His professor failed. As I said, my father was a remarkable man.

I do not remember my mother ever raising her voice to any of us once. How she managed that is to me now simply incomprehensible, especially considering I was one of those children. I never saw or heard my parents fight or argue—ever. We were always taught right from wrong, and more importantly, we were taught *why* things were right and *why* they were wrong. *We were taught to understand.* If I did something wrong, my father, who carried out the discipline for "serious" offences, would first ask if I knew why I was in trouble. If I was unsure (which wasn't very often), he would explain. Then he would ask if I knew why it was wrong. Again, if I was unsure, he would explain. Finally, he would ask if I understood why he was going to spank me or take away a privilege, and I know with me at least, the discipline dispensed, he would take me into his arms and tell me I was loved and that the matter was finished. No one was ever allowed to tease anyone about what had been said or done. Discipline was, of course, carried out in private.

I write these things because I truly don't understand why I became so fearful—what it was that drove me to such a terrible decision that morning. Perhaps it was because we had moved to a new house and a new neighbourhood and it was my first day at a new school. We had just moved from South America to Winnipeg, Manitoba, two years earlier, and then, when we moved again, it seemed something happened to me. I became afraid. Or maybe it was being run over by that car on my sixth birthday. I don't know. All I do know is that on the very first day of grade three at my new school a terrible fear took root inside me and immediately began to destroy any hope I had of a normal life. That day saw a horrible nightmare begin—a misery from which I could not wake for over 45 years.

I had arrived early that morning, and as I sat by myself on those cold school steps dreading the arrival of the other students, I felt very alone and afraid. For some strange reason I believed deep down inside that if I didn't master that fear in every area of my life I would crumble and be utterly destroyed beneath it. That thought frightened me more than the fear itself did.

For some reason, by some strange convolution of logic, I decided that I must become really fierce to overcome this fear. And in order to become fierce, I felt that I must become ... *bad*. They seemed to be two sides of the same coin. Inseparable. So that day I made the decision to become bad—really bad—and *fierce*—fierce with all the fury that this "being bad" would require of me. Unknowingly, I had made that decision an unspoken vow, and as I felt it sink to the very core of me, somehow I felt safe—protected with a shield of badness and armed with a sword of fury.

Now all of this was fine and good, but I immediately discovered I had some serious hurdles to overcome. You see, I was only seven, and at that age I did not know how to be bad, or fierce, for that matter. I had known nothing but goodness and love all of my life. I thought carefully about my predicament for some time as I sat alone on the steps that morning. After quite a bit of serious puzzling, I was suddenly struck with what I thought was a wonderfully good idea about how I could become terribly bad. I needed a mentor—someone to show me the ropes, so to speak. I decided to accomplish this task by carefully observing all the other kids, picking the one who always seemed to be in trouble, becoming his friend, and then watching and learning all there was to know about being bad.

So I did exactly that, and by the end of that day I had found my new teacher. My progress right from the start was outstanding—amazing, really. I found that I had a truly exceptional genius for this particular field of endeavour, and so I quickly surpassed my mentor.

He had given me all the basics (lying, stealing, talking back, how not to get caught, mess making, and sticking to my story). By the end of the following year I had taken things to a whole new level. I had added to my craft stealing smokes, school skipping, and its companion, note forging (a true art, for which I was paid). At the end of my third year I was the "Holy Terror" of the entire school, and it was thoroughly exasperated with me, never mind how my parents were feeling. They were hurt, confused, and exhausted. By the time I hit grade five, the school was going to kick me out for the second time. The only reason they didn't was because it was just a couple of weeks till the end of the school year.

But to my dismay and confusion, the fear—it hadn't really gone away. It continued to fester deep inside me. No matter what I did, I was still afraid, and I didn't know why, and I felt like a coward for it. Yet there I was, at no more than eight years old, hopping on and off freight trains— sometimes hanging on to the side ladders and digging my boot heels into the gravel, skiing alongside the train and timing my hops to skip over the railway ties. By age 11 or 12 I was skipping school, riding long-distance railcars, howling into the wind, and jumping off high train trestles into the river—smoking, drinking, staying out way past curfew—and then, if my folks would try to ground me, I'd just slip out a window and be gone the minute I wasn't being watched.

Yet I can see now that God's hand of mercy, protection, and care seemed always to be on me. I clearly remember sliding down a long banister at school (which was strictly forbidden) and, at the bottom, flying through the air a good six or seven feet and smashing through a 12 by 8 foot sheet of plate glass for a nature exhibit. I also remember very distinctly feeling as though underneath me was a great cushioned hand, and it seemed as if I was almost floating through the air—to the point where when I glanced around I half expected to see the Pillsbury Doughboy's fingers wrapped around my waist. This was all done with a detached observation or, at most, a mild surprise.

When I crashed through the glass I felt it as it closed in all around me. I had no fear of harm at all. Even while getting up amidst the great thick shards of plate glass and putting my hands into tiny splinters, I remember looking at the glass all around me, and all I felt was like "Well, that was odd." Nothing. Not even one scratch. I never even thought twice about it.

Had you mentioned God might have been protecting me I'd have probably looked very gravely at you, shrugged my shoulders, nodded my head, and said something like "I know ..." then turned around and in no more than five steps have some new mischief bubbling away in that endlessly diabolical imagination of mine. In my young mind, the whole not getting hurt by the glass thing was normal. I never got hurt, so all was simply as it should have been—as it always was. Everything had gone as naturally as things like that always did.

This bad behaviour was not kept to myself. By the time I was 12 years old I had gangs of my buddies skipping school and taking off downtown with me. There I would organize them into pairs, give them their lines ("Excuse me, ma'am, but I have to call my mom, and I don't have a dime for the phone"), and send them out with an exact number of dimes to panhandle. We would then meet at the agreed upon location, where they'd give me what they had collected. This coin I would change into bills. Then I would watch all the people going into the liquor store, spot the person in the crowd who I knew would go in and buy beer for me (my accuracy at this became legendary), and then take the beer and get drunk with the boys in an alleyway. Simple, really.

The first time the cops brought me home I was about eight, and by 10 years old I'd had a few run-ins with them. By the time I was 12 or 13 I was dropping lots of acid, sometimes 10 to 20 hits of the good old White Blotter. (This was only barely out of the sixties, so the acid was powerful and uncut.) I was smashing out liquor store windows for booze and popping stolen morphine pills like they were candy. I was smoking dope, oil, and hash and drinking Lysol with my back alley Native buddies in the middle of Winnipeg winters—basically doing anything that spelled trouble.

By age 14 I'd been sent to Vancouver by my parents to escape threats on my life for stealing some very bad drugs from some very bad people (that's when I became a Christian). After that, my parents tried to place me in an expensive private school (St. John's-Ravenscourt)—I had to wear a uniform and tie!—to get me away from all the bad influences at school. What my dear parents didn't realize was that *I was the bad influence at school.*

I didn't last the year, but because my grades were quite high, they passed me anyway—on the condition that I never come back there again (that meant even setting foot on their property). The next year I was kicked out of four junior high schools in six months (that would be all of them), so really, after that there was just no more school. I rarely came home for long. By the time I hit 16 I'd already been to California twice. My folks knew some people down there who were in the middle of some kind of revival. I guess they hoped some of it would rub off. A whole chunk of my life was spent going back and forth between Winnipeg and Bakersfield, California. It's all a bit of a blur as I made the trip three or four times. That was when I got into smoking PCP. The last time I went I just didn't come back again. It's hard to keep things straight in my head. I was young and there was just so much happening.

But long before I stayed in California, I had overdosed several times on strange combinations of weird psychotropic, psychogenic, and psychoactive drugs, as well as some other kinds of brain chemicals, the names of which I have no idea of. (I took them all at once and downed them with a 26 of vodka.) I wasn't trying to hurt myself; I was just curious to find out what would happen.

On one of these overdoses I woke up a few days later in my father's psych ward with some whacked-out character's face planted against the glass-walled observation room I was in, euphorically cackling in hysterical glee, "THE SNOWFLAKES! THE SNOWFLAKES ARE EVERYWHERE! CAN YOU SEE THEM? THEY'RE EVERYWHERE!" That was just the first time. Hell, it's no wonder I can hallucinate whenever I want to. That was not to be the only time I was in his ward for overdosing on strange pills. (I think I was in there three different times.)

When I went back to California for the fourth time, what followed was an insane nightmare of heavy IV drug use, drunkenness, and degradation I cannot even begin to describe. Now it's mostly a dark haze, from which, from time to time, come horrifying memories that emerge to torment me—things I so much wish I could forget—*terrible things.*

I know now that at the end of my time in the States I was demonically driven and oppressed (my father's friend John Wimber told me he got rid of at least seven or eight) and had several dangerous run-ins with some extremely nasty black witchcraft and occult stuff.

I eventually wound up getting kicked out of the States for good after I was thrown in jail for stealing that Burmese python. It was there that I was to learn real quick all about respect and survival. Cook County Jail (the Chicago city bucket) taught me a lot of brutal lessons. But even there, God's hand was on me, protecting me and giving me favour with some of the heaviest members in the entire jail system. I was … untouchable. Someone stole from me—once; that same day I received back almost three times what I'd lost.

When I got out of jail I returned to Canada (well … let's just say the USA asked me to leave quite pointedly) and began a long 24-year stint of hitchhiking all over the country. I'd just turned 26 years old. When I wasn't couch surfing, most of the time I was sleeping outside (often in the winter) or in stairwells, on heater vents, or anywhere else warm that I could crawl my way into. It would take extreme conditions to drive me into a hostel or shelter. I hated them … despised would be a more accurate term.

After a time, I could no longer tolerate the insanity of the larger cities and usually just stayed on the outskirts of them, drinking anything and everything every waking second of every single day, just moving from town to town, city to city, coast to coast, and back again, not knowing where I was going or why. I was just running hard from God knows what and using anything and everything I could to feel nothing. The loneliness I felt during this time was simply overwhelming. Often I would grab a bottle and sit alone, crying to God for some kind of solution—anything to fill that horrible hole in my soul.

I know this chapter seems to jump around a lot. I apologize and ask for your patience.

It is not my intention to give you a chronological picture but rather to give you a quick sketch of the kind of kid I actually was. My life during those early years was so insane I myself can scarcely believe I survived it. Really, I should never have lived long enough to even see the beginning of my teens. I was, in short, completely uncontrollable and desperately trying to prove to myself I was without fear. That meant I did a lot of incredibly stupid and dangerous things. As I look back now, I literally shudder and shake my head at God's mercy and protection.

It has only been as I reflected on my past that I have realized that throughout my whole life highly unusual things kept on happening to me—almost like they were chasing me. Unexplainable things. Amazing things. Events I had to understand. What follows is every word the truth to the best of my ability. I know it's the truth—I was there. Sometimes others were too. I'll try to just stick to the facts, but believe me, there were a whole lot of feelings involved as well. I had to look. *All I wanted was to understand—to make sense of what had happened to me.* What I found was more than my heart could contain.

Do I regret the decision I made as that seven-year-old? Think about it. Did I really have any other choice? I was "set up" … remember? (And I'll leave that for all you predestination hounds to bark and howl at!) But no matter what your conclusion is, you've got to admit that God always has a plan … doesn't he?

3
KNOWING

As I mentioned earlier, I was playing with freight trains by the time I was eight or nine years old. We were doing things around them, in them, and on top of them that give me nightmares every time I look at my son. When I see how small and vulnerable he is, I find it almost unbelievable (astonishing, really) that no matter how I slice it, I did the insane things I did on those trains when I was his age. (It's the only thing that makes me grateful my son is into video games.) As I think about it, I'm amazed that I even survived into my double digits! That's around when we started taking the longer trips on them. I couldn't have been more than 11—maybe 12 at most.

We did a few short runs from Winnipeg, Manitoba, to Regina, Saskatchewan, and back, and once we accidentally found a real sneaky way into the States. (I think we wound up in South Dakota.) I'm not sure where all we went—it's kind of lumped together. Of course, this was all in the late sixties and early seventies when people weren't so paranoid. It was simpler then. No electronics, no cellphones, very loose security, and riding was much more common back then. I guess it was because people weren't running about trying to blow everything up like they are these days. Seems to be going on a whole lot more as time goes by.

Anyway, we just poked around on them and took them whichever direction they were headed. I did get lost a few times. Imagine an 11-year-old boy walking up to you and saying, "Excuse me, sir, but do you know where I am?" HA! (I shouldn't laugh. Now that I think on it, I remember clearly doing that very thing.)

Getting on was the fun part—hiding out, chasing it down, the timing and all. Sometimes getting off when you needed to could be a bit tricky—knowing when and how to jump, how to land, how to roll. I never really got hurt, but I sure had the wind knocked out of me a few times. Got a few good scrapes and bruises too.

We actually did the things you see people doing in the movies. You know, running full tilt, jumping from car to car on top of a freight train that's going well over 60 miles an hour (that's like, fast, for you youngsters). Shoot, we were waving at the cars the train was *passing* on the highway as we ran along the top of the railcars. It's actually easy to do. TV just makes it look all dramatic and stuff. Just don't trip is all. I did. I don't recommend it.

Doing it though, at 12 years old, howlin' right into the wind at the top of my lungs, owning that train—it's a hard memory to forget. I think railing is actually a form of … madness? It took about 20 odd years after I stopped riding before I could cross a rail line and my stomach didn't pull all kinds of weirdness on me. Personally, now, at my age, I think the moment any child can both walk and talk at the same time they should be immediately declared legally insane and put under guard until age 20!

Anyway, two things happened to me on one of these trips that I'm still trying to understand. One thing's sure: like the rest of what's coming, they were pretty strange. Both had a huge impact on my life and played a major role in shaping me into something I certainly don't understand.

When I was just turning 12 some guy about my age I'd never in my life laid eyes on before called my name as I was walking home from school. He walked right up to me out of the blue just like he knew me and says he and a friend of his were going to run away from home and did I want to go with them.

Now why in the world this character figured I'd go with them I'll never know. It was only my second day at that particular school, so I knew that this guy couldn't know too much about me. I was just a little puzzled as to why he would ask me in particular. I mean, did I have a blinking neon light on my forehead that read *"Complete Total Whack Job"* or something? But what surprised me even more (and I remember this very clearly) was how quickly I said, "Yeah, sure! When do we leave?" Just like that! I didn't even think about it—as in, zero hesitation. (I was just like that in those days ... hormones, maybe?)

Perhaps it was because I'd never done anything like that before—I mean run away for real—and at that age there really wasn't very much I wouldn't try to add a little drama and adventure to my life. What I couldn't have known was that on this little adventure I would discover things about myself that would forever change my whole way of thinking and, in a very real way, define my existence for many years ... well, for the rest of my life actually. *Again, and I want to be crystal clear about this—I didn't have any choice about what happened. I did nothing to seek this out.* It was like all of it was there already, just waiting for me, marking time till I was ready for it to pop up.

At any rate, we all met and started to chew things over. After we had hashed things out we came up with what we figured was a good plan. It was bold and decisive, and the proof was in the pudding. It worked. This scheme of ours involved Greyhound buses, stealthy backtracking to throw off pursuers, hitchhiking, and hopping two different freight trains (by moonlight) and was just complicated enough to placate three young boys' thirst for intrigue and adventure—a secret mission, to which we all swore undying allegiance. At its end, it would leave us on the outskirts of a humble northern Ontario town called Malachi (which I thought was very cool). Once there we would hop our last freight to a small isolated cabin on the shore of a frozen lake. That this was in the middle of February didn't even enter the equation. We were Winnipeg boys! We didn't even sneeze in Ontario weather!

Now, at the time I didn't know it, but God caused the weather we encountered on this little odyssey (my very first time hitchhiking) to suddenly and quite unexpectedly turn unseasonably warm. Everyone we met kept commenting on it. "Well, we sure weren't expecting weather like this right now!" I was, of course, completely oblivious to this little coincidence. All was simply as it should have been, as it always was. It was in fact a beautifully enchanting night.

It was perfect out, with not a single cloud in the vast night sky, and that far north the heavens indeed proclaimed the handiwork of God. All was black and white and sparkling silver. Not a breath of wind stirred, and the tall evergreen forest lay silent on all sides. Quiet. Still. Peaceful in a way I had never before known. The stars shone brilliantly all about us. Even the asphalt highway sparkled with every colour of the rainbow, reflecting in tiny treasures the bright moon above us. Diamonds—everywhere I looked! Riches beyond my wildest dreams! All I could hear was the muffled breathing of my companions and the quiet scrape of our boots on a black highway that stretched, it seemed, for an eternity before me. And oh! How that road seemed to call to me, stirring inside me a sense of freedom I had never before experienced and suddenly realized I had always longed for. That night the highway bore a child ... and that naked soul was me. I had been reborn and belonged heart and soul to the road—like I was bewitched, enchanted in a way that moved me to my very core. For the first time in my life I felt freedom! And it was this feeling that kept me returning to the highway like my lover. It was as though I had been unchained, free to explore a vast new world.

Or so I thought ... as things were to turn out, the highway was to become a most horribly cruel and diabolically treacherous mistress, and I would be lashed down that insatiable road into a deeper and deeper bondage, year after year—to my very death, and then back again. Hindsight is always 20/20.

At that time, Malachi had no population listed. The only thing that even gave it a name was a train station situated about 15 feet away from the rail line. So, with no roads into my friend's cabin, the only way to get to us besides train would be by ski plane, or so we thought. Antarctica was overpopulated compared to this place. As I think on it, if any of us had been hurt up there ...

I have no idea what in the world we were thinking. Three 12-year-olds way north in the deepest part of a northern Ontario winter with nothing but a few canned goods and an old .22 rifle? I think we actually had some hazy idea we were going to hunt all winter. The great woodland hunters! We actually did shoot a squirrel (with a .22?!), triumphantly carried it home, skinned it, and tried to eat it. I think we scraped the pitiful bits of flesh that were left on the poor thing into a can of beans and tried to convince ourselves how good squirrel stew tasted. Yep! We nailed that varmint's hide onto what we finally declared to be "Squirrel Wall" (after much debate) and vowed there would be many more to join it. I put the tail in my cap, of course. Somehow, I think that as mighty woodland hunters went, we were just a tad short.

Now you know how we got there. What comes next is where it starts to get really interesting.

Remember the plane crash that killed everybody? That my brother, my mother, and my father all knew would happen? Well, I think I probably knew when I was inside my mom, 'cause this story is kind of like that only there's no airplane in this tale—but there is a helicopter.

We'd been there about four or five days. One morning I was awakened out of a dead sleep by a very powerful jolt, and suddenly I knew beyond any shadow of doubt that "they" were on the way. I had no idea who "they" were, but I was absolutely certain they were coming *for us* and that whatever was going to happen was going to happen quick! ... It almost felt like some sort of emergency shock buzzer alarm button got pressed somewhere way down inside me—an extremely urgent feeling that left absolutely no room for doubt that whoever was coming for us was already headed our way at top speed that very moment! I remember jumping wide-eyed out of my bunk in a complete panic and *immediately* yelling really loud at my pals, *"Get the heck up, you guys. They're on their way for us ... RIGHT NOW!"*

They thought I'd gone starky—that I'd completely lost it. I started rushing wildly around the cabin, stuffing clothes in my bag, madly hopping around on one foot getting my boots, hat, and gloves together and trying to figure out how to erase all evidence we had been there all at once—and was still screaming like a mad man at the boys the whole time, *"Wake the heck up ... NOW!"*

They thought I'd gone mad with cabin fever. At least that was the response I got. They told me more than once, "Cabin fever, Kev! It happens!" And then began telling tales of trappers gone insane, killing and eating their buddies and running madly off into blizzards naked, never to be seen again.

They just didn't understand, and I had no way of explaining it to them. All I knew was that they were on their way. By the time I was ready with my hand on the doorknob my pals were still talking about breakfast!

The certainty I was feeling was getting stronger every moment, and I was becoming frantic because no matter how many times I told them "they" were coming—*now*—the two of them kept dawdling around and asking stupid questions I couldn't answer. By the time they were finally ready I was screaming that I would leave them behind, "'cause I'm going, with or without you!"

I told them to shoulder their packs, opened the door just a crack, looked out, and then shut the door real quick. I remember very clearly looking at my two pals and shaking my head with a frustrated sigh. Then I threw the door wide open. Racing across the frozen lake straight toward us was a black and white helicopter. It only took a few seconds to make out the OPP markings. A few more and all of us could hear the megaphone blaring, "It's no use running, boys! We have the rails blocked off at both ends. Stay where you are until we land!"

As I stepped through the door, I recall looking over to the woods and the rail line. I knew it wasn't blocked, and that day I cussed myself out for being an idiot and not leaving. I knew that had I left when I should have, they would not have found me. Not until I wanted to be found. Now they knew we were in the area, and there was no place to run. It really didn't matter anymore. Me being me, I would have run anyway, but I didn't need to. Knowing that I could have was enough (for the time being). Of course, the OPP returned us to Winnipeg, first by helicopter to a city, then by plane to be met by our folks.

I don't remember exactly what all happened, but I know I was gone again within a week.

Even though what I had felt was urgent and powerfully alarming, it felt almost normal. Natural, like it was a part of me and not from outside of me. I didn't even question it. Not really. Once recognized, it seemed somehow as if it had always been there.

The others wondered. After the OPP brought us home, my friends asked how I knew the cops were coming. I had no more idea than they did, so I just told them I could feel my nose turning red when cops were around. After a while my friends started thinking I was kind of weird, and they didn't want to hang around me too much. I think it made them uncomfortable.

I learned later that I could kind of control it. I experimented with it for a while and I was pretty accurate every time. It was easy. All I had to do was extend my spirit. Just push it out there and check things out—

sometimes over quite some distances, sometimes over several hundred miles. Then again, some of it was just common sense and intuitiveness. But there was far more to it than just that. This knowing was not just limited to police. I could sense other things as well ... in people.

I think after a bit I just got bored of it and stuffed it into the kit of survival skills I would come to accumulate over the years. But this ... "thing" that had so suddenly popped into my life did not lie dormant. As time passed, it became far more refined and much more—useful.

Here is just one example of exactly how refined and how useful it could be. By this point, I'd had years of practice, though.

Before you read this, please try to understand what I'm trying to do here. I'm going to take only one example from each kind of weirdness in my life that best describes what it is I'm trying to comprehend. I'm trying to figure out what in the world these things are, where they come from, and what they're there for. You know, the reason for them—why they happen. I have ideas, but that's all I have.

Anyway, anyone I ever hitchhiked with knew about this little ... oddity of mine. For quite a few years I travelled around Canada with a road partner I will call Bruce. He could keep the pace and was good for his word. A real hard one, he was. We had already hiked coast-to-coast trips several times and made more quick trips over the Rockies (Vancouver to Calgary, or vice versa) than I can keep track of. Nine or ten years we blew around the highways all over Canada together with not much in the way of downtime at all. On one of our later trips we picked up some baggage in Ottawa. Bruce went and found himself a girl, tough as he was.

The three of us were all hard-bitten highway trash (rather rare really), a peculiar breed, preferring the highway and the life and quietness it afforded to the crowded filth of the cities with their violence and insanity. Personally, at the latter part of my hiking I rarely ventured past the outskirts of any place unless it was pretty darn small.

We had been kicking it around for about four or five months when we decided to hole up at an abandoned cement factory on the outskirts of Regina. We thought we'd take a break, rest up, and get good and drunk for a while. Believe me, we made a pretty curious looking trio. All of us were road-hardened, well-seasoned hikers, and let's just say we looked it.

Bruce and Norma made a rather unusual couple. He was a six-foot-six lanky Scotsman, with long curly reddish-brown hair, from which he was forever pulling various twigs and grasses, and Norma was a short stocky Native girl who prided herself on being stronger than most men. (She was, too!) She would just laugh in derision when guys would try to shoulder her green army duffel bag, full of our wet dirty laundry, she so proudly toted. Norma pulled her load and asked no quarter. A few years later, though, our lifestyle finally drove her almost out of her mind—literally. It made me very sad to see it. Actually, it drove two women half-crazy. There was nothing we could do about it. I ... we ... lived in a very strange world where strange things happening were simply a part of the whole. You had to accept things as they were. There were only a few who could handle the kind or amount of stress our life created.

Even though I had more experience on the road than the two of them put together, they were still top-notch highway folk. Far better than most I'd travelled with. The facts were, I couldn't afford to travel with lightweights. The highway had been my path for many years by the time I ran into Bruce, let alone Norma, and I couldn't afford to babysit. That could get real dangerous. Unless you could completely trust your partner to keep aware, it could get a guy dead.

It was hard all the years I travelled alone. You see, I loved people, but there just weren't a lot of folks who could keep up or could even stand it for that matter. Believe me, I've had a number of folk try to travel with me only to watch them get hurt, tossed in jail, or just fade out on me. As I said, real road trash are kind of a dying breed. They're almost extinct now. It was all in the temperament I guess. We were folk who knew how to sleep in a snowbank and not freeze to death. You got real creative on the road.

One of the most important attributes any highwayman can have is a real good sense of humour in real bad situations (among other things I won't mention). Norma was always easy to be around—funny, smart, tough. She could see a bright spot on the dark side of the moon and would be quick to point it out when things got tough.

She had an infectious grin and, once you got to know her, a cheerful easy-going manner. I must say though, I'd seen her knock a couple of girls right unconscious (and a man, too). I guess it was the getting to know her part that was kinda hard.

Bruce was very intelligent, an actual card-carrying member of Mensa, *extremely* cunning, and well trained in some of the more brutal forms of combat. Yet despite that, he had a sense of humour that was priceless and had a way of cheering a guy up quick—a good man to have at your back. Trust was implicit. We had all paid our dues—road tax, if you will. Then there was me. That I'll leave to your imagination.

The main thing was, we all got along really well. We understood each other, and we knew how to function as a unit very effectively. In almost any given circumstance, everyone knew their part and what was expected. We could read a play coming down, and each one of us knew exactly what to do and had respect for the special gifts and abilities of the others. We could also laugh together, and we did—often.

The factory was one of our regular stops. Sheltered from wind and rain, unexposed to the public, yet still close enough to all amenities (most importantly the beer store), it was an oasis in the middle of a prairie desert. We were also well known and liked by the locals. A lot of them looked on our arrival as an annual event and would actually worry if we were late. They would often bring "beer, blankets, and bongs" in the evening and then sit around and listen to Bruce and me play guitar and tell tales of our latest crazy adventures across the country.

At any rate, we had been there two or three days when it happened. I had awoken before the others and as was my custom had begun casting about, sniffing the wind, and sensing ... other things as well.

Norma woke up, and when she saw me, she knew exactly what I was doing. Bruce always had a hard time with it (I think it scared him), but it seems for some reason Natives have a much easier time handling ... what I was doing. "What's out there, Kev?" she inquired. Bruce began to wake up.

I was about to say "Nothing," as I was usually only concerned with anything in the immediate area that could be a real and direct threat, but on impulse I focused and pushed a little harder. It was like a combination of seeing and knowing all at the same time. These are the words I that morning.

"In about fifteen—no ... in about twenty minutes there cop cars—no ... four cop cars are going to roll up on us. for someone, but it's none of us. They are going to give

They will make us scatter our clothes and bags out onto the concrete—I mean spread them right out, but they'll find nothing they are looking for. One of the cops is going to have his gun drawn. It will be pointing at the ground. After they ask us a whole bunch of questions, they'll leave us alone and go their way. Everything will be fine. The trouble is coming from over there." I then indicated a group of houses across the field from us. I repeated what I said about the gun and the clothes at least two or three times.

Norma got up immediately and started picking up all the empty beer cans and organizing the cases. (We had a heck of a lot of cases.) Bruce was listening, but he just looked at me sideways and said nothing, shaking his head a bit.

When he saw what Norma was doing he asked her what she was up to. Replying over her shoulder she said quite confidently, "You heard what he said!" and kept right on working. Like I said, Natives are just better with this kind of thing than most white people. Unfortunately, this blessing can also be a curse for them. Shamanism is tricky business.

Between us we got the camp organized. I advised both of them to keep any weapons in plain sight and to stash all contraband. I also warned them to telegraph any moves and be slow and deliberate if they had to move at all. I knew this was going to happen and that there would be a sidearm somewhere in the picture. When we were done, we all cracked a beer, sat on our backpacks, and basically started enjoying the morning.

All of us had plenty of contact with highway RCMP in the past. They were generally a good bunch—cops doing their jobs. Most of the ones we dealt with knew all of us, either personally or via reputation. We stayed out of trouble. They knew what we were and never really gave us a hard time at all. We _____ nd expected the same.

___ t I said unfolded right in front of our eyes. ___ ree cruisers rolled up and stopped about 25 ___ but no one got out. They seem to be waiting ___ cruiser pulled up and parked a little off to ___'s when the other three officers walked over

___ our clothes out all over the concrete, and ___ ff, and us, right down to our shorts. They actually stuck me in a poncho, raincoat, a pair of shades, and a bandanna (I guess they were trying to make me look suspicious) and told me to stand apart from the others. Then while I was standing there all dolled up, still yet another cruiser rolled up with an elderly woman in the back. She gave me a good look and indicated a negative, and the car pulled away. That's when I saw the gun. Through the crack of the open door of the cruiser that had parked at a distance I could see that the officer behind it was holding his gun with both hands, pointing it at the ground.

As the cops were pretty much finished with us I walked slowly over to the older cop and smiling asked, "What were you going to do with that?" He never took his eyes off my partners but smiled very nervously in return and said, "I'm too old to take chances!" I agreed. Then I asked, "What's all this about anyway?"

"A lady over there," indicating the buildings I had pointed to earlier, "had her place broken into, and she saw who did it."

After a bit of radio work the cops went their way, and Norma and I started talking about what happened. That's when I saw Bruce looking at me real quiet like as he drank his beer. I don't think he quite trusted me after that. Like I said, it scared him a little.

That was all right. I'd gotten used to folks looking at me strange over the years. People had been looking at me funny since the first time it happened, so I had a lot of years of practice dealing with it. I was often looked at as a bit odd. "Whacked," I call it. I can tell you whole bunches of stories just like this one. Some of them a whole lot stranger, but the content is, well … unhelpful.

And what would be the point? I could tell you how I knew from over three hundred miles away, after not speaking with him for a couple of years, that this same Bruce was making a move from BC to Toronto, raced all the way across country to intercept him, and missed him by *less* than 10 minutes. People witnessed that. But that's not the point.

The point is—I'm the one who has to live with this crap! It's all part of this big mess of things I'm trying to figure out—that I want to make sense out of. The hard part about stuff like this is trying to find somebody who's not a witch or a warlock to talk with about it. I have found very few mature Christians who really understand how this stuff works. I myself am just beginning to understand the difference between the godly use of spiritual gifts and witchcraft. I'm pretty sure it has to do with using the gift under the anointing and direction of the Holy Spirit for the building up of the body of Christ and the furtherance of the gospel (instead of accomplishing my own agendas and gaining power and influence). I may not be able to explain it right, but I'll tell you one thing—I'm a heck of a lot more careful with it after tangling with a few covens! (I'll get to that as well.)

And I was a Christian through 98 percent of what I'm about to tell you. Do you have any idea what that does to a guy's head? I had already been trying to get sober for years by then. Every time I'd give up, God would do something crazy to get my attention. He never let me go. I was his child. But I'll let God speak for himself on that score. He sure spoke to me enough about it.

Like almost all the stuff that's happened, every single time *it came looking for me.* This "thing inside me" happened on its own accord without any help from me, and I'll tell you for sure, I certainly didn't go looking for it. I had no idea anything like it existed. It was something already there. God put it in me. And how do you tell God to get lost or start complaining about it? I've noticed he's a tad deaf at times. After much prayer, he has finally spoken clearly to me about this little oddity of mine, and for now I am to leave it alone.

4
THE FACTS

I need to stop a moment and explain a few things that are very important.
If you haven't figured it out yet, I'm an alcoholic, "type four." That's
the hopeless kind. If there were a type ten it would describe me to a T.
Whatever it is that makes men, women, and many children (such as I was
when I started) drink to the point of insanity, deprivation, degradation,
and death—whatever that quirk is, I have it in spades. (You will notice I
use the present tense.)

Alcohol took my life before I even had a chance to have one. I started
drinking way too early to know anything different. It simply never even
occurred to me to *be* any different. It seemed I'd always been that way.
I just assumed that drinking was simply part of the "being bad" thing.
There was no childhood, no graduations, no girlfriends, no nothing for
me—not even any childhood friends. Not really. From age 10 on I began
to live alone and apart, isolated from my peers. Any relationships I did
have were built upon principles of mutual convenience. The person had
to have skills or tools I could use to get us both more alcohol and drugs—
that was it. There was only booze—booze, drugs, and the search for a
more effective way to get both.

Looking for, obtaining, and drinking alcohol became the most
important things in my life from the very first time I drank—right along
with getting every other kind of drug I could get my hands on. The moment
I had my first taste of alcohol, something in me clicked on like a long-

buried switch that had been just waiting for the right chemical sequence to activate it. My reaction to it was immediate and almost violent.

I had seen my father having a glass of sherry one evening while he was reading a book in his study. That damnable curiosity got a hold of me, and I decided I would try some. I snuck over to the liquor cabinet, found the sherry (Dry Sack), and had a good long pull. A couple of minutes later it seemed as though the heavens had opened up! It was wonderful. I had to have more—and man oh man, I got more, all right! After the first taste, I waited for my parents to go to bed, snuck downstairs, and drank just about the entire liquor cabinet's contents. I think there may have been one bottle of wine left. My father said I'd have drunk the cabinet itself were it possible. He woke the next morning to find me unconscious, covered in my own vomit, lying on the living room floor, surrounded by empty wine bottles, with an almost-empty jug of brandy in my hand. All I can remember is looking up at him and hearing him say, "Kevin, I think you may be alcoholic" (an astute comment from the director of the Chemical Withdrawal Unit at the Health Sciences Centre in Winnipeg). I had no idea what he was talking about. I found out in a quick hurry.

Now when you mix the physiological reaction of my body to alcohol with its psychological effects, the sense of confidence and security it brought to a frightened and insecure child, you can easily see why it's no small wonder that alcohol and I immediately became the very best of friends. Alcohol seemed to take away the fear that I was so afraid of. It wasn't that I was afraid of anything in particular. I was afraid of fear and felt I must eliminate it from every aspect of my life—or else I'd have to consider myself a coward. This I went to great lengths to do. I had to prove to myself that I was afraid of nothing. This self-imposed insanity almost killed me many times. For me, this saying was so true: "There is nothing to fear but fear itself." I started drinking at age 10. After that, the only life I knew was the one alcohol and drugs dictated. I would do anything, whatever the cost, to not feel that fear hammering at my chest, and for me that meant I had to "drink with a vengeance."

Experts define alcoholism as a bio-psycho social disease. Seems a nice, tidy, and informative sort of diagnosis. I'm sure it beats "insane drunken sot … ism" or any of the other more descriptive titles for an alcoholic. I personally prefer "he's an angel—with an amazing capacity for whisky," but that doesn't seem to fly with a lot of people I know. What it actually means is that its effect impacts every single aspect of a person's life. Physically, mentally, emotionally, and socially the alcoholic becomes gravely ill. The main thing left out in that description is how it affects a person's spiritual life. Mildly put, it poisons the soul and brings death to everything and everyone it touches.

All I know is that the moment I drank it, I never stood a chance. I was simply unable to defend myself against it. I didn't even know I *should* have defended myself. I knew that it was part of the "being bad" package, but that was it. I had no idea the first day I drank alcohol that the course of my entire life had been determined.

As I look back, it is amazing to me the ingenuity, audacity, and tenacity I showed at that age in obtaining it. As I mentioned earlier, I ran crews of my own panhandlers in the streets by the time I was around 11 or 12. They brought me the money; I got the booze. When the liquor stores went on strike, I simply smashed their windows out with a shovel, took all the Texas Mickeys (that's the really big bottles), and created my own parties. I stole everything that wasn't nailed down. I would pretend I was walking into a liquor store with my dad by striking up a conversation with a total stranger as he walked in and then leave with a stolen bottle to pretend I was waiting outside for him. I also was an amazingly good pool player by the time I was 15 and could sneak into the back of bars, where everyone would have to buy my beer, and then there was always panhandling—the list of how to get booze was as vast as my imagination. Not to mention, booze was only four dollars for 18 beers when I started to actually buy the stuff. Drugs were much easier to get, so for a time the balance shifted, but alcohol was always my first love. So it began. A lifetime full of pain and confusion, both for me and for everyone my life touched.

There is another definition not so tidy as a bio-psycho social disease. I once heard an unusually wise, educated, and godly man—a long-standing member of Alcoholics Anonymous, with many years of solid sobriety—define it like this: "Alcoholism is the most complete, horrifying, and destructive disease on the face of the planet. It is like no other. Of all terminal illnesses in the world it is the most terminal. It is complete sickness of the body, mind, emotion, and soul brought about by the compulsive use of ethyl alcohol. It results in the total and utter annihilation of body and soul."

The "Big Book" of Alcoholics Anonymous agrees and supports this definition completely: "with it there goes annihilation of all things worthwhile in life. It engulfs all whose lives touch the sufferers. It brings misunderstanding, fierce resentment, financial insecurities, disgusted friends and employers, warped lives of blameless children, sad wives and parents—anyone can increase the list."[5]

This nightmare is what I must wake up to, acknowledge, and accept every single day for the rest of my life. It will never stop until I am dead, and there is absolutely no known cure for it, now or in any foreseeable future. Until very recently, alcoholics would either die, go insane, commit suicide, or be committed to sanatoriums, jails, or asylums for the rest of their lives. Before AA came on the scene, alcoholism was a death sentence. There was really no hope for any of them ... for any of us.

It sounds pretty grim, and so it is. Its effect on humankind has been—is—incalculable. But had I not had this condition I could never have come to know the incredible love, mercy, and kindness of God as I do now. It is a price I would gladly pay again. I doubt, however, that others in my life would say the same thing. The toll it took on my loved ones has been horrific.

What I have found is that alcoholism, while being incurable, can be managed, but oddly enough it can only be *effectively* managed by an ongoing, vital, constantly growing and ever-expanding relationship with God. It is the only physical disease I am aware of that requires a relationship with God as its primary management tool.

What is so amazing about this, and what I have now come to believe, is that God somehow built a fail-safe right into my system, ensuring that in order for me to survive (and that means to not die in every way) I must seek to grow and remain in intimate relationship with him, always, in every single aspect of my life, in every single way, every single day, for the rest of my life, or I'm as good as dead or wishing I were. There is no middle path—and there can be no reservations. *For me ... to drink is to die.*

---

[5] *Alcoholics Anonymous: The Story of How Many Thousands of Men and Women Have Recovered from Alcoholism*, 4th ed. (New York: Alcoholics Anonymous World Services, Inc., 2008), 18.

Over the years I have slowly come to see what an incredible blessing my alcoholism has turned out to be. God loved me so much that he has not only kept me alive but designed me so that in order to stay that way I must have genuine closeness and intimacy with him. If I walk in the freedom of loving him and in the joy of doing his will instead of my own ... if I love others as a way of life, what a blessing to myself and to them! God is the only strength that can relieve me of the obsession to drink. I cannot afford secret sins or unyieldedness in any area of my life that he puts his finger on—besides, who wants to carry around the stench of rotting sin? I must remain in the sunlight of his Spirit, or I will drink again, guaranteed. In a very real sense this illness binds me to God in a way I could never have otherwise experienced.

I tremble before such love. For so many years I have cried out, asking, pleading, for God to help me, desperately begging for the strength to resist, to overcome this terrible addiction and all the sin that always goes with it. But it wasn't until I began to see how much God actually loved me and felt the impact of that knowledge begin to slowly break over my understanding that I finally felt a surge of hope spring up in my wounded heart, and my soul began to heal and come alive.

Until that happened I had been desperately, hopelessly, agonizingly lost. I could see the shore. I could smell the deep rich soil of God's love, but I could never seem to reach it. I could never draw any closer, no matter what I did. All of my efforts ended the same way—complete and total failure every single time. I was blind and hopeless—and freedom, it seemed, lay far beyond my reach. That was, until very recently. Having tasted utter defeat, there was more I was to experience. I was to come to see that God's love and faithfulness was far, far greater than my failure—so, here goes ...

5
THE CHALLENGE

I've spent an awful lot of my life just hiking from one place to the next. There was never any real reason for it. I guess I just loved being on the road is all. I was good at it. I think it was the struggle—the sense of doing the impossible—hiking coast to coast without a penny in my pocket when I'd start. I loved the sound of it—of the tires fading to nothing on an empty highway—and falling asleep, wrapped up in my bag and tarp, listening to the rain pattering down on me, gently loving me to sleep. As I think back, it seems I've always been headed somewhere—with nothing but me, my guitar, and one backpack. There were a few times I tried to settle, and I would for a short time, but I just couldn't stand it. Every time that road beckoned I would answer and leave behind everything I'd hoped to build.

I guess what drew me most was the not knowing—not knowing who I was going to meet or who I was going to see again—and not knowing what would happen next. And the people ... no matter where I stopped there was always some kind of character full of surprises. It was not knowing what in the world I would see this time or where in the world the road would take me next. All of it was part of the sense of freedom I felt so profoundly that first night on the highway long ago and that eventually came to drive me mercilessly for so long.

Now being a long-haired, hitchhiking, guitar-playing, hillbilly freak took me to a lot of places that they don't really advertise in travel brochures. If they did, there would be a box at the bottom of each one to tick for how much money you'll send and another box for how many days of fasting and prayer you'll commit to the place. I could go on for hours about all the bizarre places and strange situations I've found myself in, but I'd just get lost real quick if I did. But there was this one place ...

I probably would have been in my late twenties at the time, so I was still young and spry enough to cover a lot of ground without stopping, but every once in a while, some "thing" or some "one" would catch my attention, and I'd hit the binders to linger a bit.

I was drifting through the Rockies to the Okanagan Valley and passed through a little place called Falkland. It's nestled in a mountain pass off the main highway just about halfway between Kamloops and Vernon. The entire population of the town and its environs was only about two hundred souls. That's in tourist season. Its claim to fame was a surprisingly large bar at which the Hells Angels held their annual biker rally—that, and the local witch, who had a bi-weekly question and answer radio show broadcast over most of BC. I didn't find any of this out till after I had been there a while.

Anyways, I had some cash, so I figured I'd stop at the bar, drink a few beers, play some pool, and meet a few of the locals—perhaps maybe do some picking. That's pretty much how I supported myself already over the years. I could play the mandolin, harmonica, and guitar, and I sang pretty well too. At least that's what people told me.

The pool table was at the front of the bar, which was pretty crowded, so I couldn't help brushing up against a girl who was standing at the table playing. I said "excuse me" and lightly touched her with my hand to let her know I was passing by.

Well, literally the instant I touched her she just sort of crumpled up and went down on one knee to the floor. She glanced around behind her at me, startled, and exclaimed, "Knocked me over with a feather!" (I've often wondered about what she meant by that.) Then she straightened up and had a good look at me. I apologized immediately, even though I hadn't the slightest idea what had just happened, and said, "So sorry, I didn't mean to!" and then carefully made my way over to the bar. I was intrigued now by what had just happened, so I ordered a beer and then moved to a spot where I could look but not be looked at.

My ability to assess people is huge when I focus. For the kind of life I lived, it really had to be, or I could be in real serious trouble, real quick. I've spent many hours observing and analyzing people's motives and behaviour over the years, and as I watched her, I knew intuitively there was some sort of strong spiritual component in her life. I've always seemed to be able to sense stuff like that in other people and was always drawn to it. I was also rarely wrong about it either, for good or bad.

She was quite a skilled pool player, so I decided to challenge the table. At that time in my life you had to be very, very good to beat me. I won, so as is customary, she bought me a beer and invited me to sit with her and her friend (an interesting looking lady a few years older than her) and shoot the breeze for a bit. As soon as I sat down, this other woman set my alarm systems ringing like crazy, so now I was even more curious and wanted to know why. I very quickly found out.

Over the years I have found that one of the fastest ways to really get to know someone is to listen for clues as to where they stand spiritually—what their belief systems are. It's surprising, if you listen carefully and know the right questions to ask, how much people will reveal about themselves. Folks like to talk about themselves, so genuine interest in them is always welcomed. Then there's the old adage, *in vino veritas*, right? That's why bars can be good places to talk. I've found, over the years, the best way to get to know a guy is to either get drunk with him or get into a good scrap with him. With my best friends, it's almost always been both. (Most of 'em are almost as crazy as I am.) My advice on women? Don't fight; *run!*

As things turned out, I was seated with the "Wild Witch of Pinaus Lake," the one with the radio show, and her cohort and aspiring pupil, a Jehovah's Witness I shall call Lee.

We talked and played a few more games, and as we did I told them a little about myself, where I'd been, where I was going—stuff like that. After we talked a bit more they invited me to stay the night at their house instead of out in the woods, as I had grown accustomed to. I think they could see that I was pretty road weary. I hadn't slept indoors for months that year, and a hot shower sounded real good to me after jumping into lakes and rivers first thing in the morning (if there were any nearby). Besides, any place with beer and good company was better than sitting alone in the woods at night. I gratefully accepted the invitation.

This was not an unusual happening. I've received many such invitations over the years. People, I think, could sense that although I was quite capable of creating serious trouble, I was honest and had a good heart. I also think they felt they were in some way becoming a part of something—some story yet to be told; they were right. Plus, almost everyone enjoys a for-real wandering minstrel.

Tales of the road were just as big a part of what I did as music and song were, so I played and sang and told my tales as we chatted and drank a few more beers at their place. Late into the night, right out of the blue, the witch asked me if I would consider being the male counterpoint for her female coven. I found that quite disturbing. I declined her offer, politely but firmly. I also began to suspect that God was up to something. Trust me on this: God is a *very* busy person. He is literally always up to something. I'd seen him work in unusual ways many times by then, and I was seeing his fingerprints beginning to materialize in this situation.

It seemed I had always been running into witches of some sort or another my entire life, and this was not the first time this kind of offer had been made. I used to be puzzled as to why this was so. (I've learned an awful lot since then, and I now understand why.)

As things would have it, Lee had her own place, and she said she really didn't mind if I stayed on with her for a bit. Well, seeing as how we got along real well, I accepted her offer. I think I was simply lonely. You must understand I had no real friends, no wife or girlfriend, no home, and had been travelling hard and alone on the highway for years by then. This was long before I met Bruce or Norma. We both knew I wasn't going to stick around for long, but it seems that emptiness echoes to emptiness a curious call.

Besides, it was beautiful up there in the mountains, and with such sweet company and plenty of beer, what tired and lonely hiker wouldn't want to linger awhile? I had spent so many years on the road going from province to province, never really staying anywhere very long, swapping music and tales for company and beer and then just moving on. I'd pretty much done that my entire life up to that point.

Sometimes it got real painful, and sometimes it could get terribly lonely. It was always tricky (and dangerous), but by that time I had met so many amazing people and seen and done so many wonderful things that the highway's claim on me was absolute and unchallenged. It was bittersweet really, but it was also the only life I'd ever really known or was any good at.

Now I'd always known I'd been running either to something or from something, but I just never seemed to be able to escape it or catch it, no matter how fast I ran. I supposed it was God, but I had no idea what would happen if I ever outran him or he ever caught up to me.

I had always been roving hard, but this time I decided I'd stay a bit for a change.

Over time Lee and I found we really enjoyed talking together and had covered a whole multitude of topics in our discussions. Late one particular night we found ourselves discussing religion, and the Bible seemed to be the focus of that evening's inquiry and debate. We were both surprisingly well versed in the Scriptures, and as people often do when discussing such topics, we found ourselves disagreeing on a few things, particularly the deity of Christ. We had been battling this question back and forth for quite some time, and it seemed that neither of us was getting anywhere with the other. She kept insisting that Jesus wasn't God but rather "a god," and I kept insisting he was God and the only one at that.

I knew this was so for several reasons. First, I knew what the Scriptures said about him (never mind what he said about himself); second, he and I had been battling back and forth for years by then; and third, I had seen him with my own eyes on two different occasions. (No worries! I'll get to that later.) Our fight had to do with this power struggle we'd been having for many years. He thought he was Boss Universal, and I disagreed. Also, he wanted to love me, and I didn't know how to handle that. Nope. I was too afraid to allow that to happen. Funny thing though. I've found that God just seems to do whatever he wants, regardless of how I feel about it. It gets annoying after a while. But what's a guy supposed to do? He's bigger than I am.

Anyway, speaking of power, there just comes a time in every … difference of opinion, if you will, when after all concessions have been made, all arguments have been exhausted, and decorum and dignity have gone the way of the wind; when neither side is willing to budge one more inch, and all further discussion amounts to no more than two hoots in a wind storm and a hill of beans—that's when things always boil down to that one simple thing: power. Yep, that's right—power—and who's got more of it. Lee and I had found ourselves at an impasse and had both settled back to eyeball each other and see which way the wind was going to shift and what would come next. You see, we were, both of us, real fussy about this particular issue, so neither one of us was going to let the sweat dry on it.

Now I don't know if you've ever locked horns with a Jehovah's Witness in a theological discussion before (try a fight to the death, more like it!), but they are notoriously stubborn. I had sat back on the couch to gather my wits and prepare myself for the next foray into heavily fortified positions, and as usual when discussing God with Witnesses, I was finding myself somewhat frustrated. The rubble of my exegeses and soteriological barrages (never mind my badly wounded ego) lay strewn, impotent on a battlefield of endless circular debate with an implacable and bitterly determined foe.

I could tell that Lee hadn't really thought this thing through herself but was just parroting propaganda that had been drilled into her head by somebody who had it drilled into his head, by somebody who had just been flat-out lied to, so I had a hunch there really wasn't any point in further argument. I was stymied, but much like her, I was stubborn and unwilling to admit defeat. Especially when I knew for sure I was right.

As I was analyzing her theological weaknesses and considering my options, for some reason the story of Elijah and the prophets of Baal popped into my head. At the same time, I remembered a sermon I had heard my father preach many years before. It was about God being jealous of his name, about what folks thought about it, about him. I remembered reading many times in the Bible about things like "to the praise of his glorious name" and "that your name would be praised" or "that your name would be glorified," and all the other times that it mentioned stuff like that. I also just kind of had this hunch he liked to show off—*a lot*. I mean, look at all the sunsets and sunrises we've all seen. Come on! Blatant exhibitionism if I've ever seen it. And then, he even wants to know our opinion on all the stuff he's done, what we think about it—about what he's done—like it actually *matters to* him.

Suddenly, bingo! I came up with this great idea! So I quickly turned to Lee and said, "Lee, I've come up with this great idea!" She looked at me, dubious but interested.

I said, "If God is God and we both believe what we believe, then only one of us can be right, right?" She agreed.

"All right then. Instead of us sitting here arguing about it all night, why don't we just do this instead? We both join hands together and pray, each of us to our own God, and tell him all about our argument. Then we ask him to send one person to the door in the next fifteen minutes for just one reason. That's to say, whose god is the right God."

She looked at me and raised her eyebrows. "In the next fifteen minutes?"

"Yup!" says I.

"And for just one reason?"

"That's right."

"In the next fifteen minutes?"

"That's right, fifteen minutes."

"And for only *one* reason, right?"

"That's right. One reason alone."

She looked at me sort of funny, and then she got a kind of funny smile on her face and said, "OK … let's do it." So we did just that. We joined hands, explained our situation to God, and asked for *him* to settle it. To bring someone to the door in the next fifteen minutes to say whose god *is* GOD. Then we said, "Amen." Simple, really. Then we each cracked a beer, sat back, and made small talk for the next five minutes.

Now I'd better reiterate some things for you. First, Falkland's entire population was 200, maybe 250 at the most. (That's being way generous.) It basically had two buildings: a bar and a gas station/restaurant/grocery store, both of which were closed. Second, Falkland itself is off the main highway in the middle of the Rockies, and the closest city is at least 65 kilometres away. Oh yeah, third, it was also about two thirty in the morning (no joke). There simply wasn't any reason for anyone to even come up that road, let alone stop and settle an argument between two half-drunk theologians. In spite of all this, for some reason I just had this real strong hunch God was going to pull this one off somehow. I don't know why; I just did.

After another five minutes we were both sneaking peeks at each other, taking covert glances at a clock that kept on ticking, and both of us were getting more and more fidgety.

You know, an empty highway is a funny thing at night. You can hear a car coming from a long way off before it gets to you, and with less than five minutes on the clock we could both hear the tires ringing on the asphalt. A car was coming, and we sat listening as the tires grew closer and louder. Then, whoever was driving slowed down, turned into the driveway, idled a sec, and then shut the engine down. There was *less* than two minutes on the clock. (I kid you not.)

After a few moments of silence, we both heard the car door slam and the sound of footsteps crunching up the gravel driveway. Then came the knock at the door.

Lee looked over at me, and I remember just gesturing with a shrug and a wry grin. "It's your house." Lee got up off the couch and walked down the hall to the door. I couldn't see, but I heard some low murmuring at the door for about 30 or 40 seconds. As I sat listening to the footsteps walk back down the driveway, Lee came in quietly and sat down beside me. She didn't say anything, but she had this real strange look on her face. As the car drove away I asked her, "Well, who was it?" Lee never looked at me once while she was talking, but these are the words she said.

"That was my ex-boyfriend. He said he was driving down the main highway and started thinking about me. He said he really felt like he had something he wanted to tell me, so he turned off, hoping that I would be at home and awake. Then he said the only reason he drove up here was to tell me that he had left the Jehovah's Witnesses and to tell me that they were wrong and that I *knew* they were wrong too. He said he has left them and has become a Christian and now serves only Jesus Christ, the one true God. Then he said, 'They're wrong, Lee, and you know they're wrong,' and then he just said goodbye and left."

Then I watched as a veil fell over her eyes. It was just like a thick curtain closed shut. I have often puzzled about that. I think perhaps it may have been the spirit of blindness the Bible talks about. It was like seeing a little red light suddenly turn on, only this little light just said "TILT"[6] real quiet like.

---

[6] *Tilt* is a term used in the '70s that refers to shaking a pinball machine too hard while trying to guide the ball, triggering the tilt mechanism on the machine, instantly shutting it down and losing all points gained during that round.

So, what then? Me—I wish I could say I was … amazed? Thrilled? Astonished? I would be lying. I really wasn't. Yes, I could only shake my head in wonder that God had listened and answered our prayers, but not because he had done this amazing miracle. The only reason I was surprised at all was because he had answered a prayer that had come from such lips and hearts as ours—*from the likes of us!* Who in the world were we, anyway? We were just a couple of drunks arguing about God. Drunks argue about God all the time. We were flat-out stone-cold sinners … with a capital S, *and we were right smack in the middle of sinning.* This is the God of the universe we're talking about here, right? You know … the "Red Sea Guy"? Why should it matter to the God of Abraham, Isaac, and Jacob what two people like us thought? I almost felt guilty for not feeling more surprised.

But really, should I have been surprised at all? This wasn't even about me. This was about him, about *his* name. Is it really so surprising that the God of heaven and earth should stick up for himself or for his name? Again? Even to such small and messed-up people as us?

This is about not only how important we are to him—but even more how critically important it is that we understand precisely who and what he is. Pure, white hot, burning, powerfully ravenous love. *God is love!* I already knew he was powerful. He sent that guy out at two thirty in the morning to straighten everything out—whose god *is God!* But it was also to show me, one of the most wretched creatures on the face of this planet, how deeply and passionately he loves me. That not only causes me to shake my head in wonder but also sends legions of angels and demons reeling in amazement! I know now it wasn't a miracle that I needed. I already knew God did miracles. He does 'em all the time. No big deal, right? But for me? Who in the blueberry muffins was I?

What I really longed for and the only thing that could have possibly satisfied my heart was *him.* The Miracle Maker *himself!* Joy inexpressible and beautiful beyond compare! He was the "What" I longed for and the "Who" I needed to fill the aching emptiness in my heart. He was teaching me what the most profound miracle of God truly is. *That only he, and all the love that he is, can quench the raging thirst of the parched soul that had been driving me madly down a highway that led to nowhere but death.* And every time I forget, he does something amazingly kind and generous just to remind me that I belong to him, that he loves me and he will never ever stop loving me!

Miracles are great. I truly have witnessed some amazing things in my time on this planet. Real miracles. But not one of them even comes close to the incredible joy and wonder I experienced when I finally began to grasp and understand just the tiniest fragment of how much God loves me, us, you—his people! That is the real miracle. A miracle is done once, and it's over. The Red Sea parted and closed again, but God's love for us is deeper, richer, and fuller every single day! That is why he has had to shake me again and again to my very core. So I could see it—grasp it. And just that one little fragment was enough. I don't think I could bear more.

As I think back on what happened that night, several things strike me.

First, that man had absolutely no idea he was the star of an amazing story. One that ended in the God of heaven and earth glorifying his name—again. I pray one day he will know how powerfully God used his obedience.

Second, the all-around lowly nature of the characters involved. Think about it! A half-drunk hillbilly, a very stubborn Jehovah's Witness (do you know any other kind?), and a brand-new born-again son of God, played out, no less, before an audience of angels and demons, all watching as God's remarkable plan unfolded once again in space and time.

You see, I don't think it was just Lee and I that were impressed. As I said before, Falkland was known for two things, the Hells Angels and a witch with a radio show. Just a ways beyond and above the town there is a gigantic Canadian flag set in stone right into the side of the mountain. I believe God planted a flag of his own there that night. I think maybe he just wanted to remind the powers that be exactly who they were dealing with. The God who was, and is, and will forever be "the god who *is* God!"

Last, but definitely not least, I am struck by God's ridiculously amazing timing. I mean, *come on*! He wired that thing down to almost the very last second! He even got in the whole ticking bomb thing! It was so close I couldn't even tell! Blatant! Brilliant! Really! I told you. He just loves showing off. And what's really great is that he's just so damn good at it. What an amazing God!

I spoke with Lee again years later, and I asked her, "Do you remember what happened that night a long time ago?" You see, when I saw that curtain fall over her eyes, I could see she was having a real hard time digesting what had happened—processing it, so to speak. It was too much for her. I think it would have been kinda hard on anybody, so I never pressed her after that, and she never brought it up. I just left it alone and let her puzzle on it.

When I asked her that question, she needed no explanation. She just lifted her head up, looked straight into my eyes, and said, "Yes Kevin, I *do* remember ..." and then she looked away. Nothing more was said. Perhaps nothing more needed to be said.

Ode to My Brothers

I was unusually blessed to have been brought up in the family I was born into. Ever since I can remember I was surrounded by a swirl of different languages and colours the likes of which perhaps only another missionary child could fathom. I am sure should you ask one, you would find it so.

Yet even then, it was different for us. Our family moved around so much and to so many different countries, I don't think I really ever understood where I was. My oldest brother, Scott, born in Bolivia, my sister, Liana, and I, both born in Argentina, and the twins, Leith and Miles, born in Peru, would all tell you the same thing. There were dark-skinned Africans in colourful dress, Polynesians with their grand enthusiasm, Chinese with their Pappa John (what they called my dad) and their incessant questioning, Eastern Europeans with their thick accents, and Japanese, cultured and humorous, and then, of course, my beloved Latins, from both North and South America—not to mention Spain as well. In other words, I grew up in a vast mixing bowl of cultures from around the world, a child, it seemed, of many nations. For me it was all normal, as things always were—and I knew only respect and curiosity. It was sometimes a bit strange but always exciting to listen to the stories told around the dinner table.

Because of my father's work, we spent much time in the small outlying villages of different South American towns. Many did not even have running water. My mother has told me tales of me as a half-wild, half-naked child running with all the other boys trying to catch chickens. That our skins and languages were different was of no consequence to us ... we all just wanted to get that cotton-pickin' chicken! (They are really hard to catch!) This was my life for as far back as I can remember. People from Egypt or Israel or Czechoslovakia were all guests in our home or we in theirs. So, to me, everyone was ... someone. Maybe different, but fun to learn about and listen to. Everybody was a person.

Now, I've said all that so you'll understand why I say this. The Indigenous Peoples of Canada hold a place in my heart that is as strong and straightforward as the love I carry in my heart and the blessings I pray for them as a people and a Nation. I've fallen madly in love with some of them, fought like crazy with (and for) others—I've hunted and fished and learned how to make fish stew with roe and bannock from them ... and when no one else in the world would accept me, they took me in and made a place for me among them. I've lived on many different reserves across Canada, and for a while I didn't even like white folk anymore. (There's a lot I still have a hard time with!) They lived in a different world, and, as far as I was concerned, they could keep it, 'cause I sure didn't want it.

I learned how to get on with being busy with life. Our topics of discussion were about which Chinese guy was going to buy the pine mushrooms we picked, who was giving the best price for the spring salmon, and who had the best pack of hounds for moose or deer.

As far as boozers went, no matter where I went in North America, I found the hardest drinking crew I could find, fought my way in, and then made a name for myself. I did the same when I lived among and around Native folk. And if you couldn't keep up, you got left behind, simple as that. Even during my Stateside time, I preferred drinking at Mexican bars where most didn't (or wouldn't) speak any English at all. At first, they couldn't figure out what in the world this crazy white guy was doing, hanging out in such a precarious place—but these were the kind of folk I grew up with as a child, and honestly, I just felt more comfortable there.

When I was first back in Canada from the USA, I met a beautiful and wonderfully talented Ojibwe Cree girl. It was as though we shared one soul, and I would have happily married her in a split second. I was deeply and *truly* in love with her, but somewhere I must have blinked—she got so badly messed up on crack and heroin I just couldn't stand it, and we would have both been destroyed. By that time, I had only just quit using IV drugs and was no longer seeking out any drug other than alcohol (*and alcohol is a drug!*). I really hope to see her again someday, free and clean, but the way she was going, I wonder now if she's even still alive. I have lost so many good friends to opiates and cocaine since the insanity of my addiction began.

Because of my lifestyle all these years, I have crossed paths with Natives of many different Nations, and honestly, I have a deep and abiding love for every one of them. I am instantly drawn to them, and I think they understand me better than any other people on earth. They make sense to me. My heart aches when I think of the times I had with them. I felt like an adopted child whom no one else would take ... till them, and I miss them deeply and dearly.

So, in my tales, when I speak of Natives or Indigenous Peoples, know that I speak as one who knows, loves, and deeply honours them, as I try to do with all men. My heart is with them still. It is a piece that will never come back to me again but will rest there among a people who took me in and understood a part of me no one else on this earth could have.

6
THE LEGACY

God teaches us in many ways. Not all of his lessons are readily apparent. Sometimes it takes years to discover the real meaning behind all the small little journeys we are constantly going through. It's how he shapes us—our outlook and understanding of life; everything we are, all of it, is a glorious collage of intricately woven experience designed and crafted by the wise and loving hands of our master. It is what makes us *us*. He is constantly birthing us into something so beautiful we will never grasp its fullness. Nor will we ever see the end of it. So learn then. Live extravagantly. Savour every experience without fear, knowing that all things (that means everything) work together for our good. All things are in his hands, and he is the one who loves us and calls us his own.

I remember once winding up on a Native reserve way deep into the mountains. I'm pretty sure it was the one across the Fraser River from a little town called Lytton, but wherever it was, you had to take an old pull-rope ferry manned by two Native brothers across the Fraser River. If they didn't like you, you didn't go. Once on the other side of the river, you then faced a 22-mile hike up a winding dirt road even deeper into the Rockies. This was one of the poorer reserves, where a large percentage of the population was alcoholic, and with all the hunting going on up there, almost everyone had a pack of dogs and a loaded rifle in the house or on the front porch. Get the picture?

Two of the guys I was headed up there with were friends of some distant relation I knew. I had met them in a small bar on the "tourist" side of the river earlier, and when I first saw them I got real curious right away. The one had terrible burn scars covering a large portion of his face and body and half an arm that looked as if the other half had been burnt right off. His companion had what looked like a nice sized chunk of his skull and a small piece of his jaw missing. There was a story here, and I (as usual) wanted to hear it.

I bought them a double of whatever they were drinking and then sat down for a chat. It turned out they were brothers. The one had been caught in the fire when his house burned up. He went on to say he erroneously thought his brother was the one who started it to get even about some argument they'd had earlier that day. So, before any help could arrive (it had to come in by helicopter), somehow he managed to grab his rifle, make it to his brother's place next door, and shoot him right in the head. The bullet went straight up through his jaw, then the skull, and took a good bit of that with it when it left. When the helicopter arrived, to their astonishment the medical team found the two of them still alive and flew them both to the hospital. There, they recuperated together. Neither said a word. The mountains kept their own secrets it seems ... and "accidents" were pretty common up around there.

It also seems grudges never last long in the mountains. It was kind of like you either got dead or forgiven—or both. So the misunderstanding was all sorted out, all was forgiven, and there they sat, the best of friends— brothers, having a cold beer together and enjoying the afternoon.

For a second, I didn't know whether to laugh or cry. Then suddenly, *Now that's what I call real "Canadian Hillbillies!"* popped into my ridiculous brain, and I just couldn't help it—beer sprayed everywhere when I burst right out laughing, hard! They started howling too! That's when they invited me back up to the rez. I guess they liked a good sense of humour, or a real twisted one at any rate!

I was the only white guy up there, but it made no difference to them. First off, I pretty much lived my life like I was dead already (helps take the fear out of living), and second, I drank, fought, and thought like most of them anyway, so I fit right in. Besides, I'd been crossing those mountains for many years by then, so I knew lots of folks up around there.

I had hooked up with a bunch of them to hike up to the rez when an elder who was with us stopped me and asked, "Wanna take a shortcut?" It was a challenge, plain as day. I knew he was up to something, but it kinda sounded like fun, so I was all in.

"Sure!" says I. "Beats walking along a dusty dirt road with this drunken rabble," indicating the well-lubricated crew around us (and also incidentally complimenting my elder at the same time). I should have paid more attention to the knowing smiles of the "drunken rabble."

Elder immediately turned around and started walking in the direction we had just come. He had this kind of a funny smile on his face (which got me real curious), and following him closely, I watched as he abruptly turned off the road and started climbing the side of the steepest shale mountain I'd ever seen in my life (which immediately sent my curiosity scampering back, whimpering for forgiveness). Just looking at it made me wonder why the whole mountain didn't slide down and bury every living thing in the entire area. It wasn't that it was so big; it was just that it was so cotton-pickin' *steep!* The thing just seemed to stand there, utterly indifferent to the laws of gravity and common decency.

Well, climb we did—for two straight hours on the slipperiest black shale I certainly had ever encountered. It was like walking uphill on a down escalator. Just before we crested the top, Elder stopped me and indicated he wanted me to sit down with him. Believe me, I sat down quick. Then he looked real hard at me and quietly spoke. "I'm going to show you something precious to us. I'm glad to show it to you in this way. It is the only way to see it. Had you gone down the road that was easy with the rest of them, you would never have seen what I am going to show you now." Then he stood up and indicated for me to follow him, and together we crested the top of what I called "Black Shale Mountain."

What I saw first was a grove of what looked to be oak trees, ancient, with enormously thick, gnarled branches that covered and embraced a small circular clearing of soft velvet moss. It was cool and quiet, and as we slowly entered the small "wood" I saw in the centre of the clearing a rectangle of fine ornate black iron fence. I recognized immediately what it was.

As we approached, I could see the ancient headstone of a well-tended grave at one end. I knew then to walk quietly, for this was ... a sacred place, and I could tell by the care given it and the feel of it that it was deeply loved and to be respected. Then, lifting my eyes, I beheld a wonder that I will remember for the rest of my life.

Running below us, stretching out it seemed forever, lay the most beautiful valley my eyes had ever seen. Green it was, running crosswise to us, and on each side it was guarded by magnificently high snow-capped mountains, powerfully stark against the crystal blue sky. There was what looked to be a large well-kept big-house backed up against the side of the mountain with several outlying buildings and a tractor just emerging from a large two-storey barn. The whole valley was covered in lush thick grass, and from our high vantage point it looked like a quilt of soft, green velvet.

A good-sized river flowed through it, gently winding its way along through the middle of the valley floor. There were free-roaming horses grazing peacefully throughout the valley, and as I watched in wonder I saw seven or eight more at least, running along the riverbank, all tossing and snorting.

Not in any movie or in any picture had I ever beheld such vast, powerful beauty. It seemed to have no end. I stopped and could not speak for a time. It seemed too beautiful to be real, like I was dreaming. I could have gazed down on that valley forever and been happy.

"This is my great-great grandfather's grave. Now, I am grandfather. This is the place where he first stood and looked on this valley. All of this is his land. We take care of it for him."

I walked over to the headstone surrounded by the beautiful iron fence. I wanted to reach out my hand and touch it, but I dared not. Everything about the place seemed quietly powerful. Peaceful in a way I cannot describe. All I could do was to think on a man who could give such a priceless gift to his children, and I was both humbled and deeply honoured to share for a moment such magnificent beauty and such a powerful legacy.

"There are more than five hundred acres running between these two mountains. I wanted you to see it this way first, so you would understand what it is that we love here—*why* we love this place." For a time, we both just stood, and the air was rich with silence. Then, after a bit, we walked together down to the big-house in silence, each carrying that quietness within.

I knew that very shortly there was going to be one heck of a wild gathering, but for a time I walked in the peace of that beautiful valley, beneath crystal blue skies, just on the other side of Black Shale Mountain, and as I walked I thought of a man from long ago and the legacy of what he had left behind.

I learned a precious lesson, too, that day. One I could have learned in no other way—a lesson in beauty and of the hard way, taught to me by four generations of one family, deep in the heart of the mountains.

I will tell you later of other wonders I have seen—visions far more beautiful and far more powerful than the one I saw that day. I could, if I chose, also speak of places I have seen, places that if I told you of them, you would think my words were just the fading echo of a beautiful dream I'd had or that I was reading to you from a fairy tale book. But they are not a dream, and they are no fairy tale. They are very real, and I have been there and seen them with my own eyes. Secret places of unimaginable beauty ... but again, I would just get lost if I did.

Please, forgive my lapse in focus. As I said, I never knew where I would wind up. Perhaps now you can understand why I must stay on track, and why, out of all the places I love to roam around in, British Columbia is my favourite, and why the Rocky Mountains in particular are my greatest stomping grounds ever. Don't get me wrong—I do love the high desert too, but there's something about being smack in the middle of those mountains that does something to my soul. It seems to stir my blood and coax my spirit out of hiding somehow. It's kind of like ... being able to breathe again.

7
THE AWAKENING

Now the whole cotton-pickin' reason I'm writing this is because I just can't help it. You see, there are so many things God has done for me, in me, and to me that I have to say something—*to somebody!* It wasn't until I actually started writing this stuff down that I began to connect the dots and see clearly his love for me over the years. How patient and how kind he has been—how he has always been with me in spite of myself and has never left me once.

I've had a rough life. Although God and I were formally introduced when I was 14, I had been yakking away at him long before that. I know for sure the first time I actually prayed was when I was six years old, and, like most of us the first time we talk to God, I was in a whole world of trouble. Notice I said *I* talked to *him*. He's always talking. We're just deaf is all.

Now you may think a six-year-old can't get into too much serious trouble, but six-year-olds *are* trouble (at least I was), so by my reckoning, six-year-old trouble is almost always exponentially greater than, say, five-year-old trouble or even seven-year-old trouble for that matter (which is trouble of a different kind, as I have already explained). Nope, the kind of trouble I'm talking about is the life-and-death kind of trouble. Serious trouble. Six-year-old trouble. You go right ahead and listen to all the old-timers. Somehow the story always seems to begin with "Well, it all started when I was around … ooh, 'bout six years old I'd say." Sound familiar?

Now, as I was saying, I may have only been six, but even for a six-year-old I was in serious trouble. It was my birthday and I had just turned six. (See what I mean?)

At any rate, where was I … oh yeah, it was my birthday and I had just gotten a brand-new sled. It was Winnipeg in November, so I bundled up all nice and warm and happily waddled off to show my new friend, whom I had just met the day before, my new sled. I wanted to see if he wanted to go sledding, because he had this really great hill just back of his house. I was pretty excited because, at the time, he would have been the very first friend I'd had in my whole life. I never got the chance to talk to him again.

The one street I had to cross was a quiet one, at the bottom of a large hill. The hill was quite steep, and I was quite short, so I couldn't see over the top and neither could the driver of the car that hit me. He nailed me bang on. I got kind of tangled up under a bit, and then the car just spat me out and kept going.

Now I was pretty sharp for a six-year-old, and as I lay in the middle of the road I very quickly became aware of the precarious nature of my predicament. I was stunned, unable to get up, and lay at the bottom of a steep icy hill with the car that hit me still moving away.

I knew that at any moment another car could come over that hill, and even if the driver were able to see me, he would never be able to stop in time. Then I would be run over for the second, and probably last, time. That was the very first time I was consciously aware of praying, and, as I said, like most of us, I was in a whole world of trouble.

My prayer, as such prayers often are, was real simple. It went like this: *"GOD! PLEASE HELP ME!"*

That prayer seemed to be the format for almost all of my other prayers—for a *very* long time. I know it sounds familiar. Seems to me like it's almost always everybody's first prayer. Funny thing is, I don't think God ever gets tired of hearing it. (For some reason I just saw a heavenly restaurant with a big heavy-set angelic short order cook with a great big smile on his face whipping a dinner plate across a counter with me on top of it. DING! DING! "SMALL FRY UP! *TROUBLE* ON THE SIDE!" Sigh … go figure, eh?)

As soon as those words were out of my mouth the car that ran over me stopped immediately, turned around, and came back. I remember taking careful note of this, and I remember knowing my prayer had been both heard and answered.

I wound up with a broken femur, some scrapes and bruises, and half a body cast, but I was alive, and more importantly, I had prayed. I'm really starting to think that the devil tries to kill me every four or five years. I'll explain that later as well.

Actually, perhaps I should do it now and just get it out of the way.

8
WAR WOUNDS AND BATTLE SCARS

I think it only fair that I give you some idea as to exactly what kind of wing nut you're dealing with here. I've had to pay a very heavy price to get this ... weird? In the course of this little journey I've been on, I have sustained a whole lot of injuries in my life—at least a lot compared to most people I know. Actually ... now that I think on it, compared to everyone I know!

I'm blind in my right eye after being knocked unconscious by having a rather well-constructed guitar smashed up the side of my head by a rather well-constructed whack job in a downtown Toronto back alley. What began as a small cut over my eye got terribly infected from lying face down for a few hours in what was basically a gutter toilet. At the time I was sleeping in stairwells, parks, back alleys, and the like as well, so it was very hard to stay clean (which was why I didn't like cities—the human filth of them).

The infection spread, but I didn't go to the hospital till I was literally screaming in pain and had green pus dripping out of my eye socket. There they popped my eyeball out in three operations over two days to burn out the infection before it spread along the optic nerve to my brain. Had it reached my brain, well ... I think what they did was shoot a laser beam a couple of micromillimetres away from my brain and worked their way backwards to burn it all out. It was the first operation of its kind and gained worldwide attention. I was told the case was presented to ophthalmologists from all over the world at a conference. It was some kind of new medical breakthrough. I don't know what all the fuss was about. All they had to do was pop my eyeball out, shoot a laser beam at my head, and hope they missed my brain—which my AA sponsor said really shouldn't have been too difficult. They thought it was though—they thought it was *crazy* difficult! Some days I wonder if they got it all; actually, that would be so cool! "Oh, no, I'm fine. Just fighting this darn brain infection—you know how it is ..."

I have only sustained three skull fractures, which is amazing considering the things I've been hit in the head with (beer bottles, whisky bottles, wine bottles, rocks, hammers, crowbars, pipes, knees, elbows, fists, boots, brass knuckles, trains, boats, cars, sticks, trucks, guitars, ummm ... oh yeah! Lots and lots of good hard thunks on concrete ... I hate that sound! It's so hollow sounding—especially in my case, and I think ... yep, that's about it for those kinda things); three fractures in the orbit of my eye, jaw broken two times in four places, the skin ripped half off my skull, one broken clavicle, four broken ribs (each one a different time, different place), sternum cracked two times, femur broken, tibia broken (that one almost killed me), five broken bones in my hands, two tendons cut in my fingers (loss of use), both wrists broken, three broken toes, coccyx broken—twice (that's *very* painful!), two broken scaphoids, umm ... that's about it for bones; roughly four hundred (that's when I gave up counting), and some odd scars and stitches on various parts of my carcass, all done at various times from various injuries, and puked up blood too many times to count. I once lost a third of my blood in less than four hours due to a duodenal hemorrhage—the result of drinking mouthwash, hand sanitizer, rubbing alcohol, Lysol, Aqua Velva, and pink L'Oréal hairspray on an empty stomach on and off for about 35 years. The second time I lost a little more blood than that. (I know I counted at least two bags of blood that they stuck back in me.) Oh, I almost forgot—three fractured vertebrae, scoliosis, degenerative arthritis, and sciatica, all from sleeping on concrete most of my life (or getting kicked in the back with steel-toed boots), and more grand mal seizures and *drastic* hallucinations from alcohol withdrawal than I can count, onslaughts of demonic activity, both direct and indirect, from different covens and other sources all my life, declared legally insane and committed twice (now do I sound insane to you?), fever of 108.6°F, died (and went to my own funeral), and, after they shocked me back to life, green pus squished out of my head three times a day for a month. I survived multiple drug overdoses and put more strange psychogenic, psychoactive, psychotropic, and psychedelic drugs into my system than I can possibly remember (just to see what would happen), survived an extreme form of salmonella poisoning that killed at least seven and put dozens in hospital (while I was living in the bush during the rainy season), found myself knocking on death's door more times than I can, or want to, remember, and ... that just about does it.

So, there you have it. I would say, just think of a very drunk, half-crazed, one-eyed Frankenstein monster who walks with a bad limp, a bad stomach ache, and a real grumpy attitude on his best day, and "Bingo!"—a perfect picture of yours truly. It's no wonder I'm so happy!

I hope this sheds a little more light on why I am so incredibly grateful to God and want so much to share this amazing mercy and love—the love that God has shown me ... and the love that God has for you.

9
"YOU DON'T LOVE ME ANYMORE"

I woke up in Cloverdale, BC, one morning with a bad hangover. For most people that would mean almost dead, or wishing they were. A friend had been kind enough to let me sleep on his couch for a night. It was winter, and in BC that means cold, windy, and even worse—wet.

It was just one of those dreary mornings, and as I lay on the couch in that small apartment, I looked out through the patio door and groaned. It had only been days since I'd been released from the hospital earlier that week. I had been puking up a whole whack of blood from internal hemorrhaging again, and I was weak, dangerously sick, and flat broke. The liquor store wasn't even open yet, and waking up hours before it did was—well, let's just say it's every alcoholic's nightmare. It was only 7:00 a.m., and that meant I had three hours to kill (if they didn't kill me first) before I could get a drink into me and stop vibrating.

As I was lying there, worrying about how I was going to make it through that day, I looked out at the wind and the pelting rain and groaned again. "God, you don't love me anymore." It was kind of a whispered sigh, not a prayer really—just an expression of general hopelessness and misery.

Then, without any warning, I heard it. Right out of the blue came a very unexpected reply. "Oh yeah? Ask me for anything you want, and I'll give it to you." A statement, clear as day. I lifted my head.

"What?"

Again, "Kevin, ask me for anything you want, and I'll give it to you."

I haven't gone into a whole lot of detail about this, but God and I had been on speaking terms for many years by then. I knew that voice, and I knew for sure it was God's. (Once you've heard it, there's just no mistaking it.) We'd had all kinds of conversations over the years. Besides, no one in his right mind would ever say something like that to me—especially me!

I didn't really like talking about it too much because I was a scumbag—and who would ever believe that God would talk so clearly to a scumbag (except maybe all the other scumbags)?

"Really?" I asked, suspicious now. "Anything?"

"Yep!" he says. "Anything!"

Now, sometimes God just wants to shoot the breeze, but other times he's real serious, and he doesn't just want to talk; he wants to *do*. This was one of those times. I could tell just by the tone of his voice. He was serious.

The main reason I liked talking with God so much was because he would talk about anything on my mind, anytime, night or day, for as long as I did. He'd talk about anything at all. I think he kinda liked talking to me too, 'cause even though I sometimes didn't understand, at least he had someone he could talk with as well. And, like me, he'd just talk about pretty much anything on his mind. Just—anything.

It was like (for me) I could ask him, "Hey, God! Why is the sky blue?"

And knowing him he'd probably say something like "Because I made it that way."

And then I'd go "Yeah! No kidding, but I mean, why that colour?"

And he'd go "Because I like blue! Why are you wearing green?" He'd really crack me up sometimes, but this wasn't one of those times. He meant business. Like I said, he was serious.

I sat up, sat back, and started thinking. "Anything?"

"Yes, anything at all."

"Mmph ..."

I started to think about all the things in the world I could ask for, but no matter what I thought of, my mind kept drifting back to one thing. My children. Yes, I was married for a time. And yes, we had children. Heather Anne Snow White. (Can you tell I was a hippie?) Everyone in my family thought about doing it, you know, calling their daughter Snow, but, me being me, I just went ahead and did it. Besides, Heather Anne Snow White is a beautiful name for a very beautiful daughter. And then there is Sarah Skye White, full of love and bubbles, and my son, Kevin Johnathan David White, whom I fear may be wilder than me. At this point that is all I will say about the matter. It is a subject that requires thoughtful and prayerful consideration. Now, back to God's unexpected and very curious proposal.

I did consider the Solomon thing, you know, the whole wisdom caboodle, but my needs were a bit more … immediate, if you catch my drift, and besides, who'd ever want that much grief? ("For with much wisdom comes much sorrow; the more knowledge, the more grief," Eccl. 1:18 NIV.) The more I thought about God's offer, the more I could only think about my children. They were so far away—in Ontario. I thought about how much I missed them, about how very much I wanted to see them, to just be able to hug them once in a while. I thought about how worried I was about them. The world they were growing up in was a far different place than the one I knew as a child—a far worse and far more deceptive and dangerous place. I thought about how much I loved them, but then about how broken and lost I was. I thought of how badly and how often I'd let them down, but how wonderful it would be if I could only just be close to them—even just to be near them.

That clinched it. I made up my mind and sort of spiritually cleared my throat (to let God know I was ready to talk to him now) and said, "OK, God, I want to be in Ontario." But even as I said it, it just seemed like it wasn't really … BIG enough. So I backtracked quickly and said, "No, no! Wait … yeah, OK—God, I want to be in *Toronto*, and I want to be there—*today!*" There was no hesitation.

"Right!" says he. "Get up, gear up, and go for a walk." That was it.

I looked outside, sighed, shivered a bit, and as I started dressing and getting my gear together, I began to think about faith. Funny thing, faith. Seems you always have to do something with it once you have it. Or don't.

I'm not sure that what I was doing could be really defined as faith. I knew it was God talking, and I just had this feeling he would do what he said. I'd seen him do way too many wild things already to think he couldn't. Crazy was right up his alley. I also remembered something my father had once said to me. "Faith and obedience are two sides of the same coin, Kevin. You cannot have the one and not have the other." Besides, what did

I stand to lose? I did think about how I'd feel like an idiot walking around the street at seven thirty in the morning expecting some miracle to whisk me off to Toronto, especially if someone asked me what I was doing up that early—how I'd explain it. All my friends knew I never woke up before the liquor store was open. Not if I could possibly help it. Yeah right! I can just see it. "Oh … no, ah, sorry, can't go. I'll be leaving for Toronto any minute now," while I'm walking penniless down an alleyway at seven thirty in the morning. The funny thing is, all my friends knew that weird stuff was always going on with me, and they probably would have stuck around and started taking bets on what time I'd actually leave.

To be honest, it really didn't matter to me that much. I was mostly curious to see how God was going to pull this strangeness off, exactly. Besides, I just couldn't shake this feeling …

I remember pausing outside the door and considering if I should ask him for directions, but then I thought, *What the hell, all he said was "Go for a walk." What's the difference?* So I pulled up my collar, adjusted my backpack, and started walking in the cold and the rain—a bag full of dirty clothes, an old beat-up guitar and an out-of-tune harmonica was all I owned in the world. I didn't have a nickel to my name.

I crossed the road, then a parking lot, and turned down a back alley. There was a church down there that fed the poor and the homeless a couple of times a week. Cloverdale Christian Community Church. I had a real soft spot for the place. They were genuine and sincere, real involved, and they were making a difference in the area. I also really liked the pastor, Randy Emerson. He was an unusual man, and from what I saw, they were what I considered to be "the real deal."

As I walked down the alley, a small white car drove past me, stopped, and then just sat there idling, like whoever was in it was waiting for somebody. I was curious, so I made sure to pass by it on the driver's side so I could eyeball whoever was in it as I passed. As I did, the window rolled down, and there in the car sat Randy, the pastor of the church I liked. He looked up at me with that funny grin of his and said, "Howdy, Kev!" so being polite and all I "howdyed" back, idly wondering what he was doing out and about so early.

When I asked him, he told me he had just got back from picking up this prophet guy, Brendan McCully, from Ireland, and they had spotted me turning down the alleyway. He said this character was going to be speaking at various churches in the city, but he wanted to talk to me and was now waiting back at the church office and would I come and have a chat with him.

I was going to tell him I was running on a pretty tight schedule as I was going to be headed to Toronto any minute now, but ... seeing as how they were both men of God (and one of them was a prophet and all), I figured I could probably squeeze them in somewhere—I supposed.

Honestly, all thought of Toronto at that moment was suddenly replaced by the thought of some warmth and a hot cup of coffee. Besides, I was curious. I'd talked with a number of prophets in my time, and they were always pretty good company. Also, as I mentioned before, weird stuff like this happening was a fairly common occurrence in my life, so it really didn't rattle my cage too bad. At times, though, it just got to be too much. Some days I'd get real nervous just sticking my nose out of the bush because I had no idea what weird thing was going to happen to me next. Besides, I think right there I could see this for what it really was— God's opening gambit.

Now like I said, I'd run into a few prophets in my time, and besides being a tad strange they all had one thing in common: not one of them ever looked anything like what you would expect a prophet to look like. This character was no different. I think God does it on purpose just to keep everyone on their toes.

When I got to the church office the first thing I saw was a pair of black cowboy boots. As I followed them up I found they were attached to what seemed to be a bit of a stocky fellow all dressed in black right up to a black cowboy hat, which was in turn attached to a great smiling face that said, "Sooo! Ya gooin' sum'er ar ya." More of a statement really.

Now, I have long prided myself on my poise and unflappability, and so I answered quite calmly (and I believe quite wittily), "Uh?"

"Gooin'! Gooin' summararyaeh?"

I attempted to translate and comprehend this rather curious vernacular as best I could. I believed it to be some sort of inquiry as to my somewhat, at that point, doubtful (but desired) destination (in other words, I was badly hung over and spoke only rudimentary Irish), and so began the slow formulation of an answer fit for a man of his godly calling.

Although I was very nervous, I tried to answer calmly and, this time, a little more intelligently. With great eloquence and as much grace as I could muster I bravely said, "Aaah—I think so ... maybe, yeah—well, sort of ... umm ... I think."

"Waryagoointotin?" This time I understood him and actually managed a full sentence. "Well, I was thinking about maybe going to Toronto ... I think—maybe." I was growing more nervous every second I stood there, so I glanced over at Randy for support. He just shrugged his shoulders with a shake of his head. *No help there*, I thought, and I started wondering exactly what this chap was up to anyway.

"Can e' play dathin? Ah! Donbe daft! Corsyken!" In my dazed condition the only reason I understood a single word the man said was because he was repeatedly poking his stubby finger at my guitar.

Now I wasn't exactly feeling at the top of my form, but I unslung it from behind my back and played a song I had written called "The Glory of the Lord," thinking maybe it might be prophetic enough for him.

The song had a history.

My mother had called me years before while I had been going through a particularly rough patch in Southern California and landed in a drug treatment facility. She had told me that while she had been praying for me, God told her to tell me to look up every Scripture in the Bible concerning God's glory and read them all together, and then God was going to give me a song. I thought she was a bit, well—you know how mothers are, but I figured I'd humour her, so I did as she asked. Here's what came out:

The Glory of the Lord
The Glory of the Lord shall be revealed, and all nations shall see it together. Like lightning from the east, He will light the eastern skies, and we'll sing Glory! Glory! Glory all the earth in his name! For he has worked salvation, and shown forth great love to men. Glory! Glory! Glory all the earth in his name!

And the love of our God will be made known, and all men shall praise him together! For who has loved us like the one, who gave to us his only Son? Jesus! Jesus! Your name be lifted high above the earth! You triumphed over sin, and gave us back our lives again. Oh Jesus! Jesus! Glory all the earth in your name!

The glory of the Lord will be revealed, for his people will cry out in desire! Then you will come with cloud and fire and rest upon your holy church, and the Glory! The Glory! The Glory of the Lord will be made known, and all men will fall upon their face, worship and declare your reign. Glory! Glory! Glory all the earth in his name!

After I finished we talked, casually it seemed, and then he asked me for another song. When I was done he asked me a few more questions; then suddenly, and without warning, he turned to Randy and said, "Book him on the very next flight to Toronto at the closest airport," in perfectly understandable English.

Poor Randy looked at him kind of bewildered, and shaking his head he said simply, "We don't have money for that." Brendan sounded like he was about to take his first plunge on the world's most extreme roller coaster when he said, "Neither do I! Book it anyway!" (I almost expected him to go "Yahooo!") This was exclaimed with a huge grand grin and a twinkle in his eye. It's funny, but I think I know how he felt.

I was *definitely* worried now, but I kept answering this guy's questions until Randy got off the phone. "Well?" asks my prophet.

"It leaves in two hours from Abbotsford. Actually, in just a little *less* than two hours!"

"Wonderful!" says my prophet. "Give us another song, will ya?"

Two hours? It was right at that point that I actually concluded the man was completely crackers. You see, that particular airport was about 30 minutes away. Which left just a little over one hour to raise upwards of seven hundred dollars and then get to the airport. This news only seemed to further fuel this guy's already obvious (and somewhat alarming) psychosis.

Me? I didn't know what in the world was going on! It felt like I was plunging head first down the rabbit's hole in *Alice in Wonderland*. Everything all of a sudden felt really, really strange, and I was getting a kind of a queasy feeling in the pit of my stomach. I began tuning up, but I was eyeballing the exit door *very* hard, and I was absolutely determined that no matter what, I was going to get the heck out of there right quick as soon as I finished the song.

Then suddenly, everything hit a brand-new level of weird. Almost as I tuned the last note, the door opened up and in walked an old friend of mine, Ian Greenberg. We had a long history together, he and I, and he was like a brother to me. He just stopped dead in the doorway looking real confused as he stared around the room at us all.

"Kevin? What are you doing here?" Then he looks from me to the prophet, to Randy, and all of us are kind of shaking our heads and looking like we didn't have a clue about anything—especially me!

Then Ian turns to Randy and says, "I was up all night last night praying, and I just kept praying about Kevin. God told me last night to come by here this morning and give this to you for Kevin." Then he handed him an envelope. "There's seven hundred dollars in there."

Well, I really can't remember too much about what happened next (I think I just went on full TILT mode myself), but I know Randy gave Ian back the envelope and said, "You've got one hour to get Kevin to the airport."

Poor Ian was just looking around as stunned as the rest of us. Then he looked over at me even more confused, and I just said, "I'll explain on the way!" while I was grabbing my backpack and guitar.

Goodbyes were said, with hugs all around (I remember being somewhat nervous as I hugged Brendan, slightly suspicious there may be a chance of residual psychosis transference), and about five minutes later I was on my way to the airport. We got to the security gate with less than 10 minutes to spare, and I was still busy trying to explain everything to Ian. He was listening, and while he was chuckling away and shaking his head he gave me another hundred dollars, a hug, and a warning not to get kicked off the plane (?), which earned me a dirty look from the agent. I was one of the last three persons aboard. To say I was numb was … well, let's just say I can now sympathize with a dynamited guppy.

I had a window seat, and it wasn't until we broke cloud cover and I was actually staring at the clouds down below me that the impact of what had just transpired hit me. Less than three hours had elapsed since I had that little conversation with God. *Three hours!* Three hours later and I was on a plane, ticket and all, with a hundred dollars in my pocket, winging it over the Rockies and on my way to Toronto. Just like that! All I did was go for a walk, flat broke, crossed one street, a small parking lot, and went halfway down an alley. I shook my head, trying to clear it. It had taken less than 10 minutes after I walked out the door that morning for all this to get set in motion. BAM! Just like that!

When I arrived in Toronto I walked out of the terminal and into the warm evening air. People were rushing here and there, back and forth, but I just stood there, taking it all in. I asked the time. It was 7:15 p.m. The same day! *The same day that I told God he didn't love me anymore!* And there I was, right where I wanted to be. *The same cotton-pickin' day!*

This was NOT a miraculous answer to prayer! *I didn't pray anything!* All I did was make an innocent comment. I wasn't *asking* for anything. Come to think of it, I really wasn't even talking to him. As a matter of fact, I was minding my own business, and he's the one that stuck *his* nose in it. It's like I said earlier—I didn't start any of this. *HE STARTED IT!*

I wandered over to a bench, lit a smoke, and started wondering. Why in the world would God do something like that? I was a nobody—a smelly wino. I was dirty, and I was sinful ... hell! I even smoked. Guilty of all charges.

I flicked my smoke and stared down at it, wondering what in the world he could have possibly hoped to gain by this little stunt. What was really accomplished? I had no idea at the time. Hadn't a clue. But now, I think that maybe I do. I think that after the 25th time I read my journal entry and really looked, I began to see something. I saw that no matter what anyone said, he still loved me, and he would never stop loving me—no matter what. Maybe it was to show me that he can love whoever he wants to, whenever he wants to, however he wants to, if he wants to, just because he wants to, and there's no one who can tell him he can't, or that he shouldn't, or that he's not supposed to, or that he's doing it too often, too much, or too many times! Maybe it was to show me, *sinful me*, to teach me, so I would finally really know deep down inside for real *that he loved me*, and that I'm not crazy for thinking he does, and that I'm so important to him, and that he loves me so much that he hears my secret sighs and knows all the pain and all the weariness and sorrow in my heart, and that a little plane ride to say he loves me is absolutely *nothing* compared to *dying on a cross for me*, and despite what I or anyone else thought or said, he hadn't abandoned me, and that no matter what—he never would, and that he keeps his promises, and that no matter how weak or how sinful I was he would *always* love me and would never, ever leave me, and that just makes me love him like crazy! Crazy! *CRAZY!*

For years and years I have walked hopelessly through thick black clouds of fear and guilt and shame, full of loathing and disgust for myself. I was forever alone. But from that first desperate cry of an injured six-year-old child for help, he came, and his love has never left me once, and it never will. *Ever!*

He has shown such beauty and mercy and kindness to me that everything else in this world simply pales in comparison. His love is constant. It never goes away. He is more persistent than any sin and far stronger and more powerful than death itself. Sometimes I just want to run around shouting, "Hey! Everyone! You're not going to believe this! Look! Look and see all the wonderful, amazing things God has done for me! He's done miracles ... *FOR ME!* Worked them just so *I* could see, just so *I* would understand, to show *me* he keeps his word, and that he loves *me!* Just to help me understand how great his power is, *for me!* Just to be utterly irresistible in his incredible love he has for me!"

There is this one word that keeps rolling around in my mind: loving-kindness. You don't hear it much anymore, but that's the one word that God keeps telling me—showing me—that is what he's like. What is it that I'm getting at? Simply this. Just because he felt like it, for no particular reason, he just ... gave me a present, a gift—just because he wanted to. I wanted to be near my children, but I couldn't have gotten there in a million years. I was so sick, so beaten, so discouraged, and so, so very weary I could hardly walk. I had driven myself so hard I was almost dead. God knew that. He knew I had to get away from where I was dying and catch my breath. He heard my sigh of misery, of despair, so in two sentences it was done: *"Oh yeah? Ask me for anything you want and I'll give it to you."* That plus give or take five minutes.

Who does this kind of stuff?! God doesn't have to prove his love to me or to anyone else. He already has. One look at the cross is enough! Why, then? Perhaps all to show me what he is really like—that his love for me doesn't depend on my obedience—that his love has been with me always, and never once has it been withdrawn. It has remained since the day that it came, and that was before he even made me. I guess what I'm trying to say is that he has this *kindness*, and he proved it to me right there—and he has proved it over and over again and always made sure I knew it was him! Why? Why does my opinion of him even matter? Who in the hell am I that he should care what I think? There are billions of opinions out there a lot better than mine. So *why,* then? All I know for sure is that he loves me because he does. So, *you* go figure it out.

(You know, sometimes I think it must be fun having all that power and being so nice that you just got to whack somebody with it every day. If I had it, I'd whack everybody, all at once—*all the time!* He must just have a blast!)

10
THE FISHERMAN

I'm not really sure how I feel about this one. It has kept me wondering for years. All I am sure of at this point is that it happened and it was just flat-out weird.

I'd gone out to Calgary for I don't know what reason. Probably just to roam around, or maybe to get drunk with somebody new—but this time I was actually driving. It was this little Hyundai 1800 GSL, and that thing could chirp like a bird in third and fly over mountains! (Don't ask about the car or how I managed to get a licence, and definitely do not ask about insurance!)

Gas was only 29 cents a litre because of a gas war going on all over BC, so travelling was a breeze, especially in a car like that. On my way back to Vancouver I picked up a couple of hitchhikers just before I hit the Rockies. They were young but reasonably experienced (far from road trash), having just completed their very first coast-to-coast backpack trip. I understood. It's actually quite an accomplishment. They were spoiled though—all the fancy gear, but the stuff looked almost brand new. Not tramps or ditch-dwellers—students, perhaps—out for an "adventure." Unfortunately for me they were broke. I had hoped one of them at least had a driver's licence. I was exhausted and needed to take a nap—bad. Seemed I was out of luck on that score as well. They were both unlicensed.

I was running on empty gas (again), flat broke (again), and, worse yet, out of alcohol. This, for me, was a serious problem and physically very dangerous.

We were well into the mountains before I felt there was no way I could drive any longer. I began desperately looking for some sort of rest stop, as it was an extremely hazardous stretch of road, and pulling over to the side was just plain stupid—even for a moment. There were far too many dangerous curves. I was almost positive there wasn't one on that particular stretch of the highway, and I knew that road up, down, backwards and forwards, inside and out, so with every passing kilometre I was getting more and more uptight.

To my great surprise, I was proven wrong. As we drove down the highway, on the other side of the road I saw a very small sign that said "Rest Stop." I hit the binders, pulled a U-turn, and drove down a narrow gravel road leading to a tiny rest area. Space for one car, one picnic table, and that was it. Nothing else. Not even a washroom. Small, but definitely out of the way, which would give me a chance to think.

So that's what I did. I walked slowly over to the picnic table, sat down, and started plonking my head on it. Slowly plonking—it felt good, familiar. Oh, and thinking too. I really do believe that plonking one's head on a table (rock, lamppost, brick wall, etc.) is in fact quite conducive to creative thought. Try it sometime—really!

Yep, I was thinking, that's what I was doing. Thinking …

This is where we stood, or rather where I stood. Despite their trip, the hikers were of no help to me. They were just too inexperienced and would only get themselves, and possibly me, into trouble. I had just enough gas to get to the station, but no cash for the tank. I was too booze sick to play guitar or panhandle, so somehow I had to come up with enough cash to get some gas into the car and some booze into me so I could stave off a seizure while I was driving to my Native buddies' and rest up for a while.

I stopped plonking my head. "What the hell am I going to do?" I half whispered to myself. Then I went back to plonking my head again—slooowly plonking. I overheard the hikers discussing whether they should stick with me or chance hiking the highway at that spot. I started plonking my head a bit harder.

Then I heard it again—that same weird voice in my head that always talks about crazy things. You know—God?

This time he said, "Kevin, if you stand up, turn around, and walk in a straight line I'll give you twenty dollars." I stopped plonking, paused a second or two, and then slowly raised my head.

"What?"

The voice spoke again, only this time a little slower, as if to a rather slow-witted child. "Kevin, if you stand up, turn around, and walk in a straight line, I'll give you twenty dollars." Those *exact* words. I remember noting that it had to be a *straight* line.

"That's what I thought you said." I sighed and started plonking my head again. The situation had just changed.

Now, when I was at least 60 kilometres in any direction from anything that even looked like civilization, I was supposed to say something like, "Hey, boys! No worries! God himself just talked to me and told me that if I wander off into those woods behind me there, he is going to give me twenty dollars. Oh yeah! I almost forgot. I have to walk in a straight line—in the woods—in a *straight* line; then I get the twenty." I shook my head. God! You've got to be kidding me!

I remember raising my head, shaking it again, giving a deep sigh— and then starting to plonk my head on the table again. *Damn! In a straight line?* (In case you don't know, or haven't figured it out yet, it is almost physically impossible to walk in a straight line in the woods without bumping into something ... like a tree, maybe?) *They're going to think I've lost it for sure!*

Finally, after several futile attempts in my head to try to phrase this madness in a way that made sense (not), I just stopped my plonking, raised my head, and in a voice I tried to make sound as confident as I could said, "Ahh ... well, umm ... boys, God just told me that if I stood up, turned around, and walked in a straight line ..." (sounds like something a cop would say) "he's going to give me twenty dollars" (definitely *not* something a cop would say).

There was the inevitable pause (I think the birds even stopped chirping) while everything got real quiet so as to watch the formation of the third purple head. Then, *"What?"*

"That's exactly what I said," I said.

"No! I mean, what do you mean?"

"That's what I thought you'd say."

"No! I mean what are you trying to say?!" I repeated what I said.

These boys were inexperienced, but they were far from stupid. They knew as well as I did where we were, and they also knew I stood about the same chance of running into a stark-naked redheaded female bungee jumper painted lime green from head to toe ripped on acid singing "Purple Haze" at the top of her lungs as running into a twenty-dollar bill in those particular woods. (Actually, it was the early nineties in BC, so the bungee jumper thing wasn't too far-fetched.)

"Kevin! Look behind you!" I looked.

"There's nothing back there," the one guy said.

I stood up. They both began looking uncomfortable.

"There's nothing but woods back there, Kevin ..."

I turned around.

Now you've got to understand, a hiker doesn't have the luxury of being fussy about the rides he takes. Four or five hours standing in the cold and watching the sun start sinking can make you real tolerant of other folk's little quirks and oddities. You guys have a choice who you ride with. We don't ... not really. We're the ones who take all the risks. And believe me, there's a lot of really strange drivers out there. And I do mean *really* strange. I could tell you of folk I ran into when I was hiking as a teenager—alone...

You see, getting picked up by a whacked-out driver is every traveller's nightmare. But being *trapped* with a dangerous lunatic—that's a horror story heard around many a traveller's campfire. A lunatic doesn't pick up a hiker to try to rob him. Get it? Just look at a missing persons board. That should explain things pretty clear.

(By the way, at the time I looked pretty dangerous, so these two had a valid concern.)

At this point, I'd been eyeballing the woods for a while. "He's lost it!" I started walking.

"There's nothing but woods back there, Kevin!"

I kept putting one foot *very carefully* in front of the other.

"We're not going looking for you!" I just kept staring at my feet and concentrated on putting one foot *directly* in front of the other.

I guess I walked that way for about four or five minutes, maybe not even that long. The woods were cool and quiet, and my careful steps made no sound under the tall old-growth cedar. It was beautiful, so quiet—peaceful. Besides being underwater, the woods are my favourite place in the world to be. I think it is important to note that in all the time I walked, only once did I have to deviate from my path—and then only about three inches (to allow my body to get past a tree). Had I not been attached to them my feet would've been just peachy on their own.

Now here is where things begin to get a little strange. Almost without warning, directly in front of me I found myself facing an impenetrable wall of very high tight bramble bush. There was only one small gap in it, and that gap had somehow placed itself directly in front of me. It was the only way I could have possibly gotten through the bush without getting ripped to shreds. When I stepped through it I found myself in a grass-covered clearing. Ahead of me about 20 feet was a beautiful crystal sparkling river. Not a big one—bigger than a creek, but smaller than a full-sized river—a mountain river.

The sun was quite happy and was teasing and playing with it, and as I stared across to the snow-capped mountains in the distance I gradually became aware of movement off to my right. I slowly turned to look, and there on the riverbank was an older gentleman, fly-fishing (for trout, I supposed). I stood very still as I didn't want to disturb his rhythm. I used the time to study him carefully.

I am a panhandler, and a darn good one at that. Not a sit-around-with-a-sign kind but the walking, talking, moving-around kind, and my skills of observation are way, way up there. I had to know in under five seconds what kind of person I was dealing with or all my scorecards would read zero.

What I first noticed were his clothes. They were extraordinarily clean, as fresh as if they'd just come out of a package. His pants still had a crease in them. I know this wouldn't be unusual if I was downtown somewhere, but this character was in the middle of nowhere, and his shirt, everything—he just looked way too clean to me. Even his hands were clean ... in the woods? Then there was something about his hair ...

He was calm when he turned, and, catching a glimpse of me, he gave a friendly smile while he looked me over.

"Any luck?" I asked.

"Nope, but I like fishing all the same," he answered cheerfully. Then he asked me, "Whatcha' doing in these parts?" nice like.

I gave a kind of sigh and said, "Well, I was actually asking myself the same question. I guess I'm just taking a break before I head into town to scratch up some gas."

He smiled, reached into his top pocket, and pulled out a billfold. Like magic a neatly folded brand-new twenty-dollar bill appeared in his hand.

"This help?"

I remember looking at him and mentally shaking my head in wonder.

"You know," I said with a real smile, "that helps far more than you can possibly imagine!" He waved it towards me, and as I took the bill from his hand I remember looking very hard at him.

"Thank you so much!" He just waved his hand, smiled at me, and turned back to his fly-fishing.

As I walked back to the spot where I had come out of the woods, I was shaking my head. I just thought, like, *Why? God,* why *are you being so nice to me? What are you playing at?*

You see, he'd always been like that. Yeah, there were tons of times when things were unbearably hard. The cold, the loneliness, the fights and injuries and despair ... but every once in a while, he would do stuff like this—things that were flat-out weird—and I just didn't get it.

It was crazy! *Why?* Wasn't I kind of out of bounds because I was so sinful? Hadn't *I* walked away from *him*? Hadn't I kind of "used up" my quota of grace tickets by then? Didn't I know better? I mean, we all know we gotta take responsibility for our own decisions, our own actions—right?

The problem for me was that even though I knew what was right, I had absolutely no power in me to do it. I couldn't. I couldn't stop drinking even if my life depended on it—and so very often it did. And why did he do these things the *way* he did? I could have just found the 20 dollars and said thank you, but no, he *wanted* to make a big deal out of it. He wanted to go talk in my head and tell me to do something totally weird just so I would know beyond any shadow of doubt that it was him, hands down. There really was no other possible explanation for what happened. Why was he still even talking to me? What? He's incorrigible? It has taken such a long time to find out what God's fundamental problem is—a lifetime to discover what was so simple and what had been right in front of my face all my life. God *is* love. It is really just that simple.

You see, God just doesn't quit. Once he decides to love somebody, he will not be thwarted in showing his mercy and kindness. He can't be stopped! *Nothing will dissuade him from loving us!* He's worse than the "Terminator." If you think for one moment I take that kind of love for granted, then slap your own face and give your head a shake! It's this kind of love that puts the fear of God into me!

Anyway, I don't remember looking back. I felt dazed—happy, but just kind of dazed. As I walked back to my plonking table I was very careful to put one foot in front of the other. I really don't remember much of what was said upon my return. I just remember feeling very peaceful—aware, but peaceful—and happy somehow. Something had changed. I wasn't as afraid as I was when I first walked into those woods. I no longer felt so—alone. So hopeless ...

You know, perhaps that is how God changes us, in all these small encounters—perhaps every little thing in our lives, every single one, right down to the cool breeze that caresses a cheek on a warm summer evening, reminding us, whispering mysteries—memories of all the places it has sought out and shared with our souls—or those beautiful sunsets we've all seen and so much wished we could share with someone close, someone we love. Perhaps all of it, everything, is God's way of calling to us, wooing us with his tender love and whispering to our souls, "I am the one who caresses your cheek in the gentle breeze. I am the one who whispers in your ear. I am the hand that paints the sky, the sunsets you desperately need to share with someone dear to you. I am always near you, always calling to you, and I long to fellowship with you, to share myself with you. Don't be afraid—for you so desperately need to be loved by me. Don't be afraid. You really are my child. Come—come and let me heal you ..."

I've just now, years later, found myself thinking again of this "thing" that happened that day. First off, we were at least 60 kilometres away from anything other than the highway and our little laneway rest stop. There were for sure no other roads; no cars could possibly park on the highway, and there were definitely no cars at the rest stop. No cars, no roads, no houses, no nothing, nowhere. Then there was that weird bush being everywhere but in a straight line from where I started out. I've tangled with bushes like that before, blundered into them in the middle of the night (more than once), and I always come out looking like I've been attacked by a rabid lynx wearing red lipstick with a real bad case of PMS—yet here in the middle of all this nowhere, 60 kilometres from anything but a straight line, was a hole in this stupid bush with a man inside it.

I know those mountains really well, and I know that highway even better. I had never seen that rest stop before, and that guy just shouldn't have been there—unless he parachuted in. Or flew there. As a matter of fact, I'd like to go back and see if the rest stop is even there …

11
HOW NOT TO DIE (VERY RUDELY)

I've been reading some of what I have written down so far, and I sincerely hope that I have not given you a wrong impression. Although I have a reasonable grasp of communication and the English language, that should by no means propound any idea that I was in any way civilized. I was somewhat forced into learning these skills (some were simply inherited) in order to explain to people in a very nice way exactly how much money I wanted to panhandle without offending them. These talents were also useful in being able to quickly talk my way out of trouble if I got myself into a jam. The whole purpose of them in the overall scheme of things was to obfuscate questionable objectives and inhibit any clear reasoning on the part of my prospect. They were also essential (in conjunction with certain other skills I possessed) in the creation of an intriguing tale pulled from my own experience but specifically tailored to guarantee the interest of whatever type of individual I was dealing with— all based on prior impressions and intuitions, of course. There were a lot of other skills I had, but these were learned the hard way. Most of them had to do with the cultivation of certain attitudes essential to keeping me alive. The fact that I am still here before you (in essence) bears testament to their effectiveness.

I would like to reiterate something very clearly before I continue any further. What I'm writing down here is not my fault. I didn't start it. God started it, and it's his fault. I don't know what he had in mind when he got this show on the road, but one thing is certain, *I sure as jumpin' didn't go around picking on him!* I know I've stated it before, but I'm just trying to cover my bum is all. He started this long before I even had a say in the matter. This has been something I've only now begun to realize—especially because my life has been like a mixture of *Gone with the Wind, The Wizard of Oz,* and *Fear and Loathing in Las Vegas.* What that means is, a lot of what is coming later on is pretty weird stuff, so for now, I'm going to start with something relatively easy to swallow and move on from there. This gets a bit rough, so hold on to your sense of humour. (Oh … perhaps I should mention that in my less than respectable past, I have been accused as being somewhat … "unreasonable" at times. I prefer to consider it as being "deliberately uncooperative," particularly when it came to this whole "staying alive" business. So please, think gently of me as you read, for it has been this very attitude that has kept me alive for so long.) Oh yeah, it's best for the reader to keep in mind that during most of these chronicles I was either half drunk or horribly hung over.

It was Abbotsford, BC, and it was winter.

I was busking at the time, just generally getting half snapped and kind of being a public nuisance. I could get away with it a lot more than most because people genuinely liked the music I played and sang and I was interesting to talk to. So, as long as I could hold a coherent conversation and didn't wobble around too much, everything was just peachy.

On the night in question the sidewalks were quite slippery. I was wearing shoes that were also slippery, and wonder of wonders, I slipped. Hard! The kind of arms-outstretched-feet-in-the-air-crack-your-head-on-the-concrete "THUNK" kind of slipped. As I got to my feet I realized I had twisted my ankle rather badly (or so I thought), but because I was half snapped and taking a lot of T3s (codeine), I didn't feel the pain right away.

Seeing as how I had met some new friends who were willing to put me up for a bit, I simply ignored the pain and continued to drink for the next three days. I would walk to my spot and play, get booze, drink it down, play some more, get more booze, and bring it back to share with my friends. I think that's why a lot of people liked me. I was a walking, talking, jukebox/cash machine/beer store.

On the fourth evening, however, my ankle became terribly painful and I was really not feeling well at all (meaning almost dead). When I limped into the hospital and sat down, after what seemed like ages a nurse came over and asked me what my problem was.

Now I was kind of in one of my "unreasonable" moods and was going to tell her she'd be the one with the problem if I didn't get to see a doctor real quick, but I bit my tongue and just told her that my ankle was very sore and I was having a hard time walking. As I was explaining myself to her, I noticed that she had begun to look at me rather curiously.

Now I've grown quite accustomed to this over the years, so I really didn't pay it too much attention. However, as she went from curiously to strangely (there is a difference), I started getting a tad uncomfortable and a bit irritated. I was in no mood to tolerate any judgment or criticism from anybody that night.

Suddenly she interrupted me and said, "Just a moment, young man!" (She was the kind of nurse who called everyone under 60 "young man.") "Why are you so pale?" She peered even closer and asked, "And why are your lips so blue?" (I started to feel like the Big Bad Wolf in "Goldilocks.")

I thought it was obvious because I stank like sherry, but I began to patiently explain to her that I had a very bad hangover because I drank a lot. She just kind of muttered, "Oh no! No, no!" and then she pulls this funny-looking machine over, yanks out some sort of hose, *and tells me to blow in it!*

Now I've had a lot of strange things done to me at hospitals before, but *never* have I had to take a Breathalyzer test before I got seen by somebody, and that's what started the whole ball rolling. I got right testy and real unreasonable right away.

"Since when do I have to have a Breathalyzer test before I can get into the cotton-pickin' hospital?" I demanded. I was definitely not very polite when I said it, either.

The thing was, I was confused and in a lot of pain, and with me that's definitely not a good thing for anyone or anything around me, never mind who's in front of me. I knew I was being a bit belligerent, and I'm not usually like that, but I really was in pain, didn't really care too much about any niceties at the time, didn't like hospitals at the best of times, and I definitely didn't like Breathalyzers even more than I didn't like hospitals, because unlike alcoholics, Breathalyzers tell the truth about how much I really had to drink instead of the "Oh, I've only had a couple" that I would have said I'd had if there hadn't been a Breathalyzer there in the first place, which explains why I was nervous and jumpy and didn't want to blow into the damn thing, 'cause I was in a hospital and not a police station so they had no business making me have a Breathalyzer test, as it really had no business being in a hospital anyway ... *and should be back at the police station where it belonged in the first place!*

She said it wasn't a Breathalyzer and would I please just stop talking and blow into the machine. I blew all right, but only after I put my backpack on and got my guitar handy just in case I had to get out of there in a hurry.

The second she checked the numbers on the machine she jumped on to the PA system, and everything was all code such and so, and then right away she started scribbling like mad in some sort of chart.

I was alarmed. I'd blown pretty high on the "Richter scale" a few times, but I had never got a response like that before. (Set the all-time record in my favourite jail one time. The sergeant himself came back to congratulate me!) "It can't be that bad," I muttered as I edged away from the desk.

Now I didn't like the look of what she was doing at all, so while she was busy I headed discreetly out the emergency room door. I felt safer outside, and besides, I needed a couple of good strong pulls off the jug I had stashed in my pants and a smoke before anything else could happen. For all I knew the cops were already on their way for me, and not them nor nobody else was going to get between me and my cotton-pickin' jug till I was darn well good and done with it.

I had a couple of big slugs of sherry (the four-swallow kind) and had just taken my first puff of a cigarette when, barrelling out the door, comes the nurse, who starts screeching like a crazed banshee to *"put out that damn cigarette and get back inside right now!"*

Right there, at that point, I started to get *really* annoyed. First off (as I mentioned), I didn't like hospitals, PERIOD! Then there was the stupid Breathalyzer machine, and now I was getting yelled at for smoking too? The only time I've ever had to quit smoking after a Breathalyzer was right after being slapped into a set of handcuffs and tossed into the hoosegow.

This little lady had no idea how "unreasonable" and "uncooperative" I could really get—and I was right on the sharp edge of letting her know real quick!

I was just fuming at this point, but I took one more big defiant puff, tossed my smoke, and walked into the hospital muttering, "They're *not* getting my damn jug anyway!" That's when things got *real* crazy.

The instant I set foot through the hospital door they rushed me onto a bed, were taking my blood lickety-split, then rolled me onto an elevator—and "BAM!" I was upstairs.

Smokes! I thought in amazement, *The service around here is great!* And past transgressions downstairs were almost atoned for. This impression, however, rapidly began to change. They put me off to one side of the hall, and then everybody seemed to be flying around like confetti at a tickertape parade. They were scribbling stuff down and yakking away to, at, and with everybody everywhere, but not one single person was saying one single word to me. I was starting to get right choked again because every time I would try to talk to somebody or even get their attention, they would just blow me off and keep on walking, talking, or writing and ignoring me completely. I was just about to put a real fast halt to this nonsense when I suddenly remembered I still had well over half a jug of sherry on me.

Now over the years I've found that hospitals had this very rude habit of taking my jugs away from me whenever they found them, so I determined to down the thing before this tragedy could occur and avoid the resulting chaos that would inevitably result from such a terrible lack of judgment on their part, save myself a trip to jail, and express my indignation at such shoddy treatment at a more opportune time.

After very rapidly (and discreetly) disposing of said contraband, I took stock of my surroundings, and as I did I began to wonder what in the world all the fuss was about. I certainly felt a whole lot better. However, when someone came and started wheeling me over to some doors marked "Critical Care," I began to get a bit nervous.

I'd been in critical care before (many times), and although the care was always better, I still didn't like it too much. Everybody always seemed either way too nice or way too nervous. My fears were soon relieved when we sailed right through critical care to a smaller and much more private area marked "Palliative Care." *Now this is more like it*, I thought to myself.

I'd never been in palliative care before, so I didn't exactly know what it was. I'd heard about folk being in *pallet*-ive care, so I assumed it had something to do with rest of some sort because of the story about the guy that Jesus healed when his friends lowered his "pallet" down from a hole in the roof, but at least I wasn't in critical care, and I immediately started wondering what the grub was like and how long they were going to let me stay. I was actually deliberating if I should fake things up a bit so I'd get another day or so out of this, thinking that because of the high demand for beds they'd be shuffling people in and out pretty quick.

By now the booze had kicked in pretty strong, and I remember looking around at the other patients there and, as I did, feeling kind of sorry for them. Most of them didn't look so hot, and I knew what it felt like being sick and all. (I'd been up puking my guts out every morning for years.) That's when I noticed these two doctors muttering together real low like as they compared notes and glanced over at me kind of surreptitiously from time to time.

Now I didn't particularly much like being glanced at surreptitiously. As a matter of fact, I didn't like surreptitiousness at all, and I was starting to get right irritated at it! (I'm getting irritated just thinking about it.) Plus, I was getting even more irritated because I never did have a chance to have my smoke, and everybody was still running around talking to, with, or at everybody else and ignoring me completely (except the two surreptitious doctors), and I was wanting to have my smoke, and wanting it right quick!

Finally I was able, very politely, to ask a nurse who was fiddling with some gadget or other if I might go outside and have a smoke, please, as I would only be a minute and would be right back. Well, she turned around and looked at me real strange just like the nurse downstairs had (I was really starting to wonder what in the world they were all gawking at and looking at me surreptitiously for) and said she really didn't think that was a very good idea right now, and I would have to wait for the head nurse to get back and decide.

That cut it right there! I'd had enough of this business! I'd been on a steadily rising boil ever since the Breathalyzer incident, so when that poor nurse said what she said, BAM! that was it. I went on the *warpath*.

With that one sentence, all the staff at that hospital's status changed from "Potential Source of Food" to "My Sworn Enemy" and as such I was bound and determined to escape if at all possible, and if I was unable to do so I would raise as much hell as I could until it *was* possible, and believe you me, when I set my mind to a task such as that, I am both ruthless and cunning. I have managed to escape police custody *twice*, once while handcuffed to a bed with two officers assigned to guard me (they later posted *four* officers just to keep me handcuffed hand and foot in one small hospital examining room), so as far as I was concerned, the ball was now in my court, and I was definitely ready to play.

The first order of business in a situation like that is to create a state of confusion. This I immediately set to with such fervour and inspiration I would have instantly endeared myself to the hearts of any true, dedicated, and "boney fyde" troublemaking disturbers-of-the-peace anywhere.

I began by raising my voice to at least three times that of all background noise and began by saying such things as *"ALL RIGHT! LISTEN UP, YOU BUNCH OF FREAK CRACKPOT WHACK JOBS! I AM NOT YOUR FRICKIN' PRISONER! I am a full grown man in complete possession of all my frickin' faculties and if I choose to go out and have two friggin' smokes I bloody well will and I'd just love to see anybody in this pitiful frickin' freak show tell me anything different! AND, I want to know right friggin' now just who the devil is in charge of this disaster zone and what, exactly, in the blue flamin' hell is going on around here, and if I don't get some cotton-pickin answers and talk at someone who knows exactly what in the bloody hell they're talking about RIGHT FRICKIN' QUICK there's sure as blazes going to be all hell to pay 'cause I am within one freakin' inch of raising 'Hell's Own Havoc' itself in here and rippin' this place apart with my bare freaking hands, so every single one of you frickin' sneaky little boneheaded morons in here better listen up and let me out for my cotton-pickin' smoke right freakin' fast or the damned devil himself is going to get unleashed in here and I do mean RIGHT RIPPIN' PRONTO!"*

Then I tore out my IV and started unplugging anything that stuck out of a wall and trashing everything I could lay my hands on—I twisted every dial and pulled every lever I could within reach of my bed and switched the feeds on all my machines (which started beeping like crazy), pausing only long enough to whip a half full bottle of pee at the nursing station window. This was all done, of course, with great care and calculated intent specifically designed for greatest possible impact and emphasis in mind. (It's all in the timing.)

Yeah! They paid attention all right. They could see I had absolutely no intention of letting up or slowing down but was in fact just getting warmed up, so in a quick sec the doctor showed up looking quite concerned. After a hasty but very heated conversation with the nursing staff, he started toward my bed. I glared up at him, daring him to tell me I couldn't go out for my smoke. "Mr. White," he began quietly as he was glancing over his status chart, "we have taken the liberty of contacting your wife and parents so they could be here to—"

"You did what?!"

He backed a cautious step away from the bed.

"Are you out of your friggin' mind? Why? I don't want anybody here!"

He looked at me in both surprise and confusion. "Mr. White, I don't understand … Has no one told you—spoken with you at all?"

"Told me? Told me what? *No one has told me one single solitary thing since I bloody well got here!"*

The doctor backed up a bit more, and then from a safer distance he almost whispered, "Oh … Oh dear! I'm sorry. I'm so sorry I have to be the one to tell you! You see, you are dying, Mr. White. You have almost no oxygen in your blood. Blood clots have gone into your lungs, and your blood is unable to absorb any oxygen. We notified your wife and parents because you have only a few hours—four, maybe five at best. You definitely will not live through the night, Mr. White. There is absolutely nothing we can do for you. To be honest we are somewhat puzzled as to why you are awake and coherent. If you have a God, Mr. White, I suggest you make your peace with him quickly."

Make my peace with him?! Ma …*What? Make my peace with him?!*

I kid you not. This is what this … this *cracker-box* actually said to me. (I find myself in the unusual position of being oddly limited in my choice of vocabulary at this juncture. Let's just say some of my more colourful and descriptive dysphemisms would be inappropriate as, well … my mother is going to read this, and I'm probably in enough trouble as it is!)

My first reaction was kinda like *This? This is what all the fuss is about?* (These guys obviously had no idea how long I could hold my breath.)

Then I thought, *Man! Is my mom going to be pissed at me!* (Case in point …) See, over the years my mom has had more doctors tell her more crap about how I'm on the verge of dying of this, that, or the other thing or that they are going to attempt some risky experimental such and such or I'll never be able to whatever again or I'm unlikely to survive such and so procedure and will probably die in the middle of it that I knew she was probably sick and tired of getting calls in the middle of the night from different doctors from all over the country saying I was going to die—again. To top it all off, even though I knew right away I wasn't going to die, I was sure I'd want to once my mother got there and caught wind of how I was drunk and causing all kinds of hell for the staff when I was supposed to be busy dying. I can tell you right now, I was *far* more worried about that than anything this doctor was telling me.

At any rate I clearly remember looking at him and thinking to myself, *This poor sap does not have the slightest clue what in the world is going on here.* In all honesty, I thought maybe it was something serious, like they were going to have to amputate something or other. I just gave him a kind of dirty look, shook my head, and said, "Are you out of your mind?!"

Now I was really, *really* choked! First the whole Breathalyzer fiasco, then the "no smoking" thing, then the "surreptitiousness" of it all, and now this—this (sigh …) perfectly respectable, intelligent, and extremely patient physician (upon whom I had landed like one of the 10 plagues of Egypt), telling me that not only was I going to die but I was going to die that night—*and I had better make my peace with God?!*

What this character didn't know was that not only did God and I know each other quite well but we had come to an agreement a long time ago, and our business hadn't even started yet, *so*, thank you very much for your opinion, but I have no intention of dying right now, and as a matter of fact *who in the snapping turtles does this clown think he is telling me that I'm supposed to die anyway in the first place!* Well, he left rather abruptly after hearing a few well-chosen superlatives that pointed out the questionable state of his mental capacity, his genealogy, and some detailed instructions for an extremely violent form of euthanasia, and he moved even faster after hearing certain comments I had about my great eagerness to aid him in said venture.

As soon as he stepped out he immediately started giving all the nursing staff what sounded like some pretty detailed instructions, so me being me, and not handcuffed to anything, I slipped out and made a break for the elevator while they were busily scribbling away and were still somewhat confused. (See what I mean about the confusion stuff?)

Unfortunately, just before I boarded the elevator, for some odd reason a security guard recognized me (ya think?), and after being questioned I was escorted by both arms right back to palliative care under great protest (and muttering about "surreptitiousness" and violations of Canadian civil liberties) and was *very* carefully watched by two security guards from that time on. (I wonder if anyone has actually ever escaped from palliative care … alive?)

So, seeing as how I was going to die anyway, I went right back to dying as loudly and mule-headedly as possible—so as to make sure I was remembered by all and sundry.

This must have worked because the head nurse came over, and I was very quickly told quite crossly and sternly by her to "Please! At least have a little more consideration …" and not to be so loud, as "everyone on the ward is dying!" and I had better be busy praying, "'cause as a matter of fact—*you're dying too!*"

I could not believe what I was hearing. For a moment I almost thought she was going to add, "and could you *please* at least just act like it?" I remember shaking my head in bewildered amazement, thinking to myself, *These suckers expect me to die, politely? Just for them?*

Now I'm not too proud about this, but I got very cross in return, looked right at her, and told her straight to her face that I didn't give a rat's right cheek who was dying in here—I wasn't going to be dying right now, but if I really was, who in the bloody hell was she to deny a dying man his last cigarette anyway, *and* if she didn't let me have one, and have one right quick, I was going to trash the whole place all over again!

I feel sorry for her in hindsight. I can just imagine when she got home, "Hi, honey! How was your night?"

"Oh, it was just terrible! They brought in this real jerk, *and the little freak just wouldn't die!* He drove us crazy all night!"

After a second short consult with the doctor, the head nurse came back over, and as she approached I folded my arms against my chest, narrowed my eyes, and braced myself for another full-out battle of wills.

She looked down at me, and our eyes locked for a few long seconds, both unflinching. Then she turned to the nurse with her and with a bit of a grudging sigh said, "If he's still this cantankerous and bitchy, I don't think he's going to die tonight. Get him in a chair, take him downstairs, and let him have his cigarette, but for heaven's sake don't bring him back in here! Put him in critical care and let them deal with him!" and then turning to me, "And we won't be having any more problems tonight, will we, Mr. White?"

I was as meek as a kitten. "Absolutely not," I purred.

They continued to monitor my blood every hour or so throughout the night. I was told that if they had sucked blood out of a dead corpse, I was only eight points from that (whatever that meant). The doctor said they didn't understand how I was conscious.

I suppose it would be helpful if I briefly described the nature of my injury. Compared to some I've had, it was actually quite straightforward, but like all the injuries I had left unattended, it quickly had become life threatening.

I had broken the smaller of the two bones in my lower leg very close to my ankle. The break was a bad one because although it had broken all the way through, it wasn't a clean break. The bone had kind of twisted as it broke, so there were fine splinters all around most of it, and this made it *very* difficult to set. Also, because the congealed blood around the bone had repeatedly been disturbed, the resulting clots had somehow managed to get into my lungs, making it almost impossible for my blood to absorb any oxygen. On top of all that, they couldn't set the bone because it would now disturb the blood clotted around the bone so much that the resulting number of clots created in my system would surely kill me.

So they were stumped. The best thing they could come up with was some sort of net being placed inside my leg somewhere or to design some sort of experimental cast to push the bone and blah, blah, blah ... As they were explaining all this to me I found my mind wandering. I really wasn't very interested, and I most definitely was not concerned.

You see, God had already gone through a whole lot of time and trouble to patiently teach me and show me who he was and what he was all about.

He had made some very specific promises to me, some to be fulfilled while I was alive and some after I and this carcass of mine parted paths and went our separate ways. A lot of the "alive" ones had not been fulfilled yet, so it was really all very simple to me. I knew that, once more—I was "undieable."

It was just like before I was born when I was in my mom's belly on the airplane that crashed. God had told my father some things about me, and that meant I couldn't die. Well, God had told me some things he was going to do, and I knew for sure he would keep his word to me. So—sorry, but no dying today.

I think the main reason for this certainty was because somehow, and I'm not sure how, in spite of being a very sinful man and an alcoholic dope fiend, I still knew who my God was. Both he and my earthly father knew (long before I did) the direction my life was heading, yet by some miracle, in spite of all the tremendous harm, pain, sorrow, and heartbreak my sin had brought to myself and so many others, somehow God, in his infinite love, had created in me a sense of belonging to him that has never left me, no matter what has happened.

Even those dark and terrible times of utter despair were never silent or empty but were always filled with my cries. "Father! Where are you? Don't forsake me! Where are you? You promised you wouldn't forsake me! You promised me! You said that you would never forget me! *I know you love me, God! I know that you do! Fulfill your words to me, God! Don't make your prophets liars! Keep your promises to me!*"

I know today why I couldn't follow him. Why I couldn't break free from the alcoholism that had tortured me and held me in bondage for so many years. It was because I couldn't see. I didn't understand how deep and powerfully vast his love for me really was.

This is why Paul writes in Ephesians, "And may you have the power to *understand*, as all God's people should, how wide, how long, how high and how deep his love is. May you *experience* the love of Christ, though it is too great to understand fully. Then you will be made complete with all the fullness of life and power that comes from God" (Eph. 3:18–19 NLT, emphasis added). It was only after I actually *saw* his love that I became free. And now I must have it, above all else because *nothing* in this world can compare to it. I hunger for it.

That love is what compe[...]
to share it with all my heart a[...]
it, just once, and that small glin[...]
I hope I never recover. I cannot [...]
really don't know how to describe [...]
would not keep his word to me was [...]

I simply compared what informat[...]
had told me, and BOOM! The doctors [...]
Let me have my smoke and I shut up.

Presumptuous? Maybe. Spoiled? Pro[...] [...]y
entire life teaching me these two things—[...] [...]ness and
his unending love. And these lessons could on[...] [...]g from the pain
and suffering of absolute and total failure. Tim[...] [...]d again. The complete
inability to do anything without the conscious acknowledgement of God
and my unconditional surrender to his power and presence in every aspect
of my life is now the greatest fact of my life.

Well, meanwhile, back at the Ponderosa, things took a very interesting
turn. Early the next morning my father came by with a friend of his, Terry
Lamb. We talked a bit, mostly chitchat. I remember telling my father not to
worry about me, that God was nowhere near finished with me yet. He just
smiled quietly and said, "He who began a good work in you will bring it to
completion at the day of Jesus Christ" (Phil. 1:6). It was the very first Scripture he had ever given me when I first became a Christian many years before.

Then they prayed both with me and for me. It was good to speak with
my dad again. We sometimes went years between talks.

As they were leaving, my father paused at the foot of my bed and
placed his hand on my injured leg. I looked up at impossibly pale blue
eyes that sparkled with love as he said very quietly and simply, "God—
heal my son." Then he smiled at me and walked away. I can see his eyes
even now and feel their warmth and strength in the deepest parts of me.

The nurse came and took my blood, then left. I lay back on my bed
and waited for I don't know what. I was just feeling relaxed enough to
think about a nap when I spotted Dracula heading my way again. I sat up.
She had just taken my blood less than 20 minutes ago.

"I'm sorry, Mr. White," she explained. "We have to take your blood
again." I started feeling mean but simply asked "why?" instead. She said

mistake in the test and would have to do it
and stuck my arm out. I supposed I had no other
was done, I determined to take a nap.
minutes went by and I was just starting to doze off when
er coming at me again. I was about to tell her that if she tried
king me with that needle one more time, she was the one going to be
needing palliative care, but I guess my reputation had preceded me.

She saw me eyeballing her and very quickly said, "No! No! Mr. White! Please, it's OK!" I could tell she was a bit nervous so I eased up on my glare.

"We're just confused. Just an hour ago your blood oxygen was extremely low—it was deathly low. Now it seems to be perfectly normal. We're just a bit confused." She reached over, checked through her charts, then looked really hard at me and left. I just kind of thought, *Yeah, OK … that's good, I guess*, and I rolled over to try to get my nap.

Then the doctor came over and started rustling through his cotton-pickin' charts, and I began wondering what in blazes a guy had to do to get a little shuteye. He left without saying a word.

I finally had to give up all hope of my nap when half an hour after the doctor left I was wheeled downstairs for more x-rays for this new-fangled fancy cast they'd dreamed up. After the tech took them, the doctor came out holding two pictures and looked really hard at me as well (all these hard looks were starting to get to me) and said, "This is the picture of your leg when you came in." I could see the splinters running all around the break. Then he said, "This is the picture we just took." I looked closely. Even I could see it clearly. Every single tiny splinter was perfectly aligned. Every jig, every jag … every single one, *perfect!*

"Wow!" I breathed, "I guess I won't be needing any fancy cast now, eh?"

"Nope, just a regular walking cast will do."

So that afternoon I went back upstairs and had some lunch with a brand-new cast on a leg that had mysteriously set itself, with perfectly normal blood running through my veins.

About half an hour after lunch the same doctor who told me I would never see the sun rise again (and to make my peace with God!) was standing next to my bed—again. He kept flipping pages in the chart he was holding and shaking his head from time to time. As he lowered the chart he looked over at me and said, "Mr. White, I have heard about these kinds of things, but I never thought I'd actually ever see one." I honestly hadn't the slightest clue what he was talking about. He shook his head again and asked, "Would you mind coming into my office for a few moments?"

Seeing as how he was being so polite and all (and not pissing me off and trying to get me to die some more) I acquiesced, hopped out of bed, grabbed my crutches, and indicated "Lead on, Doc!"

When we got to his office he walked over to a big board with all kinds of paper and x-rays of my leg pinned up on it. He began comparing his chart notes to the board notes. Again, shaking his head, he said, "I never thought I'd actually see one!" He seemed to be talking to himself. Pointing to his charts, he said, "I've shown these to a few of my colleagues ..." and, like a cue from off stage, another doctor walked in and took the proffered chart and seemed to be trying to make sense of it as well.

The second doctor looked up at me—"This him?"—and then without even waiting for an answer went back to comparing his chart to the board. *Rude!* I thought. After a minute, he turned to the first doctor, shook his head, shrugged his shoulders, said "I have no idea," and walked out. I really did not like that man.

As we were walking back to my bed the doctor said to me again, "Mr. White," as he slowed his pace, "every once in a while, we hear about these kinds of things, but I never thought I'd actually witness one."

I could see that for some reason this doctor needed me to understand what he was trying to say. It was then, as I thought about it, that ever so slowly it finally began to dawn on me that all this time he had been talking about me being alive—but really, even then, only vaguely.

It honestly just didn't register. My leg healing and the oxygen in my blood normalizing was—well, all normal to me somehow. Really, as I think back, I can see I was as oblivious to the miracle he had just witnessed as I had been to my own death while I sat on its doorstep the night before.

I wasn't trying to be difficult or arrogant, even if I was a bit ... over the top. (When I asked God how I acted through it all, the two words that came through immediately, and *very* loud and *very* clear, were, and I quote, "insufferable asshole.") I honestly wasn't particularly thinking about anything at all. I think it was just the way God raised me—from birth. All was as it should have been.

I remember something my father once said to me. The reason Abraham was willing to offer up Isaac on the altar was because God had told him it would be through *Isaac* (and only Isaac) that the promise would be fulfilled. That meant that even if he required Isaac's life, God would just have to raise him from the dead to fulfill his promise—the promise that was to be fulfilled through Isaac and no other. Maybe in some small way my reasoning was of the same kind. God said it to me himself, so, no further worries. I would live—no matter what.

The doctors didn't understand. They couldn't understand. God and I were working out some of the fine details that needed to be addressed, and this was something we would handle on our own.

See, I'm really thick in the head, so sometimes God would have to do things like this to get a point across. The particular point he was making is one I didn't get until I started to write all of this stuff down and then actually remembered and meditated on what had happened.

The doctor looked at me quietly. "You're a very fortunate man, Mr. White," he said softly. "We'll take your blood one more time, and if everything is in order, as I'm sure it is, there is no reason you can't leave this afternoon. I wish you the very best," and then he left. And then so did I.

I think that was an interesting evening, no? One night, one day, two miracles.

I sat outside the hospital and had my smoke.

You know, the doctor said I should make my peace with God. Perhaps I'm doing so now. I've thought a lot about this little event since putting pen to paper. Why in the world did God heal me? I know a lot of pat answers, but for some reason I went through all that stuff without batting an eyelid. I never said a word to anyone about it for at least eight or nine years, maybe more. I think it's just never dawned on me how strange it might look to others. In my mind, God and I were in the middle of something, and this was just part of it—an interesting but kind of annoying lesson—sort of. So what gives? Maybe it was all so that poor doctor could see a miracle—who really knows why God does anything?

For all I knew he was just keeping me around so he could pick on me some more. Don't think he doesn't! Yeah, that and have a good fight every once in a while. I'm not kidding! I mean, look at poor old Jacob. He was just sitting around in the desert scratching his head, and God walked right up to Jacob and literally picked a fight, didn't he? Messed up *his* leg pretty good too! Could be I know how he felt, eh?

12
EPIPHANY

I think it's important that I stop right here and explain a couple of things. I don't know how most books are supposed to be written, but I wasn't particularly "all better" when I started writing this one. Nor was I particularly methodical when I finally did begin. But I believe all was as it should have been. I wrote my thoughts about whatever struck me, whenever they happened to strike me, and it was this restlessness in my writing that kept me turning pages—seeing more—jumping from chapter to chapter, back and forth, writing bits and odds, there and here, the whole time with this sense of God's amazing grace and love growing more powerful each passing day. I've had to come back to this chapter many times to read over what seemed to be a growing depository—a distillation of all I had learned about God's love and mercy—like a pause to gather the many voices of each chapter and cause them to sing in unity for a moment. It was during this … distilling process, while listening to all those voices together, that the floodgates burst wide open, and the love of God poured into me like a great crashing wave that seemed to never stop cresting. After one taste of that distillation—one chorus from that choir, I had to go back through every chapter I had written and write more—with the deep assurance of God's overwhelming love for me growing greater with every word I typed. That love has taken root inside me now, and this book is like the "first fruit" that it has produced.

God's compassion and understanding are absolutely mind-boggling. When I least expect it, and almost always when I least deserve it, he does something so wonderfully kind that all I can do is stand in confused wonder and weep. Tears of love and gratitude and hope would pour out of me all jumbled up together, and, utterly bewildered, I'd ask him again, "Lord ... why? I don't understand!" But my heart! My heart is *not* my mind and would always betray me. It sometimes felt as if it would leap right out of my soul to answer him—such a surprised longing and hoping. And even while I loved him, as I worshipped I knew deep down what it meant to be amazed. I knew what it meant when the Scriptures said that it is the *kindness* of God that leads to repentance (Rom. 2:4). His love is so ... different from ours.

There are never any strings attached. He does these thoughtful, tender-hearted things for me, and to me, just because he feels like it. He doesn't need any reasons. He loves me because he *chooses* to. And he is tender-hearted towards me, especially when I don't deserve it. As a matter of fact, all of the kindest and most wonderful things he has ever done in my life have consistently been when I was at my weakest and most sinful self. That's what makes me love him *like crazy*! First John 4:19 says, "We love because he first loved us." I told you—he started it! (*He always starts it* ...) That's why I want to obey him—why I love him—because he has demonstrated over and over, *to me,* that he loves me. He's already given me all the "goodness" I could ever need. *I don't have to try really hard to make him like me.* I am already clean—righteous in his eyes in spite of my sinfulness—forgiven even in those times when I'm right in the midst of it and I don't know how to ask for his forgiveness anymore. When I'm so lost I can't even find my way home. Isn't that when he came for us all—when we were lost and hopeless? And isn't that when his love is most precious—and most powerful? "But God shows his love for us in that while we were still sinners, Christ died for us" (Rom. 5:8). Fully grasping the fact that he could love even me—*that* is what changes me somehow. Being fully convinced of this frees me to love him with everything in me—and obeying him becomes my greatest desire.

"When I thought that God was hard, I found it easy to sin. But when I found God so kind, so good, so overflowing with compassion, I smote upon my breast to think that I could have rebelled against one who loved me so and sought my good" (Charles Spurgeon).[7]

As this understanding has become increasingly alive in me, being "good" has become increasingly (and quite mysteriously) easy—almost natural like. I *want* to be good (here's the crazy part ...) because in his eyes, *I already am!* This is the freedom he has given me. It's when I start constantly looking at myself and worrying about "How am I doing?" that I wind up in the ditch, defeated, guilty, depressed—a slave again to the law and alienated from God by the lies of the enemy—and by the pride of my own heart. Resting in his love, trusting in his forgiveness, and knowing deep down that I am *already* fully accepted by the one person in the whole world who matters most (and who loves me the most), trusting in this— that's when I become free to truly love without fear—like him. I become like him—and I become free.

I weep as I write these words. You would too if you were me. You see, he is holy and I am not, nor could I ever be except by the blood that my God and my Lord, Jesus, gave to me at the cross—my life, no charge. *Free in every way possible but paid for in blood.* His blood.

It's no wonder we struggle grasping this. God *is* love. Just that one truth alone is so hard to hold on to sometimes. I either forget how true it is or I struggle to believe that I can't add anything to it or I just plain lose sight of it. I forget the whys and the hows of my salvation—that I need to be saved and forgiven as much today as I did when I was living in that ditch and looking to myself for life, desperately groping blindly around in circles and finding only death. (Some days I wish I had a 2 by 4 with the words "BOUGHT AND PAID FOR!" stamped on it.)

Jesus said, "You will know the truth, and the truth will set you free" (John 8:32). I have known all my life that Jesus loved me and have known the truth of the gospel ever since I can remember. I have assented to all the correct theology and believed it ... in my heart. I did everything the Bible told me to do that I might be "saved." And I was saved—*but I wasn't free.* I didn't really know the truth, or else I would have been free—right? You see, Jesus said, "I am the way, and the truth, and the life" (John 14:6).

---

[7] Charles H. Spurgeon, "Repentance After Conversion," *Spurgeon's Sermons*, vol. 41, no. 2419 (Newington: Metropolitan Tabernacle, 1895), 3. Available at www.spurgeongems.org.

The truth is a person! Coming to know that person *personally* was when my life began to change and freedom began to come. It's impossible to be the same again after knowing first-hand the love of Christ. Knowing what the rules were did not change my heart! It was tasting his love that made me fall in love and want to do his will instead of following my own selfish desires. That's what *experiencing* his love does to people. That's what experiencing the *presence* of Jesus does. It changes us. It frees us from the power of sin—and from the power of *having* to sin. It changes our hearts by filling them with his love, because God is love—and that is the only truth that matters to a broken and contrite heart. And after seeing him, our hearts cannot help but be broken. This love is something that only God's Holy Spirit can bring to life in us. Throw a thousand Bible studies at someone, and every single hour spent would be lost in the dust of even 10 seconds of knowing—of *experiencing*—God's love. I can read from a book (yes, even the Bible) and learn all there is to know about someone but never once know what it's like to be gently kissed by that person ... so sad. I wonder, how well do we know Christ ... really?

I want to share with you two of the greatest and most profound kindnesses God has ever seen fit to grant me. Their beauty haunts me in the most wonderful ways, right to this very moment. I am both astonished and deeply humbled by them (... and there's kissing, too!).

Dad in his British Navy uniform   Mom as a "vision of beauty"

Mom and a friend in the jungle   The happy
mountains on the Island of Mindoro   (but somewhat bewildered) bride
ministering to the Mangyan tribes

Dad, Mom, and older brother Scott in Bolivia

Dad many years later

Mom and Dad
(who knows where in the world!)

Dad when he was most content   *Mom saying her last farewell before burying my father*

Mom and me (I love my mother!)

Me as a punk kid at age 23

One of those extremely rare and very brief
interludes of sobriety, at age 28

Restless and ready for
the road at age 49

Me in 2018

My barn and place for detox   *George D. (one of my earliest Huntsville guides) and me in Steve's and Julie's kitchen*

Steve and Julie Hill at home (my two most dearly loved friends)

Hill's House Rules   November 10, 2013

First of all, welcome to our home. We are glad you are here and we see you as a special guest. We want to provide for you an environment that is safe and will help in keeping you dry. We are not intending to keep you against your will. You can choose to go your own way at any time, but receiving help through our home is dependent on you complying with these guidelines. This is not an exhaustive list. Where appropriate we will refer to the guidelines from the program at Hope Acres.

1. You are free to be in your room, in the bathroom, or on the main floor. To be in the attic we would like someone to be with you. The basement and other bedrooms are off limits.
2. You may smoke outside. There are two chairs on the side porch, or a few options on the back porch. Please do not smoke in the barn.
3. To go off of the property, you should be accompanied by someone from our team.
4. We collect all devices including our computers and all cell phones at night to ensure that everyone gets their sleep. (We have been doing this for years.) We will charge the phones overnight.
5. All items containing alcohol have been removed from our home. We have done this for your protection.
6. You are free to use the kitchen phone for calls across Canada.
7. Our computers are not available for your personal use at this time.
8. For your benefit, visitors will need to be approved.
9. Weapons are not permitted on the premises.

The contract between the Hills and me

We will provide your meals, a roof over your head, and arrange for transportation as required.

Our intentions are to get you safely into a rehab program, but also to be a community where you can know you are cared for and accepted. We also want you to know that our friendship is not conditional on anyone's measure of success.

We would like you to attend AA meetings regularly and the Sunday worship services at St. Andrews.

Signed: _John White_

Witness: _____

Date: _4/11/13_

YEH BABY IT WORKED !!!

WE DID IT!

I SHOWED THIS to staff, THEY WERE IMPRESSED.

The contract between the Hills and me

Celebrating my first whole year of having my own place

*John
(who saved my life more
than once)*

*Jeff and Bonnie
(two of my main pillars)*

*Accepting the Word Guild
"Best New Canadian
Manuscript" Award
with Julie*

13
JUST FOR YOU

I saw something once. Something so profoundly beautiful I could scarcely bear to look at it. I almost despair at the thought of describing it.

This physical manifestation that appeared right before my eyes—this demonstration and illustration of the incredible power and beauty of Christ's church, of his bride, and the burning intensity of love and exuberant passion he feels for her was so overwhelming, so … bewilderingly beautiful that simple words utterly fail me. How can I ever possibly communicate it? I can't. All I can do, with my so very inadequate vocabulary, is to *try* to describe it. I will never be able to explain its impact on me. What I will say is that God's love and his plans are far greater than any of us will ever comprehend. At this point, all I can do—all I can *ever* do—is try to *explain* what I saw early that morning, deep in the Rocky Mountains.

Scripture says, "No eye has seen, nor ear heard" (1 Cor. 2:9). From what I saw that day, that is far truer than any of us could possibly imagine. Again, I must say at this point, *everything* I'm about to relate is both factual and accurate to the very best of my ability—all of it.

I was driving the same Hyundai I had when I met the fisherman. (I still wonder about that one.) It may have even been the same trip; I don't know. After crossing and recrossing those mountains for so many years, things just seem to blur together. I'm only now just able to pinpoint what decade things were in. Anyway, whenever it was, I was an absolute wreck.

I don't know if you comprehend "wreck." Mentally, emotionally, physically, spiritually, absolutely, totally, completely bankrupt. Pooched, spent, terrified, alone, hurt, hungry, tired, scared, lost, guilt-ridden, dirty, sick, lonely, exhausted, and weak. Get the picture? I simply could not drive another inch, and early that morning, at the very end of my rope, I crested a hill and had to pull over onto the side of the road.

I was looking out over a valley, just trees, and far in the distance a small town. I knew the place, but I couldn't go there. I'd attract far too much attention. I looked every inch of what I just described. People would have phoned the police just for my safety, never mind their own.

I lifted the emergency brake, took the keys out of the ignition, sat back, and just stared blankly through the windshield, unseeing. Then I began to cry.

All of the exhaustion, all of the shame and guilt and remorse, all of the fighting and running and hiding, all of the being so very far away from God, all of the years and years of the highway, all of the hospitals and injuries, and all of the sin, not only my own but also that of others against me, the heartbreak and disappointment and failure—all of it just came crashing in like a thick black wave of despair, and I laid my head on the steering wheel and quietly and hopelessly began to sob. After a time, I gradually was able to slowly calm down a bit. Then, I just felt numb— completely empty—drained. I raised my head and put my chin on the steering wheel, not thinking, just staring—completely blank—completely emptied.

It was a grey dawn. The sun was trying miserably to shine, even though it was pretty much a clear sky. There were a couple of clouds, a drab grey on the pale blue backdrop, slowly drifting across the sky. Absentmindedly, I began to track one, watching as it slowly changed in shape.

Then it happened. As the grey cloud reached the very centre of my field of vision something astonishing happened—something wonderful! This is the point where I will get lost and my pitiful attempt at description will fall so very far short of what I saw and experienced that morning.

It was as though the sun, which had been barely shining before, suddenly had a veil swept aside, and it burst into brilliant life. A shaft of golden light shone directly on the cloud I had been tracking, and in less than five seconds the cloud was transformed, as though it had become lit from within, to reveal a startling and perfectly accurate vision of a man's face and shoulder.

He was incredibly detailed, in three dimensions and three-quarter profile, stunningly clear with exact and very precise proportions—perfect in every way possible. The cloud seemed to glow with every conceivable colour of the rainbow—shades that I could never possibly describe. They were shifting, changing to reveal even more colours as the cloud slowly drifted across the sky. That cloud was alive—at least it acted alive. It was the colours that gave it life—moving and shifting as if reflecting some intense emotion.

The cloud was absolutely perfect in every detail. The broad forehead, the long windswept hair, his beard and moustache, his nose, his eyes as though fixed on something incredibly wonderful. Even the crinkles at the corners of his eyes, everything was so perfect ... flawless. I could almost make out the whiskers of his beard. He was rugged looking yet majestic. I can see him now—a strong jaw and generous mouth, smiling in great joy. I could see clearly his well-defined cheekbones; even his ears were perfectly proportioned.

He was moving slowly across the sky, changing slowly, almost shimmering, but never once losing any of his amazingly precise definition. And the strength and the *joy!* I could feel it! My ears had begun ringing with the vibrations of power, heavy with the presence of the Holy Spirit. It was as though a bomb had exploded in my head. *This was not a squint-your-eyes-and-imagine sort of thing.* This was a statement! As clear, unmistakable, and understandable as it could possibly be. And he looked so noble! So full of joy and excitement! It seemed that my entire body was resonating with the Holy Spirit in every molecule.

Then slowly I became aware of something to my right. As I shifted my gaze to what had attracted my attention, the power of the Holy Spirit grew so strong on me that I can't possibly explain it. That was when my mind began to reel in amazement and my head began to swim in circles. It actually took a few seconds before my mind could accept what I was seeing. I sat stunned, frozen in wonder, and was only able to watch helplessly as this marvel unfolded right before my eyes.

Rushing toward Christ, for that was whom I was beholding, was the indescribably beautiful face and shoulders of a woman, the same size, in three dimensions, with all of the colours, all of the detail, all of the joy and passion of Christ. She was breathtakingly glorious, just so incredibly beautiful, and she was rushing towards her Lord, Christ.

She also was perfect in every detail. Her long hair was being blown about by the wind, trailing behind her as if she was running—toward him, her Lord! Glorious! She had high cheekbones, a finely sculpted nose, and her smile! So joyous, so happy, so very beautiful. Her eyes were fixed, firmly gazing into his. Her lips were slightly parted as though she were breathing deeply, and she was smiling in great joy at the sight of her Lord. She was just so, so beautiful ...

The two clouds were drifting slowly towards each other, and God's Spirit kept growing more and more powerful, almost more than I could bear. As they drew nearer each other, my wonder threatened to overwhelm me. I could see what was coming. I knew.

Each had eyes only for the other. Trembling had almost overcome my body completely, and my mind could scarcely accept what my eyes were beholding. They drew closer and closer together. With tears brimming over in my eyes, I could only whisper out in a sob, "God, they are going to kiss ... aren't they?" I watched, dumbstruck in overwhelmed silence as their lips met in the heavens—perfectly.

I began to sob in helpless amazement, wonder, and unspeakable joy as they merged slowly together to become one. As they did, the colours gradually began to dim. The clouds that had merged to become one slowly began to shrink until there was nothing left—just a few thin wisps, which soon evaporated until there was nothing left but a clear bright blue sky, not a single cloud in it. I was left completely stunned, overwhelmed by the Spirit of God, and alone on the highway.

Tears were running down my face. Sobs coming out of me mixed with unintelligible words of worship and adoration. I was shaking my head and laughing and crying and saying things like "You're so wonderful, God ... You're so beautiful; you're just so beautiful! So wonderful—I don't understand ... How? Why do you love me so? I love you so very much, God! I just love you so very, very, much, Lord, just so, so much!"

As I finally settled down a bit and was wiping my eyes and blowing my nose, I could still feel God's presence heavily on me, in the very air surrounding me, even on my car and extending about three feet out from it.

Then I noticed something else. I looked up and around me and realized I was alone on the highway. All this had taken close to 15 minutes to unfold. No cars or trucks had passed by me the entire time. All was silent, and I was alone and at peace. I got curious ...

"God?" I asked, "did anyone else see this?"

There was a slight pause, and then, very gently, "No, Kevin. That was just for you."

I burst out into fresh sobs of laughter and love, and, weeping with joy, I could only shake my head in amazement as I helplessly tried to express how much I loved him. After a time, all I could do was sit and sigh and softly smile.

I felt clean and somehow deeply refreshed. I knew for certain, once more, that I was loved and that his love is so far beyond my understanding, so vast and enormous that I will never understand it—never reach the end of it. I can only be swallowed up and drowned in it.

Finally, wiping my nose and my eyes, still shaking my head, I marked the exact spot in my mind. I have yet to return there, but, God willing, one day I shall.

As huge as he is, he took the time to once again show a tired, broken, and lonely drunk his love and his heart for him. He is so absolutely beautiful—so very worthy of praise. And not just for me, but for us! For all of us! His church. He gave me that morning a brief glimpse into the incredible mystery that is Christ and his bride, the church—perfect and without flaw. I can never again look at the sky the same way, and often as I gaze upon it and remember, tears of wonder stain my face.

I started the car and headed home with that image—that revelation—forever stamped in my heart and on my mind. I knew then that even though I was defeated, he was not, nor could he ever be. I knew then, in that moment, that his love is far stronger and more powerful than anything I will ever know and that I will never understand it or comprehend it, and once again, I can only be swept up and lost in it.

14
My Complaint

There was another time this happened, in another place—the very first time … *Whoa! Wait a minute! Just everybody hold on one cotton-pickin' minute here.* If you think putting this wild-ass kind of stuff down on paper is easy, well … you're wrong! I've probably written down enough now to get me committed to "Aunt Sally's Fruit Farm" for the rest of my ridiculous life.

And another thing. When this sort of stuff's happening, it's not like I can pretend that it's not happening, because it *is* happening, and there is no off switch or rewind or fast forward for that matter.

You know what's really scary? Many times when these sorts of things do take place, it just feels natural, normal, like it's supposed to be happening … like it's no big deal. I really mean it. I've had visions and just got up and started going about my business, and it's not till I've gone a good 20 paces or so that I realize what in the world just transpired!

Then there are the things that are not just visions. They're really real! Like with real things! Like the clouds I've just described. Believe me, I've had several visions, and manifestations are entirely different. Those times when God reveals himself, or his plans, through things that have a physical form are enough to rattle anyone down to their bare bones. You can't ever forget about those for the simple reason that they are impossible to deny. They have been, are, or have become a part of this world's reality—but visions? Those are things almost surreal—like dreaming with my eyes wide open, and suddenly they just kind of suddenly pop into focus out of nowhere. Often I'm not even sure what I'm looking at. Other times I've had my socks blown clean off by their clarity, self-evident purpose, and power—those times when things are so close and so real I can't tell if I've actually touched them or if what I'm seeing is physically present or not. It all gets very confusing. The funny thing is that I'll forget about them, sometimes for years, sometimes because I just don't want to talk about them, but mostly because I'm either too scared or God tells me to keep my big mouth shut. So, time slips by, and they don't come out till God kind of reminds me of them.

It's only when I remember them and begin talking about them with other people that I suddenly realize they're looking at me like I'm some kind of whacked-out wing nut. That's when I catch on that these sorts of things are not really a part of most people's lives very much—and don't exactly happen very often either.

And again, it's not my fault! I didn't just wake up one morning and go "Gee, I think I'll have a vision of God today." I come by this stuff honestly, you know. I could tell you at least three visions and two manifestations my father had … and he wrote about them too. *The Cost of Commitment, The Pathway of Holiness, The Golden Cow,* and *Eros Redeemed* all contain references to these kinds of things. Those are just the ones in books that I remember offhand. Then there are the ones he told only me about. Perhaps it runs in the family. I don't know … maybe it happens all the time to other people, but me being the kind of person I am, whenever it does happen, I'm scared people will just think I'm going through DTs (delirium tremens) or something. All I'm certain of is that whenever I talk about this kind of thing, people seem to get real uncomfortable … kinda nervous like. It makes me feel weird, or sort of stupid.

Visions, dreams, hearing voices in my head—knowing things? I mean, come on! Holy people maybe, or saints—you know, "godly folk"—those kinds of people; that I could understand. I don't know, somebody whom other folk might believe or who deserves them or something. But a drunk? A dirty smelly wino? Why? What's to be gained? Who is going to believe anything *I* have to say? Why me?

(Actually, now that I've had the time to think about it, maybe someone like me can let thousands of others just like me know that it's *OK!* God hasn't forgotten about you! You're not too small, and he's *not* mad at you, and he loves you so much, and you can come home now. He wants you to know that you don't have to ever be afraid of him again, 'cause he'll take you just like that, the way you are, and that he *loves* you and really misses you, and he wants you to come home to him ... *now!* I know it's so hard to believe—but it's *true!)*

Anyway ... you've got to understand. Whenever I go into a hospital and they ask me if I'm hearing things—voices, say—or if I'm seeing things (and they do ask), I always have a hard time answering. I mean, if I just said, "Oh yeah! I hear things a lot! God himself talks to me quite often. I've seen him myself a couple of times. Nice guy, but he asks me to do all sorts of stuff that's kind of strange. Yep, and he never seems to shut up either. Talk! Talk! Talk! *Jeesh!* It gets real annoying after a while. Got any Valium?"

Well, I'll leave the admitting attendant's chart entries to your imagination, but I'm pretty sure you can see for yourself why they'd get real curious real quick. Curse of Western society really. It's all touch, taste, see. Everything has to be concrete, you know?

What makes everything even worse is when you're being admitted for alcoholic seizures and hallucinations in the first place. You try convincing a doctor you really do know the difference between reality and unreality while you're watching spiders popping right out of his skin and crawling up his arm into his ear ...

I've told a few Christians things that God has shown me, done for me, or said to me, and they said things like "I find that rather hard to believe, Kevin," because they're too scared to call me an outright liar. Of course they're hard to believe! They're bloody miracles! What do you expect? It gets lonely sometimes ...

And don't think I don't go back and check and recheck my memory, not only for accuracy but because as I remember and write these things down, even I myself have a bit of a hard time with some of this stuff. My now ex-wife witnessed a few things God did, and when she told her own mother about them, her mother refused to believe her. You haven't even heard some of the really strange stuff! The things I just won't talk about. Especially those I don't understand. For them, I have only facts and theories. No real explanations.

To top it all off, how do I even begin to describe the vast bombardment of thoughts and emotions that pour through me during one of these little episodes? How does one explain the inexplicable? It's no wonder I hardly understand myself.

I have wept many times over a lot of the things I have written here, and as I've looked at them with new eyes, I have been driven to my knees, and time and again I've had to put my face on the ground in repentance and worship with every fibre in me and ask, "Why? How? God, *why* do you love like this?"

Do you really want to know the answer to that question?

Then keep reading, 'cause you're really going to like what comes next!

15
I Just Can't Help Myself

This is really a hard one (sigh). Yeah—one of those ones that left me a trembling basket case in stunned adoration and—well, worship is almost too mild a term … as a matter of fact, it is *far* too mild a term! Nothing I could ever say could possibly explain how this wonder affected me. I'm starting to weep already! Joy! Pure unadulterated, pure undiluted, endless, boundless joy! Remember this always: "The joy of the Lord is your strength" (Neh. 8:10)!

I was at a small Christian treatment centre back when I actually still believed that *I* could get sober. After some months of getting physically healed up, I began to really seek the Lord in earnest. I loved God so much and longed deeply to talk with him—just to be close to him, to speak with him again. I so wanted to sense, to feel, his presence once more.

For days I'd been fasting, crying out to God in prayer, asking for his presence and power in my life. I was eating up the Word and would often be in worship for hours at a time. God was meeting me in powerful ways, especially in worship.

I'd remembered an old Sunday school song and had taken to singing it or humming it all the time. I loved its simplicity—the love and devotion to Christ that it expressed. As I sang it one night, I started to expand it, and as I began to make it mine, I slowly became filled with the Holy Spirit very powerfully. I was singing and playing with all my heart, and as I did, gradually I became utterly lost in love, worship, and adoration of my Lord. I was ... gone, it seemed, swept up by God's Spirit, and was hardly even aware of where I was or what I was doing. I was still playing and singing to him, but his presence was so powerful it seemed unfathomable.

Then I remember that gradually the room seemed to grow warmer and brighter, till suddenly, in an instant, *He was there!* Just like that! *AND OH! HE IS SO, SO WONDERFUL!* He was there in the room—*with me!* Twirling, dancing, whirling about the room, skipping, and spreading his arms open wide! He was dancing with everything in him! Wild abandon! Great waves! He was radiating great waves of joy so powerful that they were almost physical. He was so happy! Smiling with such elation and gladness that he was almost laughing out loud. He was just so incredibly ... delighted! It all came off him, all of it, wave after wave of it, and it would have melted any heart and could have brought a dead man dancing right out of the grave ... just to be close to him. (I think now that's how he's going to raise the dead! Sheer, triumphant joy! A mighty shout of exultant and joyous victory!)

He seemed to be everywhere all at once, dancing to the song I was singing with unbridled passion, wildly free from any fear or inhibition. Perfect love driving out everything but joy—joy like I've never felt before in my entire life!

I think I must have finished singing my song because the next thing I knew he was standing behind me. He was smiling and had both of his hands on my shoulders. I knew he was smiling. Somehow it seemed I could see him, even though he was behind me. He was the only thing in the entire world I was aware of. Only him!

I have never in my whole entire life, ever, even to this very second, been so totally, completely, supremely, incredibly happy—*ever.*

I have no idea what I was doing. Crying? I must have been. Trembling? Almost certainly. All I knew at that moment was HIM! My King! My Lord! JESUS! My Saviour! My love! My HEAD! It was just spinning in circles! I was lost. Time was gone. All there was, was HIM—Jesus, my Lord.

Somehow (and I don't know how) from trembling lips I managed to whisper, "God—how? Why? How can you possibly be so wonderful?" At that, he threw back his head and gave a great laughing chuckle. The whole room seemed to get even brighter and warmer as he said to me, "Kevin, I just can't help myself!" and then he leaned around my shoulder and kissed me right on my cheek, and then, just like that, he vanished as quickly as he had come. He was gone … sigh. And all I could do was sit there. I couldn't do anything. I have no idea at all what I was thinking. I don't think I was even capable of thinking. I just sat—stunned. Jesus's love is so amazing! It's no wonder the Bible says the joy of the Lord is your strength! His joy is indescribably powerful—so powerful that nothing could ever stand it. It's his joy! *He has already won. "IT IS FINISHED!" and with a cry of victory he gave up his spirit—to snatch the keys of death and hell right out of the enemy's hand.*

The man conquered death, for crying out loud! He single-handedly beat the living daylights out of Satan and all his legions and in one move redeemed humankind from sin and death, bringing us all back to him where we belong—and after making a fool out of The Liar, he now holds the keys of death and hell in his hand. He did all of this just so we could dance with him. All of *us* are the joy he set before his eyes as he endured the cross! It is why he gave his life. For his bride. *We are his treasure—his glory!* And how we will dance (that's kind of scary for me …) *with God!* Can you imagine? Go ahead. Ask *me* if Jesus is real. (Ha!) See what kind of answer you're going to get!

These kinds of visions and the manifestations—they have ruined me now. I've often wished I'd never even seen them. To have witnessed the Lord in glory … to have been in the power and beauty of his presence— it has left me with a longing that can never be satisfied until I am at his side forever. For years all I craved was booze. Now all I want is to be in his presence. That is why I despise my sin, for the simple reason that it separates me from him, from the one I love.

God has been so incredibly gracious to me that I want to tell everyone of his power and glory … *and of his mercy.* There is no other King—none like him, abounding in love, in mercy, and tender compassion for his own, his children for whom he is coming—coming to find and bring back to himself. *And he will not lose one of them!* If you are broken, ashamed, or discouraged by your failure, just come. I have seen him, and his joy and longing for you are far greater and higher than the heavens, and his love is far deeper and richer than your sin. You can come home now! He is but a single breath away—as close as your heart.

Just come. Come to him. Don't bring anything with you but your brokenness. There isn't a single thing you can bring to this equation but yourself. It's kind of like in the movies. The high school dance. You're the guy and you're hoping against all hope that the most beautiful girl in the world will say "Yes" when you ask her to dance. As you walk across the floor of the darkened gym, you sweat bullets and your throat grows parched, and your suit suddenly fits wrong in all the wrong places, and all you can think about is the pimple you mysteriously grew the night before ... until she turns and looks straight into your eyes and, with the most beautiful smile you've ever seen (oh, wonder of wonders!), asks, "Will you dance with me?"

"The most beautiful girl in the world is asking me? To dance?" That's kind of like what God does. You may think you're asking him to come into your life, but the truth is—since before you took your first breath, he has been asking you to come dance with him. Listen to what Jesus says, "The Father who sent me is in charge. He draws people to me—and that's the only way you'll ever come. Only then do I do my work, putting people together, setting them on their feet, ready for the End" (John 6:43–46 MSG). "Every person the Father gives me eventually comes running to me. And once that person is with me, I hold on and don't let go" (John 6:35–38 MSG). That's right out of Jesus' mouth! He said it, and that's exactly what he did with me! So ... give it up! He wants you and he wants you now. Listen to this: "The word that saves is right here, as near as the tongue in your mouth, as close as the heart in your chest" (Rom. 10:4–8 MSG). It's the word of faith that welcomes God to go to work and set things right for us. "Say the welcoming word to God—'Jesus is my Master'—embracing, body and soul, God's work of doing in us what he did in raising Jesus from the dead. *That's it. You're not 'doing' anything; you're simply calling out to God, trusting him to do it for you. That's salvation. With your whole being you embrace God setting things right, and then you say it, right out loud: 'God has set everything right between him and me!'"* (Rom.10:8–10 MSG, emphasis added). So, give it up! He wants you and he wants you now. Just say "Jesus, thank you that you love me. You know all about me, and so I ask you to come and actually live within me. Forgive my many sins and cleanse me with your blood. I want to belong to you now. Please help me. Thank you for

dying for me. Now, please teach me how to live for you. Thank you so much. Please show me more about you and how much you love me every day. Amen."

Now, go tell someone who also knows Jesus. Tell them what you did. That's really important! (And you can write and tell me if you want to. I'd be really jazzed!)

16
BE CAREFUL WHAT YOU ASK FOR

This is some really weird stuff coming up. I've got to be honest; I'm not exactly sure how to communicate these "happenings" to you. It's just that—well, I don't want to scare anybody away, because honestly, I don't even know what in the world most of this craziness is. I have no idea where it comes from (which really bothers me), but I do have some theories as to how it works (which bothers me even more). I'm actually hoping that somebody out there might have a clue and give me a heads-up on what it's all about, 'cause I'm sure not going to ask the questions I have over the internet! So, with that, welcome to my world …

Strange things have been happening to me all my life. It's always been that way, and seeing as how there really didn't seem to be any signs of things changing, I guess over time I just sort of got used to them.

Now because this weirdness had been so inordinately present in my life, I've had some inordinately weird questions that needed answering. Unfortunately for me, the more information I got on said weirdness, the more particulars I needed to properly interpret and assess the conclusions they inevitably led to; long and short of it being, I had to ask a lot more even weirder questions, which naturally led people to believe *I was* weird, and no matter how much I told them that none of it was my fault and that all this strangeness was because I am the victim of an elaborately devised plot dreamed up a long time ago by a Super Intelligent Brilliant Genius Type Mastermind who wanted to show off, they would quite unfairly (at least in my opinion) think that I was even weirder than I am (which I'm not) ... (did I just say that?) ... (I never did say I wasn't, did I?). HA! I told ya you were gonna get confused. (At least I am ... sigh, I do this to myself, you know.)

Like I said, these are inordinately strange things that I need to examine and try to find some sort of reasonable explanation for. The only hindrance to this investigation of mine is that I seem to have run out of explanation ammo. Some of these occurrences are things that I can talk about even though they make people uncomfortable, some I am not allowed to talk about, and others are just so strange I simply don't want to talk about them, because if I do, first people think I'm just kidding around, and when they finally realize I'm not kidding around, I go from simply strange to straight-up crackers. This situation is both lonely and troubling.

You see, I never tried to make any of these things happen, but the problem is, I am involved somehow. When I try to speak about them, about what's going on, I mean, most Christians—just like when I was in junior high and my friends didn't feel comfortable around me—either don't want to hear about this kind of stuff or they just don't want to hear about this kind of stuff.

That being said, it's difficult to find people to talk to, and most of the people who *do* want to talk about it are scary whack jobs who do not love and are not part of the blood-bought body of our Lord, Saviour, and God, Jesus Christ.

Now, I've been dancing around exactly what these things are, so I'll get to the point. Soon. *I need to understand because these things have to be brought into some sort of discipline, just for my own sanity.* So what I've done is chosen four examples of this craziness to try to analyze and develop some sort of Scriptural theology for them. That is my ultimate goal. There is absolutely zero pretense here; nor is there going to be any exaggeration or straight out bull-pucky. You are getting straight goods.

The Bible says that life and death are in the power of the tongue. It also says that he who can control it is perfect in every way, and for you trivia buffs, it is said to be the strongest single muscle in the human body. Rightly so. It is usually the one we exercise most.

When this stuff started happening—or rather, when I actually began to notice it—I became very confused and a little frightened. I really didn't understand what it was that was going on. However, I saw that they happened far too often to be either random or coincidental. What follows are four examples of things I have said and their results in days, hours, minutes, and seconds. All I know for sure about it is that I am now far more careful about what I say and how I say it.

16.1: THE FIRE (DAYS)

It was in California, right at the very peak of my IV drug use. I knew I had to get out because the people I hung with, the places I went to, and the things I had to do to keep my habit going were way too squirrely—dangerously squirrely.

There was this one place I would go to pick up. It was OK at first, but then somehow, something changed. It became terribly dark. Sick. Wrong in a way I couldn't put my finger on, but very definitely evil. Then I found out some of the ages of the girls they were selling to, and that's when I got angry—*extremely angry*. Girls of their age couldn't afford to buy that stuff. They couldn't pay money, that is.

Anyway, I walked away from the place in a hugely powerful rage, and as I left I said real loud, "This place is going to shut down! It is going to shut down, and it's going to shut down PRONTO! I don't care if it takes a bloody fire and the whole place burns to the ground; *this place will shut down,* AND IT WILL SHUT DOWN QUICK!"

I came back a day and a half later, and there was nothing left but smouldering timbers and a chimney. Firemen were still putting parts of the fire out. No one got hurt, but the whole house was completely gutted by fire. I looked at it for a moment and then walked away. I felt nothing—only a little confused. I'm not an arsonist. It proved to be an electrical fire caused by an appliance that had been left on. Nobody blamed me at all for it, but nobody who was part of that house looked or talked to me the same ever again. Mostly they just avoided me.

16.2: THE FLOOD (HOURS)

Coincidence? At the time I thought so—but a flood? That's a little different, isn't it? You can't cause a flood ... can you?

It was BC. A Native friend of mine, Alice, came to me with a problem. She was a close friend, and I had known her for a long time. "Kevin, I really need your help with something, and you are the only person I know that can help me."

She had brought me a bottle of my favourite wine, so I knew something was up before she even opened her mouth, but I was curious, so I asked her to explain. After she did I looked at her and thought I saw the few remaining bats in her pretty little head abandoning their post.

"What in the world makes you think I can help you with this?!"

She just shook her head and said she was absolutely sure I could fix it for her—that I *would* fix it for her. She was extremely insistent and very sincere.

Apparently, her daughter, whom I knew, was getting real messed up bad on crack. Some girl had moved in on her and was getting her to hit the crack pipe really hard (as in non-stop), and no matter who talked to her she wouldn't listen to anyone, and she wouldn't kick the girl out. She was basically a good kid, but she was going down fast and in danger of losing her child, a bright little seven-year-old.

When Alice came to me I was living in the bush mostly, or wherever I could get out of the cold. I had nothing. I was just sort of tramping around from place to place and staying as drunk as I possibly could every day. Why she believed I had some sort of solution for her was beyond me, and I told her so, but she was completely convinced and most insistent. In fact, she wanted me to go to her daughter's place that day.

Finally, after much persuasion, I relented, but I told Alice several times I was promising her nothing other than to go down with her and have a *quick* look-see. We picked up a case of beer for her and a few jugs for me and then went to her daughter's place.

Her kid was living in a reasonably new basement apartment, had been there for a number of years, and never had a single problem. As we sat and visited, I watched the dynamics of the situation. I could see clearly why Alice was concerned about her daughter. She was looking pretty bad. I didn't think much beyond that, and the evening wound down to a close.

Everyone knew I was homeless, so I was invited to stay the night and have a shower in the morning. I grabbed the couch, and just as I was about to pull my sleeping bag over my head (I *always* had my gear with me), Alice came out and crouched down beside me.

"So? What do you think?"

Truth be told, I had almost forgotten about it. I was just tired and kind of grumpy. I sighed inside. *What in the world does she want me to do?* I looked at her. When I saw the eagerness, the expectant trust in her eyes, I got even more irritable, and without even thinking, out of my mouth popped, "I don't care if it takes a bloody flood! She'll be out of here by tomorrow morning!" She looked at me with eyes shining and said simply, "Good!" real excited like, and then got up and went to bed. As I pulled the covers up over myself, I thought, *Or I'll toss her sorry ass out the door myself!* (I meant it, too.) Then, almost immediately, I fell into a deep sleep.

It must have been a deep sleep, because when I woke the next morning I could hear a whole whack of commotion going on. I saw somebody walking by with a suitcase (I think) while I was still rubbing my eyes. I let go a big stretch, pulled myself up to a sitting position, and then put my feet down into about six inches of water.

"What in blazes! What in the world is—?" Just then Alice came out of a room holding a couple of boxes, with her jeans rolled up around her ankles and grinning like crazy from ear to ear. "Kevin!" she said, smiling even wider. "It flooded!" I looked around the apartment, and the entire place, all of it except for one small area at the back of the kitchen, was under at least half a foot of water.

I just shook my head, grabbed my smokes, and said, "Alice, get me a beer." Then I looked around some more and started trying to figure out just exactly what in the cotton-pickin' world was going on.

Alice came back and handed me my beer, and grinning like crazy she said again, "It flooded last night, Kevin!" Now I'm not much of a morning person at the best of times. As a matter of fact, anyone and everyone who really knows me knows better than to even talk to me in the morning, and I've knocked people unconscious just for waking me up. Peace and quiet.

Yep. No damn radio, no cotton-pickin' TV, no nothing except a beer and a smoke, and definitely no flipping six inches of water in the house!

I sat there in a daze, trying to figure out why I was drinking my beer in a house full of water while people were running in and out of the house, carrying all kinds of boxes every which way in all different directions at once. It was making me dizzy just watching them.

"Kev! It flooded, remember? You know … *it flooded.*"

I didn't like the sound of that. As a matter of fact, I didn't like any of it one bit! Waking up to a house full of water is enough to rattle anyone's cage, but now I was starting to get the distinct feeling that, somehow, I was going to get blamed for it. At that point all I could do was sit back and stare stupidly while I watched all these people running back and forth with various household items (and sip my beer, of course).

Alice could see, I think, that I was having kind of a hard time with this picture, so she leaned over and started to explain.

"Kevin, remember what you said to me last night, you know, when I asked you what you thought?" I stared blankly, not saying a word. "You said you didn't care if it took a flood, she would be gone in the morning."

"Whoa up here! Just wait one cotton-pickin' minute here! I didn't have nothing to do with anything about anything to do with any flippin' bit of *nothing!*" Then I remember blinking a few times, giving my nose a rub, and thinking, *Did I?*

"Kev! You don't understand! This is the best thing that could have ever possibly happened! She's gone! The girl is gone! Last night it rained really hard, and the drain in the driveway couldn't handle the water. It backed up so the water seeped under the door and flooded the whole place. We called social services this morning and found out the city is at fault because the sewer on the street backed up, which is why our sewer couldn't handle the water—so the city is to blame, and they are the ones who have to foot the bill. Social services is going to find us a new place to live because they have to rip this place apart to clean it up properly. They also have to buy us new beds, blankets, pillows, and some new clothing, *and* they have to replace anything with any water damage. They are really concerned about it because it's all sewer water, and they don't want any lawsuits. They're going to put us up at that hotel down the road, with the swimming pool and a hot tub, and because we can't cook in there, we can order take out three times a day and the city has to pay for all of it, *and most importantly, only family members can stay there!* So the girl has to move out and go back to live with her mother. She's gone, Kevin! She left this morning. She can't come with us! She left just like you said! You can come because we told them you are the boy's uncle."

I sat back on the couch even more dazed than before. "Alice … grab me another beer."

I went for a long swim and a sauna that afternoon. I think we ate Chinese for dinner.

16.3: ANNOYING (MINUTES)

This one will probably get me into trouble. I actually don't even want to write about it, for a couple of reasons. One, because there are aspects to it that are quite personal and involve other people whose privacy I must respect (which is just about like a bucket of glue in a confetti factory when it comes to storytelling), and two, because I "pushed" on it. Hard.

However, the whole story is true, and so herein lies another example of that which epitomizes what I'm so desperately trying to figure out. It also raises all sorts of critically important questions that I am almost crazy to get answers to. Most of them I'm afraid to even ask. You see, I am not a theologian. All I have to go on is my own experience. That probably explains why we need theologians (and why they need me?). At any rate, God and I have spoken at great length about this sort of thing, and as I have thought and prayed carefully on it, I believe he has shown me why this kind of thing can be extremely harmful (and actually very dangerous).

This story begins with my friend Bruce and I deciding to go on a "Royal Tear." I had stolen a company van, ran up a thousand dollars on the overdraft, and hightailed it to the Okanagan Valley. (This is the part where it would take too long to explain, and I have promised to guard certain people's anonymity.)

We finally got caught and tossed in the hoosegow almost a week later. It was quite the scene. We had both been tagged for years as "extremely violent, approach with caution, high escape custody risk" and were known by police pretty much anywhere we went. Nothing real serious, you understand. I think we just really irritated the daylights out of them because we were drunk every day and could go wherever we wanted to, whenever we wanted to, and they couldn't. Plus, for some reason we always seemed to come out smelling like roses every time we got into trouble. Nailing the two of us at once was a bonus, and they spared no expense. News crews, police videos, Tasers, shotguns, about eight officers, four dogs, about six cars … man, there was dust flying everywhere. Smokes, you'd have thought we were Butch Cassidy and the Sundance Kid! It wasn't that we were so bad that bothered them; it was just that we kept getting away with all the little stuff they knew we did. It was all quite dramatic actually.

Now while I was still busy using my sophisticated communication skills to try to explain that this was all just some sort of misunderstanding and a really bad case of a frightfully garbled communications network, I noticed that Bruce was being far more subdued than usual. He wasn't even lying Tasered and twitching on the ground or anything. Highly unusual … that was actually my first clue something was up. They stuck us in a holding cell until they could figure out what was what and how to proceed with charges.

Now I knew I was going to be OK. Bruce, on the other hand, was another kettle of fish entirely. He was freakin' way out. In all the years we roamed around together I'd never seen him in such a state. As soon as we were in, he immediately started pacing back and forth (which I hate) and muttering to himself (which I hate even more) and mumbling about warrants (which started smoke sizzling out of my nose). This was the first I'd heard about any warrants.

"Warrants? What warrants?" I was yelling.

He just kept on muttering about 14 warrants. "Fourteen! I've got out for my arrest, Kev! Fourteen! I'm gone! Pooched! Fourteen! I'm not getting out of here, Kev!"

I wanted to punch him right in the side of the head. Hard. I sighed instead and went to my corner of the cell and sat down. I was mad—real mad. If I'd have known this before, I would have handled everything a lot differently, and we probably wouldn't have been in the jam we were in, and honestly, you have to understand, me being angry in a closed space is absolutely not healthy for anyone, including me. Smokes, I had broken a beer bottle across the front of some guy's face and almost drowned him in two feet of water for making a grab at my beer—and that not more than a half hour before we got busted. The only reason Bruce was still talking was because we had been up and down the highway so many times together.

He just kept on pacing and muttering to himself, and I just kept getting angrier and angrier. "Fourteen! I'm gone, Kev, I'm just so gone!"

Now it's hard to explain exactly what or how this all happened. It just did. I know I had reached my absolute limit of listening and was so sick and tired of hearing Bruce's whining about "fourteen warrants" that I jumped straight up off the floor. I pushed real hard, and out of my mouth popped, "Bruce, all your warrants, all fourteen of them, are going to get dropped. They're going to let you out. As a matter of fact, they're going to let you out before they let *me* out, so wait for me!" Then I pushed again—even harder. He didn't even pay attention. I said it to him again and pushed hard—again. As I was saying it, this time he stopped and looked at me real confused like. I think because he'd seen me pull some real crazy stuff before, he was probably wondering what in the heck I was up to this time. I walked across the cell and grabbed him by the shoulders, and shaking him real hard I yelled at him, "They're going to let you go, Bruce! All fourteen charges will be dropped! You will be out before me. Wait for me!" This time I gave it all I had. Bruce looked at me funny, and then he went to his corner, sat down, and finally shut up. I went to mine and didn't say a word either.

About five minutes later an officer came in and called Bruce. "Where am I going?"

"To court," he replied. Bruce walked out looking very scared and confused. He came back less than 10 minutes later looking even more confused than before. "They're letting me go, Kev! I'm walking!"

I asked him, "What about your warrants?"

"They never came up. Like they never even existed! Absolutely nothing."

Five minutes later they cut him loose. Before he left I shouted, "Wait for me! I'll be out directly!" And so, I was. Oh yeah, the warrants? They never showed up on Bruce's record again. They simply vanished.

I don't understand how this kind of crap happens; nor do I understand how this *particular* crap happened. All I know is that it did happen and that it happened as close to what occurred as I can possibly remember. The how part of why I'll leave to the theologians, and I would really like some answers. The "why they happen" part is what I am actually more concerned than curious about.

16.4: THE RACE CAR DRIVER (SECONDS)

So far, I've covered days, hours, and minutes. Now it's time for seconds. It was BC again. There is a little town there in one of the most beautiful areas of BC called Hope. They filmed the very first *Rambo* movie there. I used to drink and fish under the famous bridge where that cop picked the worst fight of his redneck life (served him right though, eh?). I had been travelling back and forth through Hope for many, many years by then, and I was very well known by all and sundry.

Now you can't drink wine and play guitar on the riverbank in Hope for as long as I did and not get noticed sooner or later. Well, I got noticed all right. I got noticed by the entire Native population of Hope. You see, the way I drank and played, and drank and fought, and drank (did I mention that I drank?) and drank—shoot, who wouldn't notice me?! (There was a very serious alcohol problem at that time up there ... namely me.)

Now to say that you knew a couple of Natives in Hope could only mean one of two things. That you were just kidding around, or else you were flat-out lying. Nobody got to know "just a few Natives" up there. If you knew one, you knew the whole family, and if you travelled as much as I did, you knew the whole family extending clear across the Rockies. You knew brothers, mothers, cousins, second cousins, third cousins, and third cousins twice removed's mother-in-law by marriage on the second uncle's side. Catch my drift? You knew them all, and they knew you, either by face or by reputation. Word gets around quick in the mountains. I was known simply as "Guitar Man," and that's how I was greeted. There was no escaping it.

The one thing I had going for me up there was that I was pretty much crazier than all of them put together. One night one of my buddies was having a small get-together (which meant everybody), so of course, me being the entertainment, I was included.

We were all having a real good time, and I had just grabbed a fresh beer when all of a sudden a terrible cry rang out. "Last beer! We're out!" The silence was so profound that the crack my beer made when I opened it could have been heard all the way across the Rocky Mountains.

This last beer was now open, and in my hands. All eyes went to the clock. I took a looong careful swallow of my beer. All eyes went to my throat. I slowly put my beer down and carefully pushed it away from me … very slowly. There was *less* than 15 minutes till the liquor store closed. I stared at that clock for at least five long seconds, then out of my mouth popped the most ridiculous words I have ever said in my entire life: "I can get some! I'll make it!" In less than two seconds the entire household was in an uproar! It was utter chaos!

My words had precipitated an unprecedented and dazzling dialogue of scientific inquiry, faith in God, the physical nature of the cosmos, the possibilities of time travel, and its impact on our understanding of physics and overall perceptions of reality and the universe.

You see, the liquor store was close to seven and a half kilometres away. It was winter in the mountains, so there was no traffic (in other words, no hitchhiking), and the bootlegger was out of town. Even if we had a car and left that very instant, we would be very hard pressed to make it.

I had listened to the impossibility of my statement being pointed out and discussed for almost an entire minute and a half when all of a sudden something akin to a madness came over me. It was like an instant kind of wild mania hit me, and something else inside me kicked in and overrode all systems.

I stood up very abruptly and in a loud voice said, "Oh yeah? Watch this!" and without a single clue in my head as to what I was doing, I grabbed my coat, threw it on, and marched with absolute confidence out across the yard and onto the road. No sooner did my foot touch the pavement than a short block away a pair of headlights turned the corner and came racing toward me. As I reached the middle of the road, I stopped dead in my tracks, turned, and stretched one hand out to stop the car, and it came to a bit of a screeching halt. Immediately I headed around the car to the passenger door as a window was already rolling down.

"You headed to the beer store?" a shadowy figure inside asked.

My hand was already on the handle. "Yep!"

"So am I! Get in!"

Now I don't know what make of vehicle it was, but when I got in I could tell it was one I sure wasn't familiar with. I swear that guy punched the accelerator like a bank robber with a bad case of diarrhea, and *Bam!* We were off! I knew in half a sec I was in for one heck of a ride. It turned out he was some kind of driver with something experimental he was testing out in mountain roads and weather, and as I was busy unplugging my fingers from the dashboard and doing my seat belt up, I was seriously beginning to reconsider making peace with God. He was tearing around corners half sideways, flying over off ramps, all the while just yakking away. Me? I was busy praying this character would at least look at the road once or twice—just to make me at least *try* to feel like I wasn't going to die (even though I knew I was).

By some miracle we got to the beer store. I had to jump out and sprint to the door 'cause I saw the girl headed to lock up. My hand hit the door at exactly the same time the clerk's key slid into the lock. (I'm not kidding.) I gave her my most irresistible please! Please! Please! PLEASE! look and smiled. Shaking her head with a bit of a smile herself, she let me in. I bought 96 ciders. The guy got whatever he was getting and as he opened his car door said, "You coming?" Well, I sure wasn't going to walk seven kilometres on a dark night with a hundred ciders through that territory when the beer store was closed. (Yeah right!)

Now are you getting an idea of what I'm talking about? The picture, I mean? There's more. Lots and lots more. Some a lot crazier than this stuff, but what's the point? Really, that is what I'm asking. What *is* the point? Where does this stuff come from? What are the rules? What's it for? How do I handle it? Should I handle it? And please—*how do I not get into trouble with it?*

I didn't ask for it—any of it. It just happens. The only common thread I can find is that generally I'm pissed off somehow, and I'm not really even thinking about it when it happens. That's the only link I can find. Any ideas?

17
SELAH: "CHEW ON THIS FOR A WHILE"

As I continue writing, I keep seeing the means by which God's kindness, protection, and love have always been powerfully with me. I honestly didn't realize the incredible lengths he has gone to just to keep me alive until I stopped and began to add them all up on paper. I think of one, and ten more pop up. And then there are the ones that I had long forgotten and have only now just begun to remember. And I'm sure there are countless other ways God has shown me his love that I know nothing about—the incredible miracles God does for all his children, all the ways in which he keeps us safe in spite of ourselves.

Like when I was a young man and got my arm stuck in a cement mixer and was unable to reach the off switch. I'd seen what that thing had done to two-by-fours. When I asked my boss after he got my arm out of the machine "Should it have just stopped like that?" he just glanced at me real hard and nervous like and in almost a whisper said "No" and then didn't say anything else after that; he just kept staring at me real hard when he thought I wasn't looking.

Or falling through the ice in the middle of the Assiniboine River when I was about 12 years old. I was chest high in the frigid water with just my arms hanging on to some real thin ice. I could feel the river's strong current tugging at the fabric of my snowsuit. Funny thing was, even though I was in the middle of the river, there was something under my feet holding me up. What's even crazier was I found out later that at the same time I fell through the ice, my father was dealing with a powerful demonically possessed man. The demon had told my father if he didn't leave them alone it was going to kill his wife, his daughter, and his second son (me). Fifteen minutes before I fell through the ice my mother and sister were T-boned by a driver doing about 45 miles an hour (that's like, hmm … 72.5 km an hour for you youngsters). No one got so much as a scratch, and I managed to pull myself up out of the river. (At that time my father did not even believe that demonic possession was possible anymore.)

Or shooting over half a vial of 100 percent adrenaline straight into my bloodstream on a Greyhound bus with a needle that was supposed to go through your chest. I stole it out of an ambulance medical box that had momentarily been left unguarded. A dear friend of mine is a doctor, and I asked him about it. He said he wouldn't give any into the bloodstream unless the person was dead … and even then, only a little bit. Oh, yeah! It sure as blazes woke me up in a hurry! I jumped straight up, screaming, "My head's on fire! My head's on fire!" and ran wildly up and down the bus aisle until they got me off the bus. Then I ran around a farmer's field for over half an hour—full tilt! My road partner, Bruce, was not impressed. I lost our bus tickets while I was running around in circles screaming in the field.

Or travelling through Hope, BC, one time. I got into a fight with some fritzed-out character and had to get stitches from a wine bottle and a guitar being busted across the top of my head. I didn't realize it had become infected. One night I thought I was just tired and cold and kind of didn't feel very well from drinking weird stuff (mouthwash, etc.). Luckily (?) I called an ambulance. The hospital was less than a block and a half away. When I called, I lied to them on the phone and said I'd had a seizure, just so I could get out of the cold and wet for a while. The ambulance was there in under five minutes. By the time I climbed in and it got back to the hospital I was dead. (That's when I went to my own funeral, but that too is another story.) The last thing I remember was being on a gurney and someone yelling something about "He's bottoming out!" and "Temp 108.6!" I thought I was just pulling a scam to get some food and rest. Had I not called when I did, in less than five minutes I would have died that night in a snowbank on the side of a road. They shocked me a couple of times to bring me back, and then they squished green pus out of my head three times a day for a whole month before they would let me leave.

Or making the second page of the *Calgary Sun Times*. The headline read "Two Men Described as Extremely Drunk Struck and Injured by C-Train." Of course it went on to say, "Disappeared before police and ambulance could arrive." Damn right we disappeared! The both of us had warrants, and they got it all wrong. We weren't that drunk (at least not in my opinion. We were still walking), but we were carrying a wine bottle, and I was the only one who got hit. It was my buddy Bruce who pulled me back at the last second so the train just clipped my chin (still got the scar from that one) and about half of the rest of me. It sent the two of us flying a good 12 feet. I don't know for sure. We didn't exactly stick around to measure it. Perhaps that had something to do with some embarrassing questions that might have come up—like our names.

Or interrupting a murder in progress at an abandoned house in California. These two guys weren't just murdering the poor man; they were torturing him, using a knife, cutting him slow, bleeding him out, and breaking bones as they went. He was lying in a huge puddle of blood when I walked in. Some short little Mexican bandit with a shriveled-up arm came out with something in his hand. The other guy stood up off his victim and said, "You're not going anywhere, pal!" as he went for a gun. I watched as he rushed toward me, tripped, and landed on his knees right in front of me. I looked at him and was going to kick him square in the face, take his gun, and shoot him with it, but instead all I said was "Call an ambulance!" and then I turned and walked away. They did. I watched from the bushes as an ambulance came and took the poor soul to the hospital. I saw him about a week later while I was in a coffee shop. He was on crutches with a couple of casts. His head was almost twice the size as normal, covered in bandages, and he was black and blue everywhere I could see on his body. He hobbled excitedly over to me. "You're him!" he exclaimed. "Those guys were going to kill me, and I was praying to God to save my life, and ten seconds later you walked in. You saved my life!" At the time I didn't really care. I was coming down from a real bad heroin stretch and was living wherever I went to sleep— when I could sleep ... I was also real lucky to get out of there alive. He would have been the second guy just that month to get killed there. I'd have been the third.

You getting the picture? This list goes on and on, and it would just get boring. Like doing three 360s on an extremely narrow mountain road, opening the door, getting out of the car, and *literally* taking one step more, only to find myself looking about three hundred feet straight down a rocky cliff into the Fraser River. Yeah. One step from death more times than I can count ... The whole ankle thing when the doc told me I had four hours to live and I trashed palliative care ... Getting run over by that car at six years old ... Squaring off with a Mexican gang in California who were armed to the teeth and walking away, and how long can a guy keep his brain with a temperature of 108.6 F, as well as overdosing almost regularly from about 10 years old on some of the strangest drugs you could imagine? And how many times have you seen thick green pus dripping from someone's eyeball? Oh yeah ... and crashing a car doing about 45 mph smack into a tree while wearing no seat belt. (Funny thing about that one was, a guy with my first name, the exact same age, driving the same style of car and doing approximately the same speed, crashed into a lamppost not more than 15 minutes earlier. He was killed instantly—dead—*with the same name and age?!* I just punched a hole through the windshield and ripped half the skin off my skull) ... Or waking up in a hospital (not even sure how I got there) with a very angry doctor saying, "You know, if you'd have waited ten or fifteen more minutes before your friend finally got you to come in, there would have been nothing we could have done but watch you die!"

Just my days as a child playing with freight trains alone makes my toes curl and my hair stand straight up on end ... Oh, I almost forgot! As a fifteen-year-old I was taken out into the desert by a maniac bent on perversion, murder, and a shallow grave. The guy had a gun, for crying out loud! I escaped by pretending I was way drunker than I really was and puking on him and me. I vanished into the dark desert behind a sand dune while he was busy freaking, and I crawled away to the sound of him screaming, cussing, and threatening that he would find and kill me one day.

On and on the list seems to go. And again, these are only some of the ones I know about.

It says in Psalms, "Has the LORD redeemed you? Then speak out! Tell others he has redeemed you from your enemies" (107:2 NLT)! So I am, because so he has! That was my life ever since I can remember.

You know, I can really understand why a lot of Christians, and other people, are a little confused when they meet me. Anyone who's known me more than 48 hours knows what I believe and why—yet here I am stuck being a badass. But can I help it if God keeps pulling stuff like this on me? He's been doing it my entire life! Should I just shut up and not talk about God because I'm an alcoholic? It's been my experience that I'd rather talk to an alcoholic about God than to most Christians I've met. Should I just hide what I think and feel? I don't walk around telling other people what to think or what to believe. *I simply tell the truth about myself and my life.* To do otherwise would make me a hypocrite.

I have survived times of terrible ugliness and depravity when it was as if my very soul was being raped again and again, but never once have I tried to excuse or defend my actions. Nor did I try to blame anyone but myself. I have always known right from wrong, and because of that, I can spot every kind of grey you can imagine.

Many would say I have no right to even speak of God, let alone call myself a Christian. Perhaps they're right. Perhaps I'm just someone whom God has gone so far overboard in keeping alive, revealing himself to, and showering with so much grace, mercy, kindness, love, patience, and forgiveness that it's ... unbelievable? (Maybe that's the whole problem with us Christians ... we don't *really* believe the good news.)

Or perhaps there's more to it than that. St. Paul wrote to Timothy, "The saying is trustworthy and deserving of full acceptance, that Christ Jesus came into the world to save sinners, of whom I am the foremost. *But I received mercy for this reason, that in me, as the foremost, Jesus Christ might display his perfect patience as an example to those who were to believe in him for eternal life.* To the King of the ages, immortal, invisible, the only God, be honor and glory forever and ever. Amen" (1 Tim. 1:15–17, emphasis added).

I can think of no other reason. He is so rich in kindness I cannot even begin to understand it, never mind explain it. Why else would he so dramatically keep me alive, if not to share with everyone I encounter all the love and patience he has shown me over so many years? Hear me now

... I am one who can say with the utmost confidence that truly, truly it has been his mercy and kindness that have brought me to repentance ... and kept me alive long enough to see it.

You see, through all of it, everything, God has never once left me— not once. And through everything he would *always* somehow let me know (in the strangest ways) he wasn't mad at me. Surely I should be dead! Hell, I *have* been dead. And because of all this, all of it, I am learning to love other people. They—you—are why I am alive this day, so I could share with you just a few of the kindnesses, mercies, and love God has shown me and tell of how he has redeemed me and kept me. These are things that have been done and will never, ever change. Nothing can ever take them away, undo them, or separate me from them ... from him. They are matters of eternal significance.

18

THE DARK SIDE

I must now deal with a part of my life I'm hesitant to even look at, let alone write about. Times I have had to deal with things of a much darker nature than just my own sinful heart—things far more active and intelligent.

I have done all I can to not pump up, exaggerate, or glamorize anything I have written so far. I will continue to do so. Actually, I have either played down or omitted entirely certain parts of my narrative simply because I have not been able to adequately explain or express the things I have felt, seen, or heard. Others I have omitted for … other reasons. I would far rather err on the side of being too mundane than to try to glamorize my bellybutton with a whirligig.

What I write now I write after much deliberation and with great care. As I mentioned earlier, these examples deal with times in my life that were horrifyingly dark and were the source of tremendous pain and destruction to both myself and to many others. Again, these are only samplings of a greater whole that remains, as yet, largely unexamined, each one representative of a different kind of … evil—evil that is directly or very closely linked to demonic or satanic influence and direction here on earth (and for some reason—in my own life).

Like it or not, we are in the middle of an unseen battle that rages all around us each day and affects all aspects of not only our lives but the lives of every single person on this planet. We are, in fact, involved in what amounts to an inter-dimensional war. That many have chosen to close their eyes to it makes it no less real, and as in any war, the casualties and injuries are equally real. One honest look at even the last 50 years of church history should make this fact abundantly clear (never mind the changes in our society overall).

I will not dwell on this other than to say that the weapons our enemy uses are both cruel and effective, ranging anywhere from fear, intimidation, and outright physical violence to the more subtle and far more effective tactics of deception, seduction, temptation, accusation, and slander.

18.1: THE WINO

I suppose before I go into all this, I need to explain how and why I decided to become a Christian and give you some sort of insight into the events and motivating factors that led me to faith in Christ. I did not turn to him for any of the usual reasons. I wasn't fed up with life; nor was I feeling any particular need for "something more," and although I was in very serious trouble, now that I look at it, quite frankly I really didn't care. To be honest, I didn't care about anything but drugs and alcohol and how I could get more of both.

Like many kids my age, I felt I was invincible, and trouble of any sort was just something to be either mocked or, at best, ignored. At 14 years old I think I was simply too foolish to see how much danger I was actually in. My parents were receiving phone calls daily, explaining in graphic detail the beating I would receive before the callers killed their son and the pain my parents would feel as they watched my dead body being dragged up from the bottom of the Assiniboine River. This all had to do with some missing drugs and other monies owed to the callers. My folks wisely got me out of Winnipeg and sent me to Vancouver with a former New York City heavyweight boxer turned truck driver whom my father had led to Christ some years before.

I was still smoking dope all the way to Vancouver (unbeknownst to my "bodyguard") and was still as stubborn and rebellious as ever. I had absolutely no intention of changing my ways at the time, yet even then, somewhere deep inside me, at what I now think was an almost subconscious level, I knew beyond any doubt that God had his hand on me and that one day I would turn to him formally and become a Christian. I just didn't think that day was right around the corner.

I felt no particular need of a "Saviour" and was still at that point in my using where I was actually really enjoying myself. There were no real external pressures that would cause me to see my need for Christ (at least none I would have considered a problem), and I definitely was not interested in developing any kind of relationship with God at all. I found my need for him in a rather unusual way, now that I think on it—a way that almost makes me laugh aloud at the dark side of God's sense of humour. Recognize my need for him I did, although for someone as selfish and self-absorbed as I was, it was in the last way anyone, including myself, would have ever imagined.

My actual conversion was as completely a detached and unemotional affair as the changing of a burnt-out light bulb. There was zero emotion involved, and it was about as flat as four-day-old beer. Although I asked for his forgiveness, I felt neither particularly sinful nor particularly forgiven. It was like signing a contract. It had to be done. A formality. Fortunately for me at the time, I neglected to read the fine print. I had no idea at that point how very seriously God takes his contracts. However, what led to that change in my spiritual status was something entirely different. My conversion was simply the next logical step in solving certain problems brought to light by a rather odd encounter that affected my perceptions of both power and pity. The encounter itself was quite … disturbing and proved to be troubling enough to alter the entire course of my life.

The night we arrived in Vancouver, Ted, my boxer friend, signed us into an older downtown hotel. He knew of a church in Vancouver that some friends of his attended, and we were going to meet up with them and then go to the service later that day. He got up early that morning, and as I was on my way downstairs to meet him for breakfast, I saw something that changed my life forever. I have never been the same since.

As I walked down the stairs, I saw a raggedy old man standing in front of a large mirror. He looked to be around 60 to 65 years old. His clothes were filthy, and even at a distance I could smell the stench of him. It was obvious he had soiled himself. He had no shoes on his dirt-encrusted feet and was wearing about three filthy sweaters and a heavy coat, even though it was quite warm out. But it wasn't his clothes or the stink of him that caught my attention. It was what he was doing in front of the mirror that made me pause.

He was in terrible distress and was picking and wiping at his face, drawing closer to and then back away again from the mirror, as though frantically trying to see and remove some sort of invisible substance from his face. He was murmuring and whispering the entire time what sounded like some kind of desperate plea for help. Over and over, back and forth, picking and wiping and pleading, and I could only stand, transfixed by this poor creature's torment.

I had never seen a wino before. Never really even known of their existence, let alone given any thought to one. Yet there he was, and there I stood, and for the first time in my life, that day my curiosity was mixed with a compassion I had never known before. I watched him for a bit, until finally my inquisitiveness could be denied no longer, and I cautiously approached him. I can see him clearly, even now as I write, and I can still hear the desperation in his voice when he answered my question.

Staring intently, almost whispering, I asked him, "What are you doing?"

Never once taking his eyes off the mirror, he harshly whispered, "The spiderwebs! The spiderwebs ... I can't get them off my face! It's the spiderwebs! I can see them, the webs, I can feel them, but I can't get the spiderwebs off my face!" And then he went back to desperately rocking and whimpering, hopelessly picking and wiping at nothing.

That was the first moment I fully knew my need for Christ and his power in my life. I knew instinctively that the man was in DTs, hallucinating, and was pitifully, desperately helpless. I also knew that God was the only thing in the entire world that could help this man, *and I did not have him in me to give.* I had nothing! I had no way to ease his suffering. Empty—I was just ... empty. I so desperately wanted to give him some kind of release from his torment, but at that very moment I realized for the first time that I was just as powerless as he was—an empty husk, devoid of life. I could only walk slowly down those stairs with the knowledge that the man I had just spoken to would probably die alone, doomed to the misery of whatever pitiful hell was left of his broken and tortured life. I became a Christian a few hours later. I knew I had to have Christ dwelling in me in order to be of any use to anyone at all. Little did I know I was to learn in a very real way all the agonies of that man's life, and then some. The only difference between him and me was that God had a very different kind of plan for me. (Oh, that, and I had about ten thousand million billion people praying for me.) His plan was to walk with me as I journeyed through that man's hell—the stink, the DTs, everything—to walk beside me every step of the way, until I came out the other side of that terrible nightmare, carrying with me all the love, grace, mercy, and compassion of God's heart for men like the one I met that day. I was to know all the pain and anguish of the wretched and sinful man I became and all the joy, love, and gratitude of a man purchased by Christ's blood from those very same agonies.

How was I to know? I marvel as I write these words. I marvel at the depths and unsearchable ways of God's plans. But it's so much like him. And it's still all so amazing to me.

Anyway, that day, less than two hours after I became a Christian, God immediately spoke in a powerful way concerning his plans for me and what it was that he required of me. I am not at liberty to disclose what he said, but suffice it to say, it was God, and whenever he speaks, it is always powerful.

But God was not the only one who was immediately at work. Now comes the time I must speak of the other side of the coin. Satan was not about to let go of me without one hell of a fight, and that fight began almost immediately. I barely had time to suck sanctified air before I was introduced to my new and now thoroughly pissed-off enemy.

18.2: SECOND CONTACT

From day one of my Christian walk it seemed as though I had been thrown headlong into an outright, full on, sink or swim, no holds barred fight with powers I had absolutely no comprehension of. I knew there was a devil, that he was my enemy, and that he would tempt me. I knew about sin and forgiveness, but that was basically it. Given the nature of what I was dealing with, the Bible stories I'd heard in Sunday school were just not much use to me, so what I could glean from adult conversations and my father's sermons was pretty much the extent of my spiritual knowledge at the time. I was forced to learn a whole lot more real quick.

For some reason, whatever I did when I became a Christian must have po'd somebody bad, because within days of my acceptance of Christ into my heart and life I was hit by the demonic like a sledgehammer. At 14 I had no frame of reference for what was happening to me. At that age I hadn't really even watched a scary movie yet. My first real encounter with the demonic went something like this.

When I became a Christian, God spoke powerfully to me concerning his Word. So, when I got back to Winnipeg, having never read the Bible on my own before, I did what any fourteen-year-old boy would do. I sat down, opened it to the last chapter, Revelation 22, and went right to the last sentence. "Amen" was what it said. Thinking perhaps there was probably some good stuff I had missed, I backed up one sentence and read it. I immediately began to cry. When I backed up to halfway through the chapter, I began to weep in earnest. I couldn't help it. Joy! Real joy! This was something I'd never before known. It was so gently passionate, it almost frightened me.

Somehow, when I read that chapter something wonderful was transmitted to my soul. I wept, but it felt good. It was something I had never felt before—like not knowing I'd been longing for something for so long and suddenly finding it, not even realizing till that very moment I had been yearning for it all my life. It felt … cleansing and healing.

Anyway, I was overwhelmed. I picked through various Scriptures at random for a while after that, and then, placing my Bible on the nightstand, I shut the door of my room and hopped into bed. That was the first time I had ever read the Bible on my own.

Now by the time I was 14 I was a pretty experienced pot/hash/oil smoker, had experimented with LSD extensively, and was already drinking (a lot) anytime I could get alcohol.

It wasn't too hard for me to do. I was an unusually determined and innovative child. The reason I explain my drug and alcohol use is to establish the fact that even at that young age I had a lot of experience and knew the difference between hallucinations and reality. I also had never experienced what I now call a hangover. The ones I had in later years were physically horrendous and terribly frightening both to me and to anyone witnessing me go through them. They regularly would include very real hallucinations that were sometimes terrifying.

The first hallucination I had was when I woke in the middle of the night and saw a dead man who kind of looked like my father. He was sitting there in a chair, just staring at me. All I could do was scream and point. This guy was *dead* and was staring straight at me. He seemed as real as anything I had ever seen. Had he spoken, I am positive my mind would have snapped. My poor ex had no idea why I was screaming in wide-eyed terror and pointing at nothing. After a time, I just got used to them, and they no longer frightened me at all. Once I understood what was going on I became quite skilled at knowing the difference, no matter how real they appeared to be. It was the trembling and seizures I feared most.

Back to hopping into bed—I had checked the door to make sure it was closed. I always made sure it was closed because I smoked downstairs in my room, and my folks didn't want the smell of it upstairs. Then I turned out the light so it was quite dark, as I had no windows in my room. (At the time my room was painted black to enhance the black-light posters I had put up—seventies, go figure.) I felt that wonderfully peaceful feeling, which I know now was the Holy Spirit's tranquil presence, heavily upon me, and I slowly began to calm down for the evening.

Less than two minutes later, I heard my door click and swing half open, and like out of some nightmare, a completely different kind of spirit walked right into my room. This thing was big, and it was extremely powerful. Two things happened instantly and simultaneously.

First, it felt like someone had palm-slapped their hands over my ears (like in the movies), and they suddenly began ringing very loudly at a very high pitch; and second, I was instantly paralyzed with fear.

No ... no, not fear—terror. Terror the likes of which I'd never experienced before or since. I could not move. I was completely immobilized. The hair on the back of my neck literally stood up. I could feel it! (It does happen.) I could also feel the blood draining away from different parts of my body as I lay there.

This thing was *huge*—terrifyingly substantial. His presence alone was overwhelming. Oh yeah! My door? It weighed well over 150 pounds, was padded with sawdust and leather, and was perfectly balanced. My room was an old recording studio made for playing loud music in. This—creature had physically opened that door. I know. I was wide awake (and *very* alert!).

It was moving slowly around my room, and even though my room was painted black with no windows and the lights were out, I could actually see it. Not in any detail but where it was, as it moved, by the even greater darkness it emanated. This thing was blacker than any black hole. It was the emanations of it. Like it was blacker than any black in the world. I could hear it picking up and putting down various objects. I mean—I could actually hear it moving these things around. Somehow, I instinctively knew this creature was searching for anything that would grant it the right to be there—like some sort of access point. How I knew this was a mystery to me at the time. I had never heard any sort of teaching on anything demonic. I know now it was because the Holy Spirit had begun my training.

It seemed utterly indifferent to me at first—until it stood directly opposite where I lay. Then it turned and looked directly at me. Instantly, I saw in my mind a detailed and intensely graphic picture of two powerful taloned hands plunging into my rib cage and tearing it wide open. This was an immediate and horrifically real image. Then it slowly moved toward me and stood at the head of my bed, towering overtop of me.

The only way I can describe what happened next is that it "beamed" pure hatred at me. I have never felt such a powerful, concentrated, and directed hatred in my life before, or since. It was almost palpable, and it continued to direct this vicious, malignant hatred at me for about 20 seconds. Whatever else that thing was, it was hate incarnate.

I was still in shock at the size, reality, and power of this thing as I "watched" it move to the foot of my bed and sit down. I felt my mattress sink three or four inches, not as much as I would have thought but enough for me to know it sat there. It remained like this for a moment, as though thinking, and then it turned quite suddenly and lay down on top of my body, face to my face, hands to my hands, and feet to my feet. It was impossible for me to feel any more terror than I felt at that moment. I was still completely paralyzed and could feel the weight of it on top of me. I could also sense it was trying to enter my body, and I could not have stopped it had I been able to try. But I could also sense it was unable to do so because the presence of the Holy Spirit kept it out. God had taken up residence, and his Spirit dwelt in me bodily and prevented it.

After a bit, it got up off me and sat once more at the end of my bed, again as though in thought. Then it simply stood up (I could feel the mattress rise) and without pause walked directly out my bedroom door.

Instantly the paralysis left me, and, gasping in horror, I sprang out of bed and across the room, slammed my door shut, and grabbed my Bible. Clutching it to my chest tightly, I leapt back into my bed, whimpering I know not what, and stared wide-eyed around my room until I slowly began to calm down.

At no time during this event did I have any sense of what this creature was thinking or of its intentions toward me other than hurting me, hating me, and wanting to get inside me. I shudder to think of what may have happened had not the Holy Spirit taken up residence in my body only days before. This type of terror tactic went on from time to time for many years. None of them were as powerful or as dramatic as this first encounter.

Initially it was simply to frighten and intimidate me. Always these events were preceded and accompanied seconds before with the high-pitched ringing, but only one other time with the paralysis. Often several demons would come—sometimes seven or eight at once.

After I grew a bit in my knowledge of who I was in Christ, their terror tactics became less and less effective. I was learning to fight back. Eventually I no longer feared them but would actually become quite angry and not allow their presence. They then changed tactics. Things went from fear and intimidation to sexual harassment by sudden violent assaults, trying to rape me as I slept, and when that too became ineffective they eventually resorted to flat-out seduction. They would come and arouse me until I woke, then try to bargain with me, writhing, whispering, promising sexual encounters regularly—every night, either with themselves or with some agent, usually a witch of some sort or another. This I put a halt to almost immediately. I remember now becoming furious at their boldness and commanding them to leave me. I believe that was when they withdrew to the far more destructive work of deception, accusation, condemnation, and isolation. These horribly effective lies had an incredibly destructive impact on my life and caused a tremendous amount of pain and sadness for many years.

I had to go through all the early stages of this alone. I tried to talk to my father about it after that first incident, but he just told me about the state called "night terrors." I guess at that time in his life the reality of the spiritual world I was facing wasn't part of his theology. I listened carefully to him, but as I did, I felt a deep sadness slowly begin to grip my heart. I can't really explain the dead feeling that began to grow in me as I came to realize I would have to face this world alone, and I became even more afraid. I knew of no one else in the church who really had any idea about this sort of thing, and I had never heard of it spoken of before, so at 14 years old and a brand-new Christian, I was left to figure it out on my own. Like I said, I was *forced* into learning a whole lot more—like how to go from a child frozen in terror to an active combatant in an unknown and hostile world—real quick.

Of course, my dad being my father and all, I had to go back and honestly look at this experience in light of all the scientific evidence I could find. What I discovered was that night terrors, or what the *Diagnostic and Statistical Manual of Mental Disorders*, fourth edition (DSM-lV), terms sleep terror, is a sleep disruption that results from a partial waking out of a third or fourth non-rapid eye-movement stage of sleep (NREM)—being awake and yet unable to wake fully from sleep. It is practically non-existent in adults (less than 1 percent) and is rare beyond five years of age. There are many theories, but most today are at a loss to explain its cause physiologically. The best they can come up with is that anxiety and depression can cause an as yet unidentified chemical reaction in the brain, which then misfires so you see strange threatening figures or feel evil presences while you are trying to wake up, and these figures or presences can cause anything from acute anxiety to being trapped in terrible screaming fits of horror you are unable to wake from. Then, when you finally are able to wake up fully, there is no memory of anything but terrible fear—and then you have to go back to sleep … again. There *are* some records of paralysis, but these always seem to be associated with the struggle to wake up.

I have carefully read every scrap of information I could find and have now watched many videos with personal interviews about these phenomena, thinking that perhaps I may have found a less frightening explanation for what had happened to me. There are just too many reasons to list as to why I am denied this comfort. I will not attempt to address them all other than to say … night terrors, my ass! This was something different entirely! *The entity that walked into my room that night was as real, as intelligent, and as deliberate as you or me.* The time between me getting into bed and all this occurring was less than two minutes. Sleep terrors occur in the non-dreaming *third* stage part of sleep. *Neither was I struggling to wake up at any time. My paralysis was one of sheer terror.* I was fully conscious and thinking very clearly. I was in no way hysterical. Frozen in fear, yes, but hysterical, no way. I also have to account for my blood draining and my hair actually hackling up (sure physiological signs of extreme fear), not to mention that my door was carefully closed. I heard it not only click but also swing open. My door had never done that before, nor did it ever do that again. It could be left in any position without it moving. Then there was the bed sinking when the creature sat down, and me feeling the weight of it on top of me, and finally the bed rising when the thing left, and the resulting immediate release from my initial paralysis. And of very great importance is that I can remember practically every detail of what occurred that night. This is unheard of in night terrors—it just doesn't happen.

Although what I experienced was quite different, I've had a good deal of time to examine these phenomena and have had to question a few things. I think one thing that should be carefully noted is that the scientific world seems to be in a real hurry to explain away with science any possibility of spiritual matters, regardless of where they pop up—a strangely odd kind of reverse prejudice of days gone by, don't you think? Perhaps in their hurry to ignore the real significance of these kinds of occurrences (night terrors and such), the scientific community may have chosen to blind themselves to the one thing that actually makes the most sense—that there are in fact spiritual entities that are able, at certain times, to have a more direct access to our own consciousness as well as to this physical realm.

Then there is also the fact that in many cultures around the globe there is mention of this state between waking and sleeping, and it has long been held that during this period our minds (selves) actually enter an altered state of reality and become quite vulnerable to the spiritual world (much like with the use of almost all hallucinogenic drugs). I, for one, would not like to venture there unprotected, and I have a boatload of experience in that area. (Believe me!) Examine how altered states are used in almost every form of witchcraft. In the New Testament, the Greek *pharmakeia* refers to the use of medicine, drugs, or spells and is associated with sorcery, witchcraft, idolatry, and deception. Makes one pause for a second, eh? Why have these altered states been used for centuries all over the world as aids in men connecting to the spiritual realm and its inhabitants?

I have included this account because it was the first and most dramatic of my encounters with things demonic, and, as with my first encounter with God, it seemed to find me without any of my help. What really bothers me (and almost killed me) is the fact that I had to deal with this kind of thing as a child, alone, without any help from anyone. How many other kids are dealing with the same kind of nightmare—alone—right now because we think we know so much and have come so far? What we've done is become more proud, arrogant, and blind.

I guess my question is, if Christians believe in a supernatural God, why in the world are we so frightened of the supernatural world as a people? What do we really fear—God or men? Perhaps it's our own powerlessness in the face of the truth. The supernatural world either exists or it doesn't (and I do mean angels, demons, and only God knows what else!). You'd better make up your mind—and I'd do it quick!

18.3: WHO'S YOUR DADDY?

I do not presume to know a lot about witches or witchcraft. Everything I know has been learned on the fly by my experience in dealing with them—both directly and indirectly.

People who mess around with spiritual power, as far as I can tell, fall into two main categories: those who are deceived, and those who are *really* deceived. Some use spiritual gifts and power, thinking that they are in control, simply tapping into an existing power source. Then, closely related, are those who believe they are in contact with other illuminated (or evolved) beings, who are called angels, who are helping certain members of our world to evolve. But these, too, have only an illusion of control. It is an ancient deception. Probably the oldest and purest forms of witchcraft come from those who serve Satan and his minions with full knowledge, worship him as their master, and hate God and the gospel of Jesus Christ with great passion.

I remember one such individual ... (I had to stop writing and calm down for a while.) What I will speak of in the next few chapters had a hugely destructive impact on myself and others. You see, all this stuff is very real, and I knew nothing of spiritual warfare. With no one to teach me, I was forced to learn about it in a painfully difficult way. What I mean is, I got hurt badly ... a lot. And again, *I did not seek these encounters out. They found me.*

Yeah, it was California. Right—it figures—where else can you meet a nice third generation homosexual warlock off to enter into his first gathering as a full member of the local black witchcraft coven? (Oh happy day!) He was off to be accepted as a full-fledged warlock, and for some reason he stopped when he saw me, sat down cross-legged in the grass in front of me, and began zealously trying to convert me with promises of money, power, sex, and anything goes. He was even offering to introduce me to some California big shot, hot shot, coven master, if I wanted (and if I didn't mind homosexuals, of course, but everyone was bi, so who cares, right? Take your pick!).

Me? I'd just been sitting in the park with a couple of jugs, minding my own business, quietly strumming my guitar, when this clown waltzed in and started yammering away at me.

I admit I was mildly curious, as I had never spoken with a confessed practitioner of the black arts before, so I didn't tell him I was a Christian right away. I didn't want to scare him off. Instead I shared some of my wine with him and plucked absent-mindedly on my guitar as I listened to his ... theology? However, when he started in about receiving his demonic tongue, I was all ears. I had just begun speaking in tongues about a year prior and was finding it very helpful in my Christian walk, such as it was.

"Really?" I said encouragingly.

"Oh yah!" he answered excitedly, and then he started explaining how a demonic tongue gives its user more power in certain rituals and how his coven practised a deeper, more powerful form of witchcraft than other kinds of witchcraft, because most forms of witchcraft didn't acknowledge Satan as their lord and master like they did and so were unable to receive this gift of tongues.

The guy was rather full of himself, and I was starting to get bored, until he asked if I would like to hear it. Right then this idea began to burble in my brain. I hesitated a moment but then said, "Sure, why not?" I'm always curious, and I wanted to see how this would unfold. I had a hunch it would be—educational.

He sat up straight, kind of settled himself (I half expected him to clear his throat), and spoke what seemed to be four or five sentences, then sat back and looked at me expectantly. I glanced around behind me, unsure, "Umm … yeah … great!"

Then, as usual, something strange sprang out of my mouth. "I can do that too," and then I began speaking to God in my own language.

I expected something, but I was completely unprepared for what happened next. Now I'm glad he was sitting down, because as soon as I began speaking, almost instantly the poor guy flipped head over heels backwards three times in a row (I remember counting them in surprise) like he had been powerfully backhanded, then sprang to his feet a good 20 feet away with a loud howl and started running around me in circles, screaming and cursing at the top of his lungs.

I remember muttering something about a "sore spot," but then I realized I still had a jug and a half of wine left, so I had to get him to shut up quick before someone called the cops and I lost all my booze.

I had no practical experience with this sort of thing, but I knew I was dealing with something demonic, and I had to act fast. The only thing I could think of was what Jesus had done with noisy demons, so I said quite loudly and sternly, "Shut up!" Instantly he stopped running and was silent. I looked at him. "Come here!" Immediately he walked over to me and stopped about three feet away. "Sit down!" He sat. "You were being a total heat score!" And handing him my jug, I slowly sat down. A couple of seconds later he picked up almost exactly where he had left off. I gave a deep sigh and stared at him—somewhat bewildered. He had continued on as if absolutely nothing had happened. I let him go on for a while, but then, curious, I interrupted him and asked, "Do you remember anything unusual, just a few minutes ago?" He continued talking as though he hadn't heard me.

Then, just as he was getting ready to leave, I stopped him and asked again if he remembered what had just happened, about him flipping backwards. He just looked at me, strangely blank, said very certainly "No," and then asked what I was talking about. He had absolutely no memory of it. And so he left me—with a lot of questions.

Now I also need to 'fess up here and say that I knew God was with me powerfully, so I really wasn't worried too much by this character. What actually happened was, in a split second, I'd planned out exactly what I was going to do as soon as he asked me if I wanted to hear his tongue. I had expected some sort of reaction, but I must say, I was almost shocked at the force and raw power of the Holy Spirit in this situation—confrontation? As I've re-examined this matter decades later I am left with more questions than when I started.

For example, why couldn't this guy tell I was a Christian? Was this a good thing or a bad thing? Because of all the sin in my life at the time, had I become indistinguishable from the world? But then I have to ask: does spiritual authority remain despite our spiritual condition? I had it. Why else the acrobatics and obedience to my commands? I also have to notice that at no time did I use Jesus' name as some sort of incantation. I simply commanded him. I think perhaps just knowing we have authority over all the works of the enemy is sufficient. I also wonder what other gifts (besides tongues) witches possess.

Then I have to wonder if those involved in occult and New Age practices take the identification and cultivation of the gifts more seriously than we do. It would certainly make sense. The one thing they prize above all is power. And why do so many churches while acknowledging in doctrine and theory the spiritual gifts not use them in practice but severely limit them, ignoring some but not others? Or worse still, deny them altogether? Gone with the apostles!

What utter nonsense! Are we mad? The bad guys get all the toys *and instruction* on how to use them while "Joe Christian" struggles along trying to be a good witness for the Lord? (And God bless him! It's more than many do.)

If our gifts, in a very real sense, define our calling, how can we fully know what our calling is if we restrict or eliminate their operation in the church? Where in the local church do we make room for instruction and training in their use? Where is there a "safe place" created for our youth to learn about and actually use their spiritual gifts? And how can the church function at its full potential while much of the body lives in fear of them?

I have been terribly hurt by witchcraft. At the time I had no idea how it could have happened. Now that I do know, I have some legitimate questions to ask. Questions like, where are the wise elders who can guide and instruct in the use of spiritual gifts? What has happened to godly discernment in these matters? Are not all the gifts meant for the building up and edification of the church? How then can we do this if we don't know how to identify spiritual gifts, don't even know what gifts are on board, let alone how to function properly in them? I think that perhaps this is one reason the church is so crippled and lacks the power it needs for effective ministry to its own people, let alone for evangelism. Understand this in no uncertain terms: spiritual gifts exist (even the odder ones), and we are to use what God has given us. To say they don't exist, or to condemn their use, is tantamount to saying, "It is by Satan he casts out devils." Again, this is nonsense. They are being used every day, all over the world, and we need to know what in the world is going on with them instead of being upset because the topic fluffs some feathers. Believe me, I have seen all kinds of bizarre phenomena out there, and I am extremely fortunate (?) I survived it, let alone understand any of it. The gifts exist, and I know they do because I myself function in several of the ones that are not commonly used in most churches. I guess I'll have to figure them out on my own, just like I did in those times of demonic attack. This is something I really don't *want* to do. But what else *can* I do? I don't go around picking fights with the enemy (at least not any more), but like much of the spiritual stuff I've encountered, it has a way of finding *me!* Got any ideas?

18.4: HIPPIE CHICKS WITH CRYSTALS

Here's another little encounter that's still raising questions in my mind. I was in Vancouver, and I was not in very good shape. If I remember correctly, I was coming down from a coke run—a rare thing for me in those days—and I was tired, sick, scared, and desperately trying to get somewhere … anywhere safe. I was headed to the Sky Train, and then I would make my way out of the city from there.

While I was still about a block from the station, I cut my hand jumping over a broken fence, and it was bleeding quite badly. I knew that I looked scary enough as it was, so I didn't want to add a bunch of blood to the equation. People nowadays get pretty jumpy when they see a lot of blood, particularly when someone looking like me is wearing it.

That being said, I made double sure no one saw anything. I wadded up some tissue I had, put it over my cut, pulled my inside sleeve over that, pulled my sweater over that, pulled my coat over that, then stuck my hand in my jacket pocket. That done, I tugged my hat down over my eyes, looked around to be sure no one had seen anything, and then continued on my way to the station. I wanted no trouble that day.

Now before I ever go into any close or crowded area, I have a long-standing habit of always pulling up and over abruptly to check my back trail for a while, and being particularly paranoid from the coke, I was doubly cautious. That done, I went up the stairs to catch the train.

It was a typically busy afternoon—tons of people. I'm pretty sure I got off the train early, as I was starting to get freaked out from being so crowded in. As things turned out, I was about to get a whole lot more freaked out.

When I got off, I stepped into a hive of activity—people getting on and off, waiting around, each intent on their own plan for their own reasons. As I stood still for a moment, through the mass of people I saw a girl about my age scanning the crowd, obviously looking for someone. Somehow, instantly, I instinctively knew that someone was me. Sure enough, as soon as she spotted me she walked straight over to me and held out her hand.

"Here, I think you might need these," she said, looking straight into my eyes. I looked down, and in her hand was a large rectangular bandage, some Polysporin, a roll of gauze, some sterile pads, and some tape. I just stared at her, confused.

"Umm … Yeah! Yeah … aah, I really could use them …" My mind was racing furiously. Had I somehow been spotted? Impossible! I was at least a block away from the station when I cut myself. Followed? Very unlikely, and if so, why? I had nothing and was doing nothing. I knew for sure no one had seen any blood while I was on the train or at the station—and what was this woman doing here in the first place, meeting me with exactly what I needed when I myself didn't even have any idea where I was going?

Confused, I shook my head. "Who are you?" She glanced around, then took my arm and gently steered me out of the traffic to a railing.

"It's OK. We're Wiccan. Some of us go to your dad's church here. We know a lot about you, and your family. We also know about the book on witchcraft your dad is writing."

That shook me up a bit. I had just found out about that book myself a short time before. It was still in manuscript form and had not even gone to the editors yet.

"Look," she said, "I go to the youth group at your dad's church. I work with the kids there. I babysit for … [so and so]. We're Wiccan. We use love and the energy of goodness."

I didn't even know who this "so and so" was, even though she insisted I did—and by the sound of it, this girl was way more involved in my dad's church than I ever was. My mind was racing in 20 different directions at once.

She stared hard at me and then said, "Look, we own the coffee shop downstairs under the train. You look tired and hungry. Why don't you come down, have a coffee and a bite to eat. Then we can take a look at that hand of yours. After that, if you want, we have a back room where you can lie down and rest a while." Still kind of stunned, I pushed and checked things out. I felt no immediate danger and so agreed and followed her down the stairs.

The first thing I noticed when I went into the shop was that all of the staff were female, which in itself is not unusual, but now that I was clued in, I could tell that all of them were Wiccan and all of them were very aware of me.

No one spoke to me or the girl, but a coffee and sandwich (Hey! Sandwitch … get it? Witch, sand*witch*, you know—never mind, sigh …) were placed in front of me.

I asked her what Wicca was. In my exhausted state all I could gather was that it had something to do with the universal energy of love and various other energies and so forth. It all sounded pretty Darth Vaderish to me (use the force, Luke!), but I took in what I could.

She took me to the back where it was quiet and dimly lit. She then left, and a couple of minutes later, another girl came and helped me bandage my hand, then left, also without saying a word. Then the first girl came back in, told me to rest, and turned out the light. I made sure there was a back exit, checked through all my possessions, and then fell asleep on the couch.

When I woke, the first girl was gone, but another one gave me a coffee and five dollars. After thanking them I walked out and continued on my journey through what now seemed like the twilight zone.

So … *what in the heck was that?* Do you have any idea how many questions I *still* have over that little fiasco?!

First off, I didn't even know that girl! And I sure didn't know any of those people. I didn't even really go to my dad's church, for crying out loud. So who were those girls? They had money, I can tell you that much. Anyone owning an espresso shop at that location would be making money hand over fist night and day.

They had to have some sort of intelligence network to spot me, know me, know my condition, and have someone prepared to meet me with exactly the things I needed … and then be at the right stop! How? I never once took my hand out of my pocket, and I am almost positive no one saw me cut myself. They knew my family, my father, and my mother. They even knew about a book only yet half written. *Man! They were teaching the young people at church!* How could it be? What was going on? How and why could they know so much about us, and us know absolutely nothing about them?

I know why they were interested enough to go to our church, though. I have seen it time and again. They want power. For a while there was a tremendous release of the Holy Spirit's power in that church, and I have seen over and over that whenever there is a release of the Holy Spirit's power in the church, witches are always drawn to it. Just look at "Simon the Sorcerer" or the fortune-telling demonized woman who followed the apostles around town in the book of Acts. *They covet real spiritual power.*

I also have to wonder how much of the church and its leadership had been compromised. I cannot break any confidences, but I know for a fact that very soon after my father stepped down as the pastor of that church (for health and age reasons) there was a huge increase in sexual sin and division, among both the congregation and the church leadership. I can't help but wonder about that *because all of it occurred during the exact period of time I ran into that witch.*

Witches! That is what they call *themselves.* How much contact do they have with small groups, with the young people ... with our children? The one I spoke to was involved in all these levels of the church. She was a practising witch babysitting our children, for crying out loud! Not only that, but she said, "*Some* of us go to your dad's church." I wonder how much, how many, and what kind of effect their involvement has had on the spiritual health of the church as a whole. A good thing to bear in mind is that witches don't generally feel morally obligated to tell the truth about themselves.

As you will read further on, I've seen far too much of witchcraft and its power to doubt its reality. (Bear in mind that I am only dealing with the *least* complicated of events.) Witches have spiritual power ... some more than others. But spiritual gifts and laws are precisely that, laws. Whether for good or ill, that is what makes them work. The gifts are given to all people, good and evil, Christian or not. The fact that witches are not only aware of this but are also trained in the use of their own gifts is obvious. I'll say one thing—most of the witches I've met take their religion very seriously, and many work far harder at it than a lot of Christians I know.

You see, there's no free ride in witchcraft. Their whole purpose is to increase their personal power, and that only comes through study and some hard-core persistence and training. *They practice their witchcraft.* The result is that many witches are far more equipped to understand and function in the gifts they possess than the vast majority of Christians are in theirs. Most Christians don't even know what gifts God has given them.

Paul encourages Timothy to "fan into flame the gift of God, which is in you through the laying on of my hands" (2 Tim. 1:6). Are we imparting, releasing, or "fanning into flame" the gifts in our churches? By this I mean are we encouraging people to allow God, through his Holy Spirit, to bless and edify the church and aid in the function of more powerful evangelism through the use of the spiritual gifts God has given various people in the body? Paul said, "my speech and my message were not in plausible words of wisdom, but in demonstration of the Spirit and of power, *so that your faith may not rest in the wisdom of men but in the power of God*" (1 Cor. 2:4–5, emphasis added). If you say the words *witch, warlock* or *coven*, people expect the supernatural. We serve a supernatural God who is far more powerful than all the powers of hell combined! Why then is it so amazing when something supernatural happens in a church? *We have the real thing!*

I have survived direct attack from demons and covens that have almost killed me—*several times.* I still bear the scars of these attacks both on my body and in my soul, as do many of the people I know who were not even involved. Innocent people. *Both they and I were hurt because again and again no one taught me how to use correctly what God had given me!*

In the coming chapters I give two examples of the *wrong* use of gifts. In both instances, I used the same gift. The answers to the problems these illustrations raise should be obvious. And it's not "See! I told you the gifts are dangerous!"

The facts are, spiritual gifts exist, and most Christians have no idea about what to do with them! Shutting our eyes and pretending they don't exist is just plain nonsense. Perhaps the church is just too busy pretending they are not castrated by their own sin (or covering it up so the world won't see it) and are embarrassed because of their powerlessness. I wonder if this is not the motivating factor behind the theology that the gifts have gone with the apostles.

As for me? I am just sick and tired of nobody teaching me not only how to fight in this bizarre war I'm in but also *how to take the fight to the enemy!*

19
DAMNED IF YOU DON'T

I have tried to write about this chunk of my life at least a dozen times. Each attempt has wound up with me throwing crumpled sheets of paper all over my room, vaguely trying to hit any number of garbage pails I have stationed at strategic points. Once in a while I actually hit one.

What I've been trying to fathom is how God managed to keep me alive and out of hell. At the end of this particular ten-year stint (between ages 17 and 27) I had become an animal. I was full of rage and with not a single shred of hope or dignity left—savage, uncontrollable, frenziedly banging speed, cocaine, and heroin on top of drinking all day, every day. I was completely obsessed with self and frantically doing anything and everything I could to remain oblivious to the pain and blind to the horror I had brought upon myself and everyone I touched. That I was demonically driven at the end is beyond question, yet the Holy Spirit dwelt in me still, just as he had from the beginning. Questions of that, I leave to theologians. I know what I know.

I was running all over California and parts of New Mexico (I think ...) —basically just blindly tearing back and forth, to and fro, much of which is just a nightmarish blur of deeper and more anguished desperation. I was completely lost in a maze of sin, pain, addiction, and fear, no longer caring where I was, who I was, or where I was going—as long as I had something to find oblivion in.

Early into that time (I was about 18 years old), a small group of concerned Christians drove me to an induction centre for an internationally known treatment centre, probably glad to wash their hands of me. For some reason, in this godly environment I was finally able to settle down for the first time in my entire life. There was such a peace about the place, and I started to thrive as God began a slow process of healing. I had never known anything like it before.

Soon it seemed as though parts of me I never knew existed woke, slowly stirred, and came to life. I began to pray in earnest and was devouring the Scriptures like a starving thing. God commenced the work in me I so desperately needed, washing away much of the encrusted filth I had been carrying in my soul by the gentle ministrations of the Holy Spirit.

You see, in the four short years I had been a Christian, the enemy had almost completely devoured me. I had to deal with several kinds of addictions, had multiple visions I didn't really understand, and had been bombarded with all manner of spiritual attacks that I had zero comprehension of. Actually, I had no understanding of addiction either, but somehow in that place, I felt for the first time in my life a sense of peace, freedom, and connectedness I had never experienced before.

Soon after becoming a Christian I had often felt terribly alone. I was starving for God and wandering around in great pain with this horrible gnawing emptiness in my heart that I did not know how to fill. I was hurt—badly, but as I think back now I can see I wasn't, at that time, able to even tell I was in pain. It had always been with me, a constant companion, so I knew no other way to feel. I had no knowledge of what life was without it.

In that peaceful place, for the first time in my life I felt truly happy, walking with God, sensing his presence, being refreshed daily by his Spirit and his Word, and in strong fellowship with the body of Christ around me. I was almost always praying, both in tongues and with my understanding.

Spiritual gifts were becoming evident in my life, some of which I'd never even heard of, let alone operated in. And again, as per usual, I had no idea what to do with them or who to turn to for guidance. I remember one such occasion.

We had joined hands to pray about an outreach we were preparing for on the streets of Hollywood. As I was praying, the Holy Spirit fell heavily on us all. Just as I was closing in prayer I suddenly found myself looking through the eyes of a demon.

He was a spirit of the air, and it was as though I were flying with him, in him, looking through his eyes, seeing what he saw as he flew. He was gliding just over shoulder height, weaving in and out of the people on the Hollywood sidewalks. His purpose was to sense people—to search them, seeking out woundedness and sin in their life to corrupt and exacerbate further—to feed upon it. It lasted only four or five seconds, but the two guys standing on either side of me dropped my hands and stepped away from me, startled. Then they looked at me and exclaimed, *"What was that?"* I couldn't explain it. Neither did I know what to do with it or who to talk to about it.

I never wanted my time there to end.

One evening after praying I was just so peaceful and so happy I walked over and, leaning with my arms on a fence, I prayed, "God, I love you so very, very much! Lord, if you know I'm going to leave you ... to fall away again, Lord, please! Please kill me now, Lord! I just couldn't bear it! Please just kill me now! Don't ever let that happen again ... please God, just kill me! I would rather be dead than apart from you!" I prayed this way for at least half an hour. He didn't kill me. I still don't know how I feel about that. I'm just so glad I did not see the years and years of bitter struggle ahead.

After the time in the induction centre was done, I was sent to a much bigger treatment facility in one of the larger cities to continue on with the program. As soon as we arrived, as was my custom, I began to walk the perimeter, pushing out and praying as I went along. (I didn't find out till years later that this was a commonly used gift in many churches.) It didn't take long for me to find out there was something drastically wrong with the place. Within minutes I began to feel like the place was injured or ... contaminated.

"What is it, Lord?" I questioned.

The answer came almost immediately. "The leadership here is in sin. I want you to go to them and tell them to repent."

I got real nervous, real quick, and so I asked him again, thinking I could not possibly have understood properly. The answer was clear and unmistakable.

"*The directors of this program are in sin.* I want you to go to them and tell them to repent!" At this point I think I actually began to sweat, and, deeply troubled, I pushed a little and located the building they were in and then found the exact area of the building they were in at that very moment. (I know now that I was right. Much later, I was invited up to the director's apartment for dinner in that very building, and he lived precisely where God had shown me that day.) Somehow I knew without a doubt that he was telling me to go there immediately and speak to them.

That got me even more panicky, so I inquired again. He was very clear, but this time he used my name. "Kevin, I want you to go to the directors of this program, right now, and tell them to repent. They are in sin."

I looked at the building, and I became afraid. I knew it was God doing the asking. At that time I had only heard his voice that clearly once before, many years earlier, but once you've heard it, it's impossible to mistake or to forget it.

I was also frightened because this was the first time he'd ever asked me to actually *do* something. Before this, all our talks had simply been "him and me" in straightforward dialogue. I knew I should obey, so I went directly to the building he had indicated.

Sure enough, there on the outside of the building was a sign saying "Admissions."

My heart started sort of pounding. I absolutely did not want to go in there. However, even though I was afraid, I went in and asked the lady at the desk if this was where the directors were. She said yes, it was, but I really shouldn't be "in here" as I had not been through orientation yet. That was all the excuse I needed. I lost my nerve and walked away. I was too afraid.

You must understand—I was barely 18 years old and an alcoholic dope fiend wing nut barely three months clean. Not only that, but I hadn't really ever walked as a "Christian" in my entire life before that time.

This was a centre with more than 150 clients, plus all the staff. I was hugely intimidated. Who was I? I was no one. I knew nothing of Christian leadership. To me, all leaders were giants, to be respected and prayed for. I was a half wild, barely housebroken whack job, and a frightened one at that. I must have been mistaken … surely I was imagining this.

Perhaps it was all just overzealous delusions of grandeur, blown way out of proportion—I had fooled myself into imagining something that wasn't.

These were the directors not only of this facility but also for all of Southern California! Now I have God telling me to just walk up on my very first day and tell them, "God has sent me to tell you that you must repent!" I didn't even know what I was telling them to repent of! This couldn't be right. What about the chain of command? Where were the "elders"? Surely God would have spoken to one of them first! I just couldn't do it. I was too scared. Overawed. Perhaps later. I was far too young and much too sinful; I had to have been mistaken. Yet deep down I knew I wasn't. I knew that voice, and I felt miserable, confused, and guilty as I walked away to find more excuses for my cowardice.

All was well until about 10 days later when, very suddenly, everything came to light. As it turned out, the director for all of Southern California and the wife of the director for that facility had been having an affair and had siphoned off huge sums of money, embezzling every penny they could, including the money assigned for the clients' food. Then they had picked up and run off together in a very expensive sports car.

It was then that I realized the terrible consequences of my cowardice and disobedience. Whole families were torn apart. Hearts were broken. The entire organization was shaken to its foundations. The supporting churches were thrown for a loop. Faith, even among the students, was shaken and questioned. The clients, the staff, the families, the supporting churches and businesses—all of them suffered.

And I suffered, never once opening my mouth but racked with guilt and too ashamed to speak to anyone. Although I have no way of proving it now, it is quite possible that had I been obedient and delivered God's message to them, the leaders might have repented, and God would again have been glorified.

I simply didn't understand. I didn't know God's character at that point—*that it would be just like him to choose a vessel like me.* I didn't know enough about his love. I didn't know that God could use anyone he chose to carry out his purposes. Even sinners—you know, people like me. But I felt so small ... so weak and far too frightened to ask for guidance. Where was I to turn for counsel and for wisdom anyway?

I believe there are many in the church today whom God is speaking to all the time, yet they can't believe it's God who's doing the speaking or that they are anywhere near holy enough, righteous enough (old enough?), for God to speak to them like that. Some may not even realize it's been God talking to them, so fear of disbelief and ridicule shuts their mouths, and the church is neither healed nor corrected. She only suffers.

I have seen with my own eyes just a small fragment of her and beheld for only a moment the love Christ has for her. I have seen the incredible beauty that she has been given. But she is wounded and needs all the gifts, whatever they may be, to edify, strengthen, build, and guard her. I know there are a multitude of gifts—too many to count, each one unique to the one to whom it was given. And every one of them is vital to us all. *These gifts must be recognized, identified, and used under wise, godly discernment and careful instruction.* It's that, or else the church will continue to suffer as she has been for so many years—and the enemy will continue to mock the impotence of God's people.

Paul had to deal with people who were only too familiar with the supernatural.

We are a church bound by the fear of it. Why are we so afraid? Where is our faith placed? Are we just a church of science? Of reason alone? We have discipleship programs galore. Surely there must be some way of identifying, teaching, and encouraging these gifts. We are commanded to seek and save the lost, and in order to do that in these last days we must use all God has given us. Within the next two generations North America will for the first time in its existence be faced with a generation raised in an entirely godless society. It seems we are making the same mistakes as Israel. They never lasted beyond two generations of God delivering them either. Selah (chew on that awhile).

20
DAMNED IF YOU DO

If you remember, I said at the beginning that my purpose in writing this stuff down was to try to make some sort of sense out of all these odd occurrences and miracles that seemed to keep happening in my life. It is working. Even as I write this I am seeing things I have never understood before with a new and deeper insight. I made many terrible blunders in my life, and I struggle along as we all do, but now things are beginning to make some kind of sense to me. I can only pray that any who read this would grow in their own way with me.

What I write about next deals with what has probably been the single most horrific period of time in my life. I must now look at actions that bring me deep shame and tremendous sorrow. Its very nature makes it difficult to keep innocent people protected, so please excuse any vagueness or sense of disjointedness.

At the time, I was renting the top floor of a house in a large city well known for its violence and corruption. It was during a period when I was battling not only alcohol but various kinds of IV drugs as well. One of the results of this was that I had to deal with a huge increase in the amount and intensity of spiritual oppression. For me the two seem to go hand in hand. This was an extremely dangerous time in my life. I was plagued by suicidal thoughts and was fighting a losing battle with great fear and depression. Almost everyone had given up on me (including me) and wanted nothing to do with me. I would try and fail, try and fail, over and over again until I was terrified of standing one more time, lest when I fell again I should kill myself in some drunken depression ... Yet out of sheer desperation I would get up and try once more, only to fail again. Later on I would have to deal with suicidal thoughts so strong that I would climb to the top of high buildings and hang for long periods of time by one hand, with one foot out in space.

I was desperately doing everything I could think of to stop—AA, prayer, church, meditation on Scripture, treatment, crying, begging, pleading—absolutely nothing worked. I'd be very lucky if I got one or two months sober, and just that felt like absolute torture. I was dying in every way possible. The church I was going to tolerated me, but only barely. I was a pariah, and a very lonely one at that.

During my brief intervals of sobriety, I began taking long slow walks around my neighbourhood, praying earnestly, seeking answers, and often crying aloud to God in great pain for any kind of help or release at all. I could feel the hope and life draining right out of me.

As I would walk back down my block toward home, I began to notice that every time I got to a certain area on my street I would begin to get horribly edgy. It was a much different feeling than the utter defeat and despair I had grown so accustomed to. It felt like some sort of powerful darkness—almost predatory. This feeling would steadily increase in intensity and then slowly fade as I continued past the area. One day I decided I would find out what it was and why it made me so edgy.

God's gifts are irrevocable (Rom. 11:29). That means he doesn't take them away, even if we are not doing particularly well. If he did that, nobody would be doing anything. This fact has often caused great pain and confusion in the church, as well as in the world, and as I mentioned earlier, these gifts are given to *all* men, not just Christians. So when I say I was going to find out why, I mean I was going to deliberately use a specific gift that God had given me for a specific purpose.

By a process that is both boring and tedious, I narrowed things down to two houses on the block next to each other, and I tentatively pushed. What I found there was a particularly strong coven of witches who practised black witchcraft and demon worship and called Satan lord absolutely.

I can feel eyeballs rolling, but that *is* what I found, and I had a *very* good reason to trust my own judgment on such matters. Perhaps for the reader when it was just Wicca it was easier to handle—not quite as extreme. Maybe even a bit artsy fartsy hippieish—a bunch of eccentric women with strange ideas of fun playing around with crystals—even a bit enticing, titillating? But the dark arts? Witch hunter! So overly dramatic! (Tsk, tsk!) Well, tough luck; take a number and get in line. That *is* what I found.

Several days passed, and I had an opportunity to speak with a friend about it. He was spiritually mature (I had supposed) and was a solid Christian, so I assumed he had good insight and thus would have good judgment and advice. When I discussed my discovery with him, he suggested that I go back to the place and pray over the houses and against the witches, and that I mustn't worry. God was with me. (I literally shuddered when I wrote that sentence.)

Well, that's exactly what I did. Walking past the houses again (just to make sure of what I'd felt) not only confirmed my judgment but cleared up some of the confusion I had about the second house. I will say only this: one was for living in, and the other was used as a gathering place and for conducting their rituals.

As I walked back down the opposite side of the empty street, I pulled up sharply and stood behind a tree directly in front of the houses. Leaning casually up behind and against it, so as not to be noticed, I began to pray.

I can't remember what exactly I prayed, something about confusing and hindering them, among a whole lot of other things, but I'm sure, though it was very well intentioned, it was also all very foolish. I guess I prayed that way for about 15 or 20 minutes, finished up, mentally dusted off my hands with a "Well, that's that then!" and returned home—a job well done. I was a fool.

Everything was peachy keen for just less than three days. Then hell itself was unleashed on me.

I was catching a ride home after a small group meeting for Bible study. Things were going a bit better, and I felt I was making some headway spiritually. I was finally beginning to feel somewhat peaceful. I had shared nothing of what I had done with anyone other than my one confidant. I was already viewed with deep suspicion, and people were rightly questioning even my salvation. This would have definitely pushed me right over the edge. And who would believe me anyway? By what right or who did I think I was to presume that God would bother telling me such a thing as where in the neighbourhood a powerful coven that practised black witchcraft would be? My life was a mess! I was far too sinful a person for God to talk to me about such matters.

I was just a couple of houses away from home when I saw her. I still shudder every time I remember her face. You know in the movies where a guy is driving his car and all of a sudden someone is standing on the corner staring straight at him, and time goes into slow motion, and the person on the corner glaring at him is some kind of a really creepy/evil/strange/scary/weird-looking person? Well ... that is *exactly* what happened, *and I knew instantly who she was.*

An older lady, in a long funny-looking dark grey overcoat, with dark grey hair, and an extremely malicious face was staring straight into my eyes and didn't so much as blink the whole time until the car passed her and turned the corner. My eyes seemed to be horribly riveted to hers, and I was unable to drop her gaze.

This woman had not only stared *at* me but, far worse, she had stared straight *into* me. Deep into me, and I was afraid. To say that woman hated me a lot would be meaningless compared to how *much* that woman really hated me a lot. I had only felt that kind of virulent hatred once in my life, many years before.

The look she gave me was intensely and incredibly penetrating and equally malicious. The sheer force of it was like a powerful slap across the face.

Intelligent, murderous, powerfully probing, sensing, analyzing me— with a single look she had brushed aside any defence I might have had and scanned me in detail, right to the bottom of my spirit. We *both* knew what she was doing. And we were both very aware of the other. She was searching for, *and finding*, all my weaknesses, woundedness, sinfulness, and fears. It felt like I was being raped. I can still see her face clearly today, many years later. Both of us were locked together somehow, and I was powerless to stop it. All this took only about 10 or 12 seconds.

As soon as we turned the corner and parked, I looked over my shoulder. She was nowhere to be seen. She'd gone out of my sight in only seconds! *Less than five.* I got out, frantically looking in all directions. Nothing.

"Did you see her?" I asked the driver.

"See who?" was the response.

That's when I realized where she had been standing! I realized she had been doing openly, directly in front of my house, what I had done in secret in front of hers. I felt a cold, cold chill. "That woman! *THAT WOMAN WHO WAS STANDING RIGHT IN FRONT OF MY HOUSE! SHE WAS JUST RIGHT THERE!*" I was yelling, almost in panic. My ride had seen nothing.

I woke the next night to strange sounds outside my house—odd scratching, scraping noises, indefinable sounds—just strange, and totally unfamiliar. Later I would wake from horribly vivid nightmares of violent rape and murder to the sound of high heels clicking loudly on the sidewalk, interspaced with strange rhythmic tappings, like a cane beating out some odd counter rhythm. It would abruptly stop and then a few seconds later begin again, then stop again for good. No sound of a car door, no house door. No nothing. And no one I knew would just start walking on wet grass in high heels late at night. This occurred several nights in a row, almost always accompanied by the same kind of dream. As time went on, the nightmares became more vivid, more perverse, and far more violent—unbelievably violent, as in people being torn limb from limb.

When I spoke to the person who had been with me driving that evening, he said his family was experiencing almost exactly the same things. He told me that while he and his wife were changing their child's diapers, they started feeling horrible emanations coming off her.

We didn't know what was happening. We didn't understand anything.

I had no idea who to talk with about it all. I knew I should tell someone, but there was no one in the church I trusted. I had a rapidly growing fear and darkness that was very thick and oppressive settling down on me—almost to the point where it felt like I couldn't breathe. I began to be tormented by terrible guilt and shame for all the harm I had done to others in my life and became dangerously suicidal, sometimes placing a butcher knife under my chin and calculating the exact angle and force necessary to drive it through my chin, up through the soft palate, and into my brain. I would spend long moments mustering up the blind courage to do it. I also found the ribs through which to place a thin strong knife, and I held it against the counter, knowing that one quick lean in would drive it into my heart. I began to drink again, only this time in insane quantities, and I would quickly become furiously enraged for no reason at all at everything, anything, and anybody. This wasn't like me. I wasn't a mean drunk.

I began going to bars and parks, looking for fights with anyone who even looked at me the wrong way. This was way, *way* out of character for me. Later I started getting far more plastered than usual. I began painting my face with strange blood-like designs and would go out late at night with dangerous weapons and huge rage. I finally went crazy, jumped out of a moving vehicle right into traffic, and ran off into the heart of the city. I have never returned there since, and it haunts me to this day.

My pal fared no better than I did, maybe even worse. His child was seriously injured, and his marriage went quickly to pieces within three and a half months.

There were other things as well. I was continuously plagued by feelings of going mad—violently, suicidally insane. All of this happened in less than one and a half months. I didn't know what was going on until a friend gave me some information much later—far, far too late.

This whole time I was too fearful to turn to anyone for help and much too uncomprehending to explain it even if I could have. I had no idea what was happening to me. An incredible amount of damage—no, not damage—*destruction* was rained down upon our heads in diabolical proportions in an incredibly short period of time. The effects of it continue to this day. Whole families were destroyed. I wound up five times more hurt, angry, distrustful, confused, frustrated, and afraid than I'd ever been before. Terrible harm was done right across the board. Any trust I had in the church or Christians evaporated. It has taken almost 20 years and a huge amount of prayer just to begin to recover. And why?

Well, let me count the ways. Let's see … going up alone against an unknown source of unknown numbers, of unknown power, in an unfamiliar territory, with no experience, no teaching, no defences, no prayer support, no leadership, no covering, no accountability, in extremely vulnerable condition, exposing completely innocent people, and totally unprepared for any retaliation (for starters).

I would say that was pretty damn … *bloody brilliant!*

Why, you may ask? *Because these were not just a bunch of kids playing around on a Ouija board!* This was very, very real. I have much more practical experience and understanding in these areas now and have learned a little.

People have died making the mistakes I did.

What I had so innocently stumbled upon, what tore loose on me and some others even less prepared than I, was a coven that worshipped what is called a territorial spirit. Peter Wagner writes, "Unlike personal deliverance ministries, dealing with territorial spirits is major league spiritual warfare. It should not be undertaken casually. If you do not know what you are doing—and I am aware of only a few who have the necessary expertise, Satan will eat you for breakfast"![8] That was precisely what happened to me. I found an account of an encounter with a territorial spirit in a book I stumbled upon while researching this subject. I personally knew both the man and the church described in the book and was there at the same time as this man's encounter with that spirit. I lived not more than a fifteen- or twenty-minute drive from where it occurred.

The fault lay not in an inappropriate use of a spiritual gift *but in what I didn't do before I moved forward.* It never occurred to me to ask God what to do with the information I had discovered. I sure wasn't willing to go to the church with it and get either dismissed or rejected some more. I'd had more than enough of that.

Instead I went in, all on my lonesome, with both guns blazing and some hazy ideas about "We Shall Overcome" and "There Is Power in the Blood." They came back, slaughtered my ass, and hung it out to dry, along with anyone else involved and some others who were just innocent bystanders.

Launching a full blown attack against a witchcraft stronghold is flat-out foolishness. But I had no one to turn to—no one to say either 1. *Hey! Don't pray against a coven on your own!* or 2. *Don't pray against a coven— period!* No one was there to tell me. No one taught me how to pray at all, and this kind of thing wasn't exactly on the local church curriculum at the time, and even if it were, they still probably wouldn't let me attend!

The one thing the enemy hates above all else is the gospel of Jesus Christ—his incredible love for his own. Think about it. That is what defeated Satan at the cross. That is what any and all demonic forces come

---

[8] C. Peter Wagner, *Supernatural Forces in Spiritual Warfare: Wrestling with Dark Angels* (Shippensburg: Destiny Image Publishers, 2012).

against … hard. The gospel. So perhaps I should have prayed for God's powerful love to intervene in the lives of those involved in the coven—that God's Holy Spirit would come and save them. But I had a problem. *I didn't know his love. I couldn't understand it yet. I was just another walking wound.* Who was there to point out to me that I should pray *for* the people—that I should bless them and ask God to fill them with the love of Christ? Satan cannot stand God's love. He hates it and has to flee from its presence. I have seen demonically oppressed people being released simply by the Holy Spirit being asked to pour out God's love and forgiveness and mercy into and onto the oppressed person.

Believe me! I am *not* writing any sort of treatise on spiritual warfare! Shoot, I'm on spiritual *welfare* most of the time. All that I do know about this stuff is just what I've picked up as I've wandered through this life and had a lot of it mess me up real bad.

You see, I had thrown a wrench full tilt at a hornet's nest, and what's ironic about all of this is that by using the very same gift I used they were able to locate me and give me the beating of my life. That I lived through it was a miracle.

Pick up a copy of *Supernatural Forces in Spiritual Warfare: Wrestling with Dark Angels* by Peter Wagner—a very scholarly work.

So there you have it—two stories, each one including the use of the identical gift, both ending with disastrous results. In the one I didn't act and many people were badly hurt. In the other I did act and the results were equally catastrophic. The gift was very real. Guidance and maturity were lacking. Basically, it simply boiled down to the fact that I had to learn alone, again, the hard way. Think it's easy?

21
THE TAPESTRY

I've written about a few of the wonderful things God has done for me—the unmerited mercy, and the unceasing grace and kindness he has poured into my life. I have also tried to explain a few of the events I don't understand but still hope to gain some sort of insight into. I needed to understand. That was my whole motivation for picking up a pencil in the first place. This is not a book of answers. It is a book chock full of questions, some that God has answered in full, some that he has in part—and on others, he has remained annoyingly silent.

As I wrote, I quickly discovered I'd gotten far more than I'd bargained for. I was deeply and powerfully moved by what I found. Examining the miracles themselves changed me in the most profound way I have ever experienced, and I can never be the same now. He revealed his love to me in the midst of writing this. The time had finally come, after so many years, for God to open my eyes so I could see not just the miracles he had done—but him. He alone is the "who" and the "what" that I had been crying out for all of my life … and it was he whom I finally saw and now worship with all my heart.

And So It Begins

We know that God's plans and timing are far beyond our understanding. I still do not know why I had to walk for so long in darkness—why for so many years I cried out, knowing that he heard me and not understanding why the darkness in my life remained. But God knew what he was up to.

You see, never in this lifetime will we see where his plan started. Nor will we ever see its end. We are only allowed small glimpses of our part in it for the brief amount of time granted us. Once in a while we get the chance to see how he weaves together many different parts of his plan. But only once in a lifetime do we get to see how he takes one of these threads, carefully weaves it into place, and then, at just the right moment, pulls on it, and that single thread draws together what looks to be a tangled mess of chaos into a wondrously intricate and beautifully crafted tapestry of love.

Only once so far have I been allowed to see such a marvel, and it was the final step in his conquest of my heart. Now I would tear it from my breast and throw it at his feet were I able. This "tapestry" played the final role in freeing me to walk in a way I never thought possible. Until God tangled me up into its threads, I was utterly, hopelessly, and desperately lost. But he heard me and took pity on me—and he rescued me. There is no one like him! Compare him? To whom? These are not just words to me. I know they sound like I'm quoting from some old hymnal, but I can't help it! Words such as these are now the biggest reality of my life.

This tapestry, which God in his great love created, is without any doubt in my mind the most profound miracle he has ever confounded me with to this day. Threads are still being woven into it, and I have no doubt there will be many more to praise him for as I continue along in this journey. Buckle up—'cause this one's pretty crazy. (My head's still spinning!)

SCENE 1

It was the end of winter, and I was too tired in my body and too sick in my soul to run any longer. I had no money, no strength, no power. And it all showed. My condition was pitiful. I was down to drinking the hand sanitizer in the bus depot washrooms. It wasn't too bad. I'd drunk worse. Hairspray was much harder to choke down. You could get past the jelly texture of the sanitizer if you just downed it real quick—73 percent ethyl alcohol (that's the good kind). It was the other 27 percent that tore you up bad, but it was enough to stave off the seizures … at least for a while.

I was riding Greyhound back from Saskatchewan to Ontario. I had to get back to deal with an assault charge I had there. Some creep pedophile had been scoping out my two daughters every time they went swimming in the backyard pool. They were seven and nine years old. He had already been convicted twice for it, and as far as I was concerned, there was not going to be a third. That is something you can never undo. I'd punched the guy's teeth right out of his mouth. The way I'd been feeling that year, he was incredibly lucky that's all he lost.

The cops had kept his teeth as evidence, and I'd already been convicted, so I had to get back and do my time. I'd been breached at least three times on the charge. Like an idiot, I'd skipped on my bail. I was thinking of simply outrunning the stupid thing as I'd done so many times in the past, but I was just too weak physically, and it somehow seemed as if I'd lost all heart for the road. I'd been down it so, so many times—and it had left its claw marks on every part of my soul.

Amazingly this was my first assault charge. Ever. Actually, given the number of fights I'd been in over the years, it was nigh on impossible. The only reason I got away with it before was that I'd always left whatever province I happened to be in anytime the cops were looking for me. Generally, I'd just knock somebody out and leave town—quietly disappearing down the road. This time, like I said, I was just far too bone-weary tired.

I fell asleep to the familiar sound of the highway, idly wondering if I'd wind up in jail again for drinking on the bus or in the hospital for having another seizure.

SCENE 2

It was cold, and I was desperately sick. I'd been vomiting up great clots of dark-red blood. I'd filled the sink up twice. I had the sense to drink huge amounts of water so it was thinned down a bit, but nothing would thin down what was coming out the other end.

I'm dying, I thought—more of a distant and detached observation than a thought. My friend Dan was begging me to let him call an ambulance. I finally surrendered my phone. I didn't care anymore. Who gives a damn when you're pretty much dead and insane anyway?

"I haven't heard a peep out of you," I whispered as I crawled on my hands and knees to my filthy bed, "for a long time," and I rolled up onto it to wait. For what? Death? The ambulance? *Who cares? Whichever one gets here first.* I closed my eyes and carefully folded my hands on my stomach to wait. One of them was sure to come.

SCENE 3

I had just got back home from the hospital—third or fourth time in eight months. The doctor had angrily informed me that during the previous four hours I'd lost over one-third of my blood. This time they kept me under twenty-four-hour observation because I'd had a seizure right in admitting—on top of all the bleeding, so they were forced to keep me for a while. I was also hallucinating and delusional, which complicated things quite a bit. I started seeing my daughters in the hallways and fearing that somehow they were going to get trapped under a bed somewhere. I kept getting out of my bed and running around the hospital looking for them. The nurses had to sedate me very heavily. They came in every hour or so to ask if I knew my name, where I was, and what the date was. They had to back up and start with what province I was in and what year it was, never mind what month or day it was. It took a couple days till I began to get it right.

I was drinking 20 minutes after they released me, only this time I began to pray—hard. I missed God so much. I could still remember all of those precious moments I'd had with him—the wonderful sense of being in his presence, of being enveloped by his Spirit. I felt so cut off, so bitterly alone, so lost, and so very, very empty. God! How I missed him—I had to be in his presence again or I felt like I would lose my mind ... as well as my life.

After a time, I could barely choke down enough booze into me to ward off a seizure. Then I would just lie on the floor and beg through my tears, "God, please! Please help me! I can't do this, I just can't do this. I need your help, God. I'm dying! I need your help so badly! Don't forget your words to me. Lord, you promised me! Remember your promises to me. Remember what you've told me! Please! Please help me! I can't do this! *WHAT DO YOU WANT FROM ME? WHAT DO YOU WANT?*"

The answer was always the exact same four words: *Everything. All of it.* He would not be satisfied with anything less. All of it. (That meant everything.) I didn't know how to do that. I couldn't do that. I told him so. I told him that I couldn't even repent on my own. I just didn't know how. My heart was so hard. It seemed like a steel vault, and I certainly didn't have the combination.

I think it was at that point, right there, right then, that it happened. When I finally saw clearly how absolutely, hopelessly, helplessly doomed I was. That I couldn't even offer God my heart, I was so powerless—that my life was an absolute, complete, catastrophic nightmare and that no matter how many treatment centres I went to, no matter how hard I tried, how sincere I was, how much I prayed, or how hard I tried to overcome and "gain the victory"—*that no matter what I did*, alcohol, sin, and all the rest of it were going to find me, torture me even more, and finally kill me after destroying everyone and everything my life touched—and there wasn't one single thing I could do about it. Nothing. I was completely and utterly helpless.

I think right then was when God popped himself a huge grand grin, cracked his knuckles, started rubbing his hands together, and said, "DAMN, I'M GOOD!" (or something like that), "HE TOOK THE BAIT, BOYS! HE'S ON THE ROPES AND HE'S GOING DOWN—HARD! ROLL ON TWO!" and then pulled together over five decades of miracles and thousands upon thousands of prayers into one great big miraculously beautiful tapestry that I'm still backing up from just to see, never mind comprehend! Most of it I'm still watching fall into place, even as I write these words. God has pulled off some crazy-ass stuff in my life, but this—this masterpiece of intricacy and wonder—is hands down the blue ribbon, first prize, takes the cake with a cherry on top, clears the stands, confetti and ticker tape parade—coincidence? HA!—*miracle* I have ever seen him do, and it's still being revealed. So far, I'm only just now seeing the framework for it. That alone is more daunting than Godzilla with a bad case of heartburn.

From this point on things get pretty complicated, so I'll have to just stick to the bare facts. The finer details would easily fill another thousand or so pages, so bear with me as I try to explain this, his "Great Fiasco," in, well, in words, I guess (which often, as whenever dealing with the things of God, just never seem to be nearly enough).

In the Beginning

I was living in Huntsville, Ontario. It was winter, and I was too sick to move around, so I'd been sharing a cheapo place with my buddy Dan.

I am not sure why I went into the hospital that last time, but I went. Perhaps I had a seizure, or was suicidal, or both. Maybe I just had some half-baked hazy idea of getting some sort of help somehow—somewhere. Perhaps I was just hoping for a miracle (not that I actually had any hope of one).

At that point it had been 40 long years of pain and struggle since my first attempt to quit using. I had been drinking for 44 years, but I had been trying to quit for 40 of them. I had done everything I could think of, and everything had failed—again and again. So I ran—all over North America, from city to city, province to province, fleeing like some wild blind desperate hunted thing.

The AA, Antabuse,[9] church, God, religion, psychology, counselling, having demons expelled from me—I actually tried giving up and not trying *anything* anymore, but even that small peace was denied me. None of it worked. I knew too much; I had seen too much. It was useless, and all I could feel was that deadness of soul that comes with utter hopelessness, so I ran some more.

None of that failure mattered anymore. What did matter was that after days and weeks of lying face down on the floor pleading with God for my life, I just went.

The hospitals and doctors were tired of me. I'd been coming in almost dead every two or three months, and they'd keep pumping me full of Valium, fluids, and more blood to replace what I'd puked up. The last time I was at that particular hospital, it took four nurses to get an IV into me because I was trembling so hard from my withdrawal. They also had to try five or six times because my veins had so much scar tissue over them from my coke and heroin days that they couldn't hit a vein. I'd blown just about every single one within reach of a needle.

Anyway, a doctor came in and asked me the usual questions and then left. They started in with the IV fluids and Valium right away. I was relieved. This drug, alcohol, will kill you coming down from it. I don't think people really understand how dangerous it actually is.

After a bit, the same doc came back and told me he was going to admit me for a few days. This was *very* good news and a huge load off

---

[9] Antabuse (disulfiram) is a drug used to support the treatment of chronic alcoholism by producing an acute sensitivity to ethanol.

my mind. Quite often a doctor would just pump you full of fluids, give you a few Valium, and then boot your bum out the door in the middle of the night with a script you can't fill till morning and no way to get home (if you even had one). That left a guy sedated, no place to sleep, and no place to use the bathroom—all night. I'm pretty sure that's part of why I didn't like hospitals too much. That, and that almost every time I went there, they'd keep telling me how lucky I am to be alive (Oh yeah right! Live in my shoes and see how lucky you feel.), or that I'm going to die, or that I was dead but now I'm not, or that I should be dead and they don't understand why I'm not dead, or any combination of the above. It just gets real repetitive after a while.

The next day a different doctor walked in, looking all professional and busy, and introduced himself as Dr. Hill. That threw me for a total loop 'cause at first I thought he said Dr. *Hell*. (What a *great* name for a doctor, eh?! *DR. HELL ... ooh yeah!*) Well, while he started running through his doctor checklist to figure out what's going on with me, I figured (me being me), whilst he was trying to figure me out I'd try to figure him out. I was curious. Almost the instant he walked into the room I kind of had a hunch he was a Christian, so I checked him out, and "Bingo!" he came up all aces.

Inwardly I gave a deep sigh of relief. He felt like the real deal. This combination makes for a very good doctor. I had also picked up an odd feeling that for some reason or other this character might even be able to help me somehow—not that his help would actually help—but what the heck, eh? It was just a hunch, anyway.

To be honest, I'm really not sure who was sizing up who better, but I decided I liked this doctor character, and so I figured I'd cut him a break and introduce myself properly. I'm pretty sure our conversation went something like this.

"Sooo ..." (tentatively) "my dad was a doc too."

"Oh really ..." (absentmindedly).

"Yeah, he's—well, he was a shrink. Well, actually he was a surgeon first; then he became a psychiatrist." That got me a noncommittal grunt.

I could tell I was kinda dying quick so I decided to up his curiosity level just a twitch. I contemplated telling him about my various overdose trips to "Dad's Kooky Wards," but then I thought ... aah, that might be just a tad over the top and may freak him out, just a wee bit.

I knew he was a Christian, a real one, so I decided to leave the physical realm and bark up the spiritual tree awhile. I was genuinely curious. People interested me, and I wanted to find out what made this doctor dude tick—where he stood on things. Besides, what could it hurt? At least he'd keep me amused …

"Yep," says I. "He's a bit of a writer too." I saw his pen slow, just a bare fraction.

Bingo! thinks I. (*He reads, at least …*)

"Actually, he's got a few books out. He's … he was a Christian." (Can any Christian really ever be referred to in the past tense?) Then I named a couple of his books.

I watched his brain working as his eyes slowly drifted up to the top of the chart. Then, just as slowly, he looked up at me in the hospital bed.

"Your father was Dr. John White, the writer?" As things would have it, he was quite familiar with Dad's books, and I could tell by the way this doctor spoke he had a lot of respect for Dad's writings. What's more, Dr. Hill's wife, Julie, had read *The Fight* as a young Christian, and apparently it had a real impact on her early Christian walk. He was a Christian, and so was I, and that meant I was able to talk to him much more openly about my situation. It also meant I might have one more person praying for me. I knew it had been prayer that kept me alive all those years, and I valued it immensely.

I saw him again a few times after that, and twice we actually prayed together right in my hospital room, which I thought was way cool and a first for me. (Not that I haven't had a lot of prayers going up in my hospital rooms before.)

As things turned out, he was way cool, too. A real QUACC—Quiet Unruffled Absolutely Crazy Christian. You know the type. Cool as a cucumber …

We talked of me getting sober and of treatment—and about how there were AA meetings every week at the church he went to. I expressed interest, but inwardly I gave a deep sigh—very sadly. You see, I had lost all hope by then. It seemed as if all the things that God had spoken to me, all the incredible things he had shown me, all the miraculous things, what he had done … I guess I thought they were all, just, gone—

that I had blown it, worn God's patience out. I thought maybe he had just given up "striving" with me—that his Spirit was through with my rebelliousness. It says in the Bible something about him not striving forever. I really wasn't sure if I was even a Christian or had ever even been one. That maybe everything, all of it, had just been in my head— that it was all my imagination gone wild or some kind of crazy delusion or that I'd just missed the boat somehow. I wanted to have hope. I really did. But watching it, feeling it smash to pieces and drain out of me— time after time, over and over again, 40 long years of it—it was just way too painful. I couldn't do it. *I would never get my, or anyone else's, hopes up again.* I never wanted to see that disappointment and hurt in the eyes of anyone I loved ever again. I'd had a whole lifetime of it, and it hurt bad enough just being a drunk—but a hopeless drunk—*with hope? No way!* Not a chance.

"Yeah ...," I said, "I guess I could check out a few meetings." But I knew it wouldn't happen.

I wanted to get sober, to be free of it. God knew it, even if no one else did. But all that was just a pipe dream from long ago, and I knew that too, even if no one else did. But you see ... I had forgotten one thing— something very important. It was something I read in the book of Isaiah once. It was something vital that really struck my heart strong. It said, "A bruised reed he will not break, and a smoldering wick he will not snuff out" (Is. 42:3 NIV). I had memorized it.

Dr. Hill cut me loose a couple of days later. I was drinking again 15 minutes after I left the hospital. Same old, same old. But then something amazing happened—something that had never happened before in my whole entire life. Ever.

The Soup Thickens

Almost a week later I was sitting at home (such as it was), drinking a few bottles of wine with my crew, and trying to figure out how we'd manage to get enough booze for the day when I got the shock of my life. The phone rang, and to my great surprise, it was Dr. Hill on the line! On the other end of *my phone! At my home!* Yep. It was the QUACC—*himself!* Calling me! I couldn't believe it. I was completely blown away! So were all my buddies when I told them to shut their yaps.

No doctor had ever phoned me in my entire life before. He was calling to see if I'd had a test of some sort done (not) and to see how I was doing (??!).

I have been dead in hospitals. I mean I have died right in them, and no doctor has ever called me to see how I was doing. I mean, I have literally made medical history—*a couple of times*—for strange life-threatening injuries and even stranger miraculous recoveries, and in all that time I had never ever heard one single peep from any doctor anytime—*ever.*

Yet here's this doctor calling to check up on some strange wino he tried to dry out at the hospital. I was just a drunk! A very surprised drunk, but a hopeless (and useless) drunk nonetheless.

Things quickly got even crazier as our little checkup chat progressed. While we were talking he suddenly interrupted me and said, "Just a sec, Kevin ..." and the line went dead for a while. Then he came back on and said something like "You won't believe what I'm holding in my hands right now." Obviously, I didn't have a clue, and I said so.

Then he said, "While we were talking, my wife, Julie, came downstairs looking for a book she had bought a long time ago. It was about how to help parents who are struggling with how to handle kids that are in trouble." Somehow I knew what was coming, and my heart started doing funny things. "She didn't know the name of the author, but ..." This time I interrupted him.

"Yeah," I whispered, "I know ... *Parents in Pain*, right?" I sighed and, not waiting for an answer, continued, "If you look on the dedication page it says 'To John René.' That's me. All but two of the examples and scenarios at the beginning of the book are things that happened to me, to them, to my parents."

I sighed again, deeply. Things had definitely changed. God was doing the interrupting this time (sticking his nose in—*again!*), and right then something very, *very* frightening began to happen inside me.

You see, this had his mark all over it. It smelled like him. I knew his handiwork—how he did things—and to my great dismay, way down deep inside of me an old familiar flicker of hope began to stir in my heart. This was something I absolutely could not afford. Something that I never wanted to feel again ... *ever!*

Now, after struggling with it for so many years, when I was finally just beginning to accept the fact that I would be an alcoholic for the rest of my life, that I would live as one and die as one, most likely from some accident or maybe bleeding out or some infection or something, but that I would definitely die a drunk, out of nowhere this doctor phones me up and flips everything upside down, and all in an instant I start feeling that treacherously irresistible hope again. Why? Was I out of my ever-loving mind? There was no concrete evidence of this being anything more than a coincidence. I had not felt any kind of hope in a long, long time—and now, all of a sudden, I was afraid. Yet I couldn't help it. I couldn't stop it. It came unbidden, unwanted, and unwelcomed, and I was *very* afraid.

We talked for a bit longer, and as I was hanging up the phone, I could feel that damnable curiosity pick a fight with my heart again. *God ...? What are you playing at now?* Then, just before I could stop it, I whispered something to myself that began the end of life as I then knew it. "You know what, Dr. Hill ...? I think I might just go down Sunday and have a look-see at your church after all ..."

And then I felt that old familiar tug. I was just curious—at least that's what I told myself ... again.

(Zap!) Back in Time 23 Years

I have always disliked Ontario. (That's being kind.) I could fall asleep, cross the border, wake up, and without even opening my eyes know that's where I was (not kidding). I mean, I guess in the right light it's pretty enough—in some places (if you squint ... and use your imagination).

Don't get me wrong, but it just seemed like people in Ontario had no sense of humour. The very first time I stopped in Toronto, within a few hours I got jumped, knocked unconscious, kicked half to death, and blinded in my right eye and almost died in a back alley with green pus dripping out of my eyeball after being dragged behind a garbage dumpster and left for dead.

And the OPP? No sense of ha-ha at all! Way too tense. Everybody was. If I had things my way I would put the whole cotton-pickin' province on a good healthy dose of Valium! I was a mountain woodland creature, so whenever I got into Ontario, I got out of it as fast as I possibly could. Besides, the liquor store hours were simply ridiculous!

I did stop once for a while in Ottawa. (At least it was close to Quebec, where they kept rational beer hours.) Anyway, that was a little over 29 years ago. We were staying at a place where any sane person would have gladly traded their wallet for an environmental suit and a handgun—crackheads, whores, and junkies downstairs, all drunks upstairs. Those were the only rules. Other than that, it was all about anything goes.

One particular afternoon Bruce and I were beating the streets for change. We had been hiking coast to coast for years by then, and we had worked out a real good system. We each took one side of the street, always moving, keeping parallel as much as possible—no signs and sitting around for us. We decided for ourselves who to approach and who to talk to. Knowing who to pick was a real skill honed by many years of practice, and we were good at it. It also made it possible to watch each other's back in case things got out of hand, as they sometimes did. In that case we became quick and effective. Both of us knew exactly what to do—and we were good at that too. We'd already rustled up enough cash to get some booze into us that day, so I wasn't too hung over. Just as I was eyeballing another possible prospect, Bruce came hurrying over to me.

"Kev," he says, "those guys across the street there are Christians, and they want to talk to you."

I looked and saw a couple, obviously husband and wife, checking us out. Bruce knew I could both speak and translate Christianese, so he was probably thinking I could wrangle a few bucks out of them. *What the hell*, I thought. I was always curious to find out what new twist or turn life would dish out, so I figured I'd go over and have a quick look-see and find out where this little quirk would lead.

As I crossed the street I gave them a real good going over to find out what I was dealing with. The man made me a tad nervous—very aware, very intense. No getting around him. The lady was a real sweetheart. You could see it a mile away.

Now this was a long time ago, so I'm not exactly sure how it all happened, but as it turned out these two "Christians" were on their way to a big conference where my father was one of the main speakers and was talking about sexual sin. I think it was when he was travelling around with John Wimber.

When Bruce heard that, he piped up and told them I was John White's son. Now I'm pretty sure this kind of took them by surprise. I mean, discovering that this half-drunk smelly hitchhiker was the son of one of the main speakers at a Christian conference that was being held not more than half a block or so away had to have made them think a bit. That was only fair, because I was just as surprised as they were. I had no idea my dad was even in Ontario, let alone a couple of blocks away. They asked me a few test questions about my family, and as I answered I could see the man becoming even more focused. Suddenly he brightened up and asked if I wanted to go to the conference with them.

That made me think. I hadn't seen or spoken with my father for years. I had just left one time and never came back. I thought about all the pain and disappointment I had caused him over the years. I was dirty and a bit sick. Besides, I was kind of hung over, and dad was real busy anyway. I'd just be a distraction for him. He'd lose focus. Never mind that the last thing I wanted was to get surrounded by a bunch of whacked-out Christians I didn't even know trying to pray for me or kick out another demon or give me another prophecy—when I was hung over? Nope! Binder-dun-dat! Thank you very much. Actually, I was nervous just knowing he was in the same city as me. I said no.

We talked a bit more, and then they prayed for us both. Then the guy asked me again if I was certain about not going. I declined again.

Just before we were going to head out, he stopped me and said, "Then I want to give this to you from your father," and then he gave me a great big hug. It kind of frightened me a bit at first, but I could sense his sincerity, so I took it in.

As Bruce and I were leaving, I stopped and thought for a moment; then on impulse I turned around and walked back to the man. "Give this to my father when you see him," and I gave him a big hug back, then turned and walked away into the crowd of people.

Well, that was just weird, I thought, and then I promptly forgot all about it—just another weird thing in a lifetime full of weird things. It was often like that. Perhaps it was just another little "Hello" from the big guy in an otherwise empty existence—or so I thought.

(Zip!) Back to the Future of Then ...

Curiosity and determination can be a real good mix, and I've got lots of both when I want them. After I hung up the phone with Dr. Hill, I was bound and determined to find out just exactly what in the world God was up to this time. I knew for sure he had something sneaky up his sleeve, but I had no idea that this something was about to change the course of my life, and me, forever.

Sunday morning arrived, and I found myself for the first time in many a year heading to church. One I'd never even been to before! My brain kept asking my heart just what in the great blue blazes it thought it was doing, but my heart seemed to be running some sort of tactical black ops mission and was operating on a "need to know only" basis ... for "security" reasons. That made me *very* nervous, but seeing as how I had my faithful drink container of wine/rubbing alcohol/beer/mouthwash mix at my side (for emergency communion and breath freshening purposes only, of course), I felt well equipped.

Yep, I was out for answers. So, full of investigative zeal (and well-fortified by my jug of paint thinner), I set out fully intending to get to the bottom of this inscrutableness. Little did I know that this investigation of mine was only starting—and I haven't got to the bottom of it yet.

When I finally found the church, I was a bit flummoxed. This was a feeling I was to become quite familiar with in the very near future. The church proved to be two churches, right across the street from each other, both old, both beautiful, and both nameless. I guess they were so big they didn't think they needed a sign. Of course, I have been known to not see things from time to time (trains, whisky bottles, boots, fists—and the occasional sign once in a while).

I hung around the lighter coloured one with a friend, hoping to find some sort of clue as to whether I had chosen correctly. I was in need of some hint that would help me find this enigma I was coming to think of as "my doctor." (I had never had my very own doctor before.)

As I was admiring the old brickwork, I began to notice all the well-dressed super-respectable types, many of them elderly, walking into the church. All of a sudden it hit me, "God, you gotta be kidding me!" as I rolled my eyes heavenward. "Oh yeah! This is *just* my kind of place!" Now I was positive that God was involved. This kind of church was the last place in the world I would ever set foot in! It was just like him.

I was still kind of chuckling at this latest crank God was pulling on me when my attention was drawn to one lady in particular. She was it! I knew it! My inside source ...

Now I really can understand her startlement. Most people are kind of edgy and suspicious around me at first. Let's just say ... well, let's just not say, and leave it at that.

I approached her directly, looking straight into her eyes, and gave off all the body language to indicate "Hi! Please stop, I need to talk, I have a question." She did, and as I approached, she kind of unconsciously clutched her belongings a little tighter to her as she eyed me up and down a bit suspiciously.

"Hi! Good morning! You wouldn't by some chance happen to know if this is the church Dr. Stephen Hill attends, would you?"

She suddenly seemed quite surprised and looked at me kind of real funny, almost startled, but she said yes, she did know a Dr. Stephen Hill, and that this was indeed the right church. I thanked her, then watched as she scurried off into the building.

I thought, *Nice lady. Very odd reaction. Unused to stranger contact. Keep more physical distance with all future church unknowns.* (This is actually how my brain automatically functions.) What I didn't know was that she was the second thread in the vast multitude of them to come.

I later discovered that other than the pastor, Steve Hill was the only other person she knew in that church, that she didn't even attend there, and that she had only come up to do some work on their cottage and then go back to Toronto where she lived. That was the reason she had come—because she knew the pastor and Dr. Stephen Hill. Had I known this, I would have caught on to the fact that God was turning up the heat, and I was the proverbial lobster in the kettle. Anyway, the soup now thickens even more.

I never have been real shy, so, satisfied I had picked the right church, I walked in and made my way directly to the front of the sanctuary. It didn't even occur to me that I was dirty, stank like a drunken chemical factory, and was a tad unsteady on my feet—oh, or that I just didn't exactly fit in there (HA!).

First off, I was used to it. I didn't fit in anywhere. And second, the way I figured it, if anyone should feel ashamed or embarrassed, it should be them, not me. At least I knew what I was.

The service hadn't started yet, and I needed information. Now one of the things I have learned over the years is that if you ever need to find out what's going on in a crowded area, ask the person who looks the most worried, stressed, or nervous—90 percent of the time that's your man. (Sheer panic is a dead giveaway.) Having located my target, I moved in on him slowly, so as to have time to study him a little more carefully before speaking to him. I had made this a habit of mine, and it had come in very helpful many times.

This character was walking intensity incarnate. To say that he was a man on a mission would be tantamount to calling King Kong a chimpanzee. He had a feel like he might very well spontaneously combust at any moment. When I asked him, very politely, if he happened to know a Dr. Stephen Hill, he stopped dead in his tracks and, blinking violently, began glancing wildly about the chapel as if I had just told him the devil himself was in that very room and *"He's come for YOU!"* He then quickly spun around, fixed me with a gaze almost feral in nature, and said "yes" as his eyes continued darting rapidly about the room. (By now I was backing up and glancing around as well.) "I am certain he is here, but I am unsure of his exact location at the moment—*and the music is about to begin!*"

This last bit was spoken with such apocalyptic certainty, I almost gave an involuntary shudder. I thanked him and as I walked away mentally chalked up this odd behaviour as the unfortunate but inevitable result of living in Ontario (poor soul).

I was to learn later that his name was George Anderson, that he was originally from South Africa (which is almost as bad), he was the pastor of that very church, and that I would come to know him as a remarkable man. He was the first person I spoke to in that church, and to be honest, I'm not sure what I'd have done had I known who he really was. Now these details are actually quite important later. They are all part of the finer weave of this tapestry that was coming to life. Suffice it to say, at that point I knew nothing other than what my nervous acquaintance outside and the obviously troubled gentleman (poor soul) inside had both said— Dr. Stephen Hill was at that church somewhere—and I was hot on the trail. Now although I am used to churches, there was no banana-jumpin' bunch of monkeys that could've made me sit down inside *that* church, so I started bookin' it outta there as fast as the crowd would let me.

I was almost out of the sanctuary when all of a sudden out of nowhere, Dr. Steve himself snagged me from behind. When he suggested I stay in for the service and then we could have a talk afterwards, my hair just about stood on end. "Nope! *No way!* Not for me! Nice church and all, but definitely not for me!" He then suggested that maybe I sit in the foyer. I thought about it for a second. That would mean (technically speaking) I wasn't really actually inside the church, so what harm could come to me—but still, I was starting to really not like this at all.

I needed a good long pull of an extra strong mix of my paint thinner to fortify my nervous system (and quiet all the cotton-pickin' alarm bells), so I went to the washroom and re-spiked my concoction with as much mouthwash as I could fit in my jug, and then looked for a safe place where I could both see and hear without being noticed too much. Plus, I didn't want to get whomever I sat next to intoxicated. The fumes coming off me—well, let's just say I had a very good reason for calling the concoction in my jug "paint thinner." I settled for the library in the foyer.

Now here's where things get a bit sketchy, and I really should explain. Anytime God is involved with something, it's never as simple as it seems. I mean, how simple is a sunrise? So, on top of everything being a lot more complicated than what, at the time, I ever could have imagined, I was— well, let's say "a wee niggle uninhibited."

Actually, perhaps I should expound. Even though I had learned, over the course of many years, how to handle it remarkably well, the quality and quantity of my average alcoholic beverage could, would, and should turn a normally decent, hardworking, law-abiding and respectable member of society into a stark-naked, moon-barking, slobbering drunk, fall-down porch-climbing madman who wanted to pick a fight with everything and everybody in his path—*and the bigger the better too!* That's the honest truth. So, that being said, please forgive any sense of disjointedness.

I sat there, and after politely declining four or five invitations to join the main body in the sanctuary, I started getting real nervous. It was bad enough being inside a church, but when everybody kept trying to drag me way deep into unfamiliar territory, get me surrounded, and do God knows what to me, every alarm bell and instinct I've ever had in my life started screaming, "You better run, boy! And you better run fast!" The problem was, they had these two big bodyguards at the doors of the sanctuary eyeballing me and making sure I didn't steal the carpet or something, and I wanted to just get out unnoticed. I finally caught a break when it was time for the guards to take everybody's money, so the second they left their posts I was gone. This was way too close for me! I got rattled just walking into *any* building, never mind a church like that one! Besides, I had a liquor store calling my name, and I knew the consequences of not paying attention to that voice, so it was back to the slave pits for me.

The Coup de Grace

Over the next few days I just couldn't shake this feeling that God was sneaking around, doing something weird, and was up to one of his old tricks again. I knew his ways well enough to know once he starts his doings, he's impossible to stop (and they say I'm stubborn!). I could kind of tell something was rattling Steve too. He called another time and then a bit later stopped by my hovel, chatted for a while, and then left, but as he did, I could tell he had a brain full.

Now I know I've said this a few times, but once a curiosity gets ahold of me, I just can't shake it. It's like this little bug chewing on my brain and sticking it in my ear all the time. Finally, I just couldn't take it. I had to find out what in the world was going on. I got myself geared up the Sunday after Steve's visit and went back to the church. I actually stayed long enough to listen for a bit (jumping out every 15 minutes for a smoke), but the instant they started singing the last hymn I headed out the doors so I could look for Steve from a safe distance, unobserved.

Things turned out a bit different than I planned. I was only halfway down the walk when he suddenly poked his head through the front exit, called my name, and beckoned me toward him. I was instantly on my guard. I did not like being taken by surprise, and if contact was to occur, I wanted it to occur on ground of my own choosing. In my way of thinking, I always searched for a position of tactical advantage when meeting with someone unfamiliar.

Throwing caution to the wind, I approached him. As I did, I could feel his gaze as he assessed my condition, and I knew something was about to change. As we continued to chat, I could see there came a point where he suddenly reached some sort of inner decision.

I'm not altogether sure how all this came about—I know he started it, but his decision seemed to entail me getting detoxed again, thoroughly, like right away—as in, right now! I believe at that point he had some sort of hazy idea of helping me somehow but was uncertain exactly how to go about doing it.

To this very day I haven't a clue what it was that made me agree and actually go with him. I wasn't bleeding, and I wasn't dying (honestly— those are the only two ways I'm forced into a hospital), but had I not gone, I know for sure I would not be here now. (Maybe I *was* dying ...) I just thank both God and Steve's love and openness to God's prompting that I was able to make that decision. I am absolutely certain I would be dead had it not been for the love he showed me that afternoon.

Also, now that I think about it, I've always been a little strange ... so it could have simply been a morbid curiosity to see how deep this odd little rabbit hole was going to go. I really did want to get sober, even though I knew I had absolutely zero chance of doing so, and honestly, I had no idea what being sober entailed anyway.

Still, I agreed, even though I knew it could only last for a very short time. You see, I don't think I'd ever been sober for more than four months in my life before, except once in jail and almost 10 months in treatment when I was 18 years old. Definitely not after that, and I was well over 50 by then.

After taking care of a few details, Steve admitted me to the hospital. I found I was genuinely surprised when I discovered the next day that I actually wanted to stay put and not run. I told myself it was just that I was curious—again, and that "I" didn't start it, whatever "*it*" was—and that maybe I just wanted to see how badly all this would end.

After a couple of days Steve was back at his regular doctor job (which I was told by all the nurses he was *very* good at and how lucky I was to have him taking care of me), and he popped in to see how I was doing. At least that's what I thought at first. What actually happened was this.

As soon as he walked in he just kind of stood there, looking at me. I knew immediately something was up. "So," says he, "it looks like we know some of the same people!"

I immediately started getting panicky real quick. You see, the only people I knew were either real crazy or real dangerous or real both, and that meant one or the other of us was in a lot of very real trouble.

"Oh …?" says I (nonchalantly).

"Yeah!" he says, and then he launches into a tale I'm still not sure I fully grasp.

As I've already established, Steve was a church-going kind of Christian, and a real one at that. Now everybody knows every real church has a real preacher, and as things turned out he explained to me that this real preacher was the same character I had met at the church who was suffering from "Ontario Syndrome" (poor soul). Then he went on to tell me that this poor soul actually knew me, because I panhandled off him in Ottawa—29 years before!

I went completely blank. Then I remember kind of wincing inside and very quickly picturing where all the exits on that floor were. God only knew what kind of horror story he was going to lay on me, but I was preparing for the worst.

He went on to say that on the Sunday I crashed the church service, George Anderson (the preacher) went to tea with a dear lady who happened to mention to George that a certain Kevin White had been inquiring after Dr. Hill, and this same lady had also told Dr. Hill that I had just left, which was why Steve booked it toward the door to intercept me. So she was the one who clued both Steve and George in on my presence at the church.

OK, at this point I better regroup and get things straight. About a week and a half before all this, I had been down on my face for days, bawling my eyes out, sick almost to death, desperately pleading for God's help and mercy; and after days of doing this, for some half-remembered reason I decided I was going to the hospital when I wasn't even dying or anything! I then ran into this doctor who didn't normally even see inpatients (as he was actually an anesthesiologist), but that day he just so happened to be working what was termed an "orphan shift" (attending patients with no family doctor), which he only did four times a year, and this same doctor just happened to have looked at one of my dad's books, and his wife, who had read *The Fight* (which had greatly impacted her early Christian walk), had just happened to walk downstairs to find a book that she didn't know was written by my dad and was dedicated to me while I just so happened to be on the phone at the time with her husband, my doctor, who went to the church pastored by George Anderson, whom I panhandled while on his way to one of Dad's conferences in Ottawa 29 years prior, who had later been told about me by the same lady I asked for information from, who didn't even go to that church and happened to know only two people in the whole church, who were George and Steve, and that she had told Steve, who at that time didn't know I knew George (which is not surprising seeing as how I didn't even know that I knew George), that I was there, who then intercepted me, called me one sick puppy dog, and admitted me to the very hospital I was now in and who was at that very moment there trying to explain to me a ridiculous story, and I didn't have a single bloody clue what in the world he was talking about! Get it? Oh, yeah, and that when he told George he had me in the hospital, George told Steve he had often wondered what had become of me and had preached a couple of times on the "prodigal son" using our meeting in Ottawa as an example in his message. Not only that, but he had actually tried to contact me when he heard I was in the Muskoka region two years prior to all this nonsense—but wasn't able to because I had already drifted off to go somewhere else.

Don't worry; it gets a lot worse before it gets any better. This is actually the "simplified version." It's way more complicated than this, but the contributing factors are so beyond reason, I can't figure out how to put them together. So, if it's any consolation, I know how you feel. By the time I was done just listening to this madness, I wasn't sure if I was coming or going, never mind comprehending it. Try to understand—I was sitting in a hospital bed with my head spinning around in circles without any help from anything (but the absence of my paint thinner), desperately trying to understand what this good man was trying to tell me.

I was alternately nodding and shaking my head at what I hoped were the right places, accompanied by what I thought were the right noises at the appropriate times, while this guy's crazy story just got more and more complicated, and he had lost me at panhandling a preacher in some city somewhere, and I honestly didn't have a clue what in the world this guy was trying to tell me. I was detoxing, for crying out loud! *I still wasn't sure if I was in trouble or not.* I was at the point in my detoxing where I was hoping I wouldn't be talking to dead people again. (They never talk back ... thank God.) All I was really sure about was that God was up to something, and I was now as nervous as a box of chocolates at an Overeaters Anonymous convention. That, and I was quickly getting the feeling that this thing was going way deeper than I had ever anticipated or was prepared for. Smokes! I was mentally getting ready to book it out of that hospital the moment Steve left the room!

Honestly? It was all I could do to say, "Oh really? Oh yeah ... I ... I think I remember, sort of ..." and then nod my head a few more times and ask for about the sixth time what city he was talking about.

This whole Ottawa thing apparently happened 29 years before, for crying out loud. I had either panhandled or busked half drunk in almost every major city and small town in Canada. Several times. That could be anywhere from 150 to 300 people a day—for 29 years! Just cutting it in half would be around 150 per day for 20 years—that's 1,095,000 people, while I was *drunk!* And those are only the people I asked money from— while I was in God only knows what condition!

Our life was very simple. It was daytime or nighttime, hot or cold, wet or dry, summer or winter, city or highway. That was it. Sometimes I'd even lose track of how old I was because I honestly didn't know what year it was—never mind what city I was in.

The Hook

Well, I didn't get arrested, the good doctor continued doctoring me up, and finally the day came when I could get my spoon to my mouth without shaking it all over myself. I was feeling much better, and I knew I would be leaving the hospital soon. Inwardly I gave a deep sigh, kind of sadly. I knew what would happen when I left, but I cheered myself with the thought that God still knew my name and that he loved me yet.

I had seen, once again, the great lengths he would go to just to say "Hello" and that I was not forgotten by him! Oh, and that I'd finally found out what in the world this was all about. I could praise him for his faithfulness and unfathomable ways, at least, and the amazing details he would figure out just to let me know I was on his mind—and that was huge to me! It was knowing I was still his own child and that he had heard my heart crying out to him—that he loved me and would never leave me behind. He had promised me that much. That was what really mattered to me. But still ...

It was the very next day that Dr. Hill came in to see me. I put on a brave face and cheerfully asked, "So! When you going to cut me loose, Doc?"

Something about the look on his face and the way he sat down made me nervous. He crossed his legs and looked at me hard. I got definitely even more nervous. I knew right then that whatever was going to come out of his mouth next was going to give the weirdness button on this merry-go-round I'd been on a good hard triple push.

Then he just kind of sighed. "Kevin, I've been meaning to talk with you about that."

Here it comes, I thought.

"I've spoken with my wife, Julie, as well as the kids who are at home right now, Megan and Robert, and we feel you would stand a much better chance of making it into a treatment centre if you were in a place that is both helpful and supportive of you reaching your desired goal of sobriety. A place where you could be in a 'dry' environment that is both healthy and helpful to you. We are aware that you already have a place of your own; however, we think that your chances of staying sober after you leave here and remaining that way until you get into a treatment centre are minimal at best, especially given the alcoholic environment that is present in your home at this time."

It was right about then that the room all of a sudden began to shrink inwards on me. I could hear the words, but I was disconnected from them, like they were coming from a TV set in the background. I couldn't seem to connect the dots. I began shaking my head, trying to deny what I knew was coming.

"We have carefully discussed this and prayed about it just as carefully, and we would like to know if, after I release you, would you consider coming to stay at our home? Both of us feel strongly that this is what God would have us do. We have already removed everything that contains alcohol from our home, and we would like to see you continue to attempt to get sober and give us the opportunity to help you achieve your goal of getting into treatment and remaining sober. We also want you to know that we are not only willing to do this but it is something we really want to do. We want you to know we are willing to do all we can to facilitate your plans of treatment and sobriety."

Now you've got to understand, Steve actually talks like that all the time. I don't think it's his fault. Maybe it's because he has to talk to his doctor friends every day—at least I hope that's what it is.

(Good God! I just had a *horrible* thought! Maybe he actually thinks like that—ALL THE TIME! *Can you imagine?* I wonder how he would manage to cuss? "Oh ... BOWEL EXPULSION!" Let's just say our communication styles are markedly dissimilar and leave it at that.)

It's funny, but even as I was severely panicking, I was kind of chuckling at his way with words. I actually briefly considered responding with something like "Well, Dr. Hill, given that things are as they are and circumstances actually are what they appear to be, I would most likely be very open to examining this option you have presented to me to its fullest extent and, in my humble (but somewhat considered) opinion, would, after close, thoughtful scrutiny and careful reflection, be likely to concur with both your analysis of my chances of staying sober (given the unhealthy and riotous nature of my present living arrangements with all their inherent opportunity for unhealthy distractions), and given my obvious penchant and long-standing proclivities toward severe alcoholic indulgences, with all the ensuing difficulties that it inherently presents, I would most likely have to bow to the overall wisdom of the alternative you are proposing as quite probably the route most likely to successfully address and facilitate, in a most timely manner, my overall goal of treatment, continuous sobriety, and further integration into a loving and supportive church family and, quite foreseeably, eventually even into society itself, and so I must acknowledge that by following such sage wisdom and counsel that you are proposing, I would also be, in essence, able to heal a long-standing and bitterly painful alienation from God in a process that could quite foreseeably culminate in my lifelong objective of overcoming a devastating alcohol addiction that I know now beyond any possible shadow of doubt is, and has long been, in fact, the main antagonist in both my societal and my relational exigencies and is the primary culprit in the terrible consequences that it has demonstrated upon my body, mind, spirit, and soul, and I would therefore look with the glad hope of expediting these processes with all due haste and diligence."

I didn't.

Instead I felt the few remaining hairs I had left on my head almost stand straight up on end, swallowed hard, and from a very dry throat half whispered, "What? Doc—*are you out of your freaking mind?*" as I mentally considered appointing a lunacy hearing at that very hospital (complete with recent blood work). I jest, but he was not kidding. He repeated what he said, only more "Dr. Hillishly."

The entire time he was laying this craziness out, I was mentally shaking my head and thinking things like "I know this man means well, but he really does not have the slightest clue what he's saying."

I liked this doctor friend of mine, and I was grateful and thankful for his care and his prayers, but as far as I was concerned, the best way to maintain any sort of positive relationship with him was to thank him and then have as little to do with him as possible. Never mind his home and family. No way!

He didn't know. He couldn't possibly know. Just being my friend was dangerous, never mind me living in the same house as his family. There was no way I could risk it. I could very possibly put them in grave danger … it was out of the question! Just thinking about it gave me a chill. What if the booze madness got going? Nope. No way.

I have had many people at different times in different places think that "now" was the time for me—beautiful, well-meaning Christians, men and women all over North America, praying for me. Actually, there were people from all over the world praying for me, for my deliverance and freedom, and once in a while I would actually believe some of them, only to later watch as things crashed into chaos because I got drunk. Then I would have to see again the pain and disappointment in the eyes of a lot of people who were hurt and angry because I had stolen something in order to get drunk. I never wanted to go through that again or to put one more person through it again. I never wanted to harm anyone ever again.

Well, that wasn't all this QUACC (who was sure earning his credentials *that* day) said. He went even further and proceeded to tell me that he had brought this nonsense up at some sort of church thingy and that close to 20 men had volunteered to help him keep an eye on me till I could figure out what I was doing—where I was going to go.

Smokes! I hadn't had that much attention since I manipulated Bruce out of the custody of a downtown Calgary jail extension with nothing more than a mover's hat and a clipboard! (The cops were *really pissed* about that little scenario.)

A 24-hour watch! Over me? All so I could make it into a treatment program sober. I didn't bother telling him that unless they added handcuffs, leg shackles, a tracking chip in my bloodstream, and a Taser gun, they'd be hard pressed to keep me anywhere. No, no ...

At this point I simply could not assimilate what he was saying. He didn't know it then, but my heart was pounding like a trip-hammer, and I was getting real dizzy all of a sudden. This doctor, this "orphan patient" doctor, was going to take me to his *own home* and keep me there for an unknown period of time and had already gotten rid of all the booze in his house—ta-boot! He had even got some bodyguards to keep an eye on me. To live and eat with his family—*in the same house.* With his wife and children? With me? This character had only known me a couple of weeks! He had no idea what I was really like.

I wanted to get real mean and snarl and curse at him real bad—I don't know, maybe pretend I was demonically possessed or something, scream at him, and mutter "Re-drum!" in a weird voice repeatedly under my breath. I wanted to scare him away from me—*for his own good.* He had no idea the ramifications of his words.

I can only wonder what his co-workers would be saying. "Hey Steve! Don't you think you're taking this orphan shift a little too seriously? You're not supposed to be taking them home to play with your kids!"

I had to hold very steady, for I was fighting a whole range of emotions, some I'd never felt in my life before. We talked a bit more, and as we spoke I knew I had to get out of that hospital fast. I made up my mind, and in order to plan my escape from the hospital I told him I needed a day or so to think it over. I knew I had to run, and run quick. But then—did I really want to run, again?

After he left I sat on my bed, still trying to figure out what had just happened. What was happening ... I was in at a state of complete confusion. The whole panhandling some preacher 29 years ago, and then how I ran into Steve on his orphan shift, and Dad's books? All that was strange enough—but now this? I sat back shaking my head and fighting things I didn't want to feel—or face.

I literally used to leave *any* town if even 10 people knew me and could call me by name. I'm not exaggerating. I would jump right back onto the highway at any time of year and usually not come back for several years. Now a whole cotton-pickin' church knew my name! Eighteen of them were going to keep six on me—and they were praying for me too.

As I thought about these things, I began to gently weep. I felt this sudden huge surge of hope, fear, and desperate longing all mixed up together well up inside me all at once, and there was just no stopping it.

"God … is this you? Could it be? After so many years—is it now? Could this actually be? God! After so long? Is it time now, Lord? Please! Is it really my turn? Please God, don't tease me! Don't play with my head, God! I can't take that—please, don't get me hoping again. Don't play with my mind, God! Don't break my heart—please! So many years—so many bloody years … is it time?"

I'd been in situations similar to this before, but none were so real or near as evident. It was so obvious to me that this was God's hand, but every time before all I'd managed to do was screw things up and really hurt people I loved—people I'd grown to really care about—just folks who were trying to help me. I never ever wanted to do that again, but still I could sense God's hand in all this. It was just so plain to me. This was just like him, and I'd be a fool not to see it.

Once again came that sliver of light, that gleam of hope in the midst of all the great brokenness and darkness that had been my life until that day.

Finally, I broke down and just let go of a gigantic chunk of fear and pain. I wept for a long time. I loved him so, and I longed to be a free man, just for once in my life, even if it was for only a little while. Then, somehow, very gently, I kind of slowly drifted off into sleep.

I don't know how long I slept, but when I woke, my heart was set. The next day I agreed to give it a shot, and so began a journey into discovering, in a new way, a very real way, the love that in all those terribly dark years had never once failed me. The love that had been with me, yes, even in the very midst of my sin, showing me kindness after kindness, mercy after mercy, and never once leaving me. I know him now in a way I never dreamed possible. In all the time I was out there, he never stopped teaching me … one kindness, one comfort, one miracle at a time. All of this began at that moment—with that one decision.

I did go to treatment, and it was there that I picked up a pencil—just on a curious whim—and I began to write down some of those things I had never taken the time to think about. It all came to me as I wrote—and it comes even more, right now as I write these very words. The result of all of it is now in God's (ha! and your) hands. Truly, truly, it was the love of God that led me to repentance.

I now attend the same church that gave me such a chuckle that day. It seems so long ago now. So much has changed. I was deliberately surrounded, adopted almost, by an entire church—by elders, very wise and good godly teachers who love and care for me. I am in a wonderful community of believers. God has placed me in a church I would never have dreamed I would go to. But I would not have made it had I been anywhere else. I have, at St. Andrew's, experienced incredible love and support—every day—twenty-four hours a day! People there have gone so far to help me in this battle. They have actually gone and learned about addiction and what addicts need to overcome their struggles. They ask me questions about how they can best support me. All I can tell them is how *not* to get sober. People in church actually know me now, *and I don't run away!* I have a function there, and I watch and wait with growing curiosity as I see this remarkable plan unfolding further. Yeah, curiosity is all. Can't help it, can I? I guess he just made me that way. (So what's your excuse?)

I see him moving from one day to the next—always up to something, he is—and I never know what to expect, never know where he's going to go next … so that means I don't know where I'm going to go either. But you know, as I think on it, it's all good! Man, I was *trained* for this. I was always moving; I just caught a better ride this time is all.

You know, I remember once kicking my partner awake one morning in a park in downtown Calgary. "Get up! We move!"

"Where? Why?"

"Why not? And how about Fort St. John?"

"Which one?"

"I don't know … which one comes first?" And so off we went, with not a penny but what we could panhandle on the way to that old familiar highway. I really have always been curious, and I'm telling you the truth when I say this: God has a lot more surprises up his sleeve than that highway ever did.

Oh yeah! And that time when I kicked Bruce awake in Calgary? We went all the way to Halifax, and if I'm not mistaken (and I'm sure I'm not), that was the trip where I first met George Anderson (poor soul!).

Things are different now. I'm experiencing for the first time the close and abiding love and presence of the God who broke all the rules and defied all the "That can't be God! God just doesn't work that way!" (They don't know half of what he's done.) He has shown me consistently that he loves me and that he knows the names of *all* those whom the Father has given him, and he has not lost one!

Nothing can take his love away, and nothing can separate me from it—*nothing*—for I am, *and always have been*, firmly clasped in the very hand of my God. He who loves beyond measure! The Faithful One ...

22
ABOUT FALLING DOWN ...
AND GETTING UP AGAIN

In short, get used to it. As a very polite French teacher I once knew put so eloquently, "Poop occurs." And it occurs to us all. I think that is part of the reason I love AA so much. Alcoholism levels the playing field. It's one of the few places where you'll ever hear a plumber advising a psychiatrist on how to handle his life and relationships—and the psychiatrist actually pays attention! Everyone comes in on different ships, but there, everybody winds up in the same lifeboat. Alcoholism does the same thing to all of us. No exceptions. And there is only one way out.

Sin does exactly the same thing. Like alcoholism, we are born with it, and we'll die with it. That means everybody. No exceptions. And sin affords only one way out as well. If I've given you the idea that my life has been a peachy keen happy bowl of strawberries since I've come to a deeper understanding of God's love, I am truly and sincerely sorry. I mean that with all my heart. Things have been far from easy! It has only been by God's loving grace and forgiveness that I have survived this long. Trusting that I am forgiven and placing my hope in Christ's work on the cross, *for me*, has been the arena of countless battles. If the enemy can destroy my hope, then I have no hope.

Knowing that God loves me allows his perfect love to drive out all my fear. I had been afraid all of my life. Every fear I have ever had, have, or ever will have is because I don't believe that he loves me like he says he does. When I began to believe him—trust him—that's when things started to happen. I discovered that all of my heart's desires, all of my unexplainable yearnings, and everything good and beautiful in this world, all of it, is in him or *is* him. I mean, name one good thing that doesn't have God as its source. Try it. It really boils down to love or fear—take your pick. That's all we've got. When I finally saw—was gifted with the grace to believe—that I was fully loved and completely accepted, that's when I began to taste true freedom.

The investigation I undertook, when I began to write, changed something in me. I can't explain exactly what. Nor do I have any name for what it did, but I am never ever going to be the same again. God's love is like that. Once truly tasted, there is absolutely no substitute, and there is absolutely no turning back. It has been tasted, and nothing tastes the same anymore. It is the freedom that only love can bring. But this newfound freedom that came with my discovery did not remove the struggle that raged both in me and around me.

No, my life continues to be quite the battle, even as I am writing the words you are now reading. Who then am I to write anything about God at all, you might ask? I have asked myself that very same question many times. Actually, Moses asked it at least four times. "Who am I to speak ...? I can't talk very well ...!" He used every excuse he could think of not to do what God was telling him to do. Believe me, I am not equating myself with Moses, but God has commanded me as well, and so I too must also speak. And I must also ask, who am I to disobey what the living God is telling me to do? He has told me to proclaim his love and kindness to every person I meet. And because of that one simple directive, my life has changed in ways I cannot even begin to describe. I am bought and paid for, purchased by the blood of the very same God that Moses was also compelled to obey.

I know an awful lot about falling down—I'd been doing it all my life. But after I began to understand and experience more fully the freedom Christ had given me, I was ecstatic and figured I was done with that old life forever. All those years of getting up and falling down, time and again, had sucked my heart right out through my stomach till I had nothing left and was just empty, soulless, and broken. So when I found myself falling right back into that life, just like I had always done before, I was confused, demoralized … and what—utterly heartbroken and bewildered?! I was a hundred times that—and a *hell* of a lot more! *How could I possibly do such a thing?* I thought I had been freed from that bondage! How could God take me out of that miserable hole knowing I would just fall right back in again? I was on the verge of walking straight out into the highway traffic with my eyes shut. But then I remembered something very precious— something I learned as a child that has only just recently returned to me. I am going to tell you a wonderfully instructive (but rather embarrassing) story, but before I do, there is an extremely important matter I must address first.

What I am about to share with you is in no way intended to trivialize either sin or the nature of forgiveness. Sin is always a very serious thing, and it is always to be taken seriously. Because I am an alcoholic, it can actually kill (me or someone else). It is the cause of all the terrible heartbreak, pain, death, and destruction that is done to every part of our being, never mind what it has done to the entire planet—or what it did to God himself. It is horrific in nature. I can only understand its true essence when I understand the cost of its inevitable demand. It was our sin, yours and mine, that led to the spilled blood of the Living God—the God of Abraham, Isaac, and Jacob. And it is this loving sacrifice of Jesus Christ on the cross that is the reason we stand in the grace and righteousness his brutal death bought for us. That being made clear, I must also say— *we have a mighty Redeemer! His love and mercy have triumphed over his righteous judgment! It was his love that fulfilled the law and has brought true freedom from slavery and death, to myself, and to countless others.*

Now I will tell you my tale.

I was perhaps five years old—a big boy now. I knew how to go potty on my own and needed no help doing it. I was actually quite proud of the fact that I knew all about going by myself and was secretly pleased (and a little proud) every time I flushed the toilet on my own. I needed no one to remind *me* to flush, ever.

One afternoon I was out playing with my friends when I suddenly had to go "number two." I was quite some distance from home, and having so much fun at the time, I tried to hold it back. Nature, however, cannot be ignored (or denied), and by the time I realized the seriousness of my situation, it was too late. I made a mad dash for home, running down the alleyway, trying to hold back with all that was in me, all of what was so urgently trying to get out of me, but, as I said, I had waited just a little too long. Only about five or six houses separated me from home when, to my undying shame, things just let go.

I was absolutely mortified! Shame and embarrassment flooded over me like a terrible wave as I kept running down the alley—tears of my dishonour streaming down my face. When I burst into the backyard I saw my mother, sitting quietly, reading. In tears of shame and blushing to my very toes, a terrible story of disgrace burst out from the depths of my heart in a flood of embarrassed, anguished defeat. I was a big boy now, and I had done what big boys ought not do! *That's just not what "big boys" do. Ever!*

After I had poured out my desperate tale of dreadful woe, my mother spoke the 12 most freeing and wonderful words I had ever heard. I can still hear her voice to this day.

"Well, dear, just go upstairs, clean your bum, and change your pants!" Just like that. *Like it was nothing at all.* The freeing effect of those words hit me like the warm rays of the sun dispelling the gloom of a cold miserable morning. Almost instantly, all of my shame and all the embarrassment—all the mortification and anguish in my soul—melted into the freedom those 12 little words brought to my tiny heart, and all was right with the world again. No shame. No guilt. *No nothing!* "Well, dear, just go upstairs, clean your bum, and change your pants." *Freedom!* And so I did—and then I went back out to play, with all the world around me right again—a happy little boy.

She had no idea of the impact her words had on a defeated and shamed little child. (I did tell her about it almost 50 years later.) But the freedom of the simple act of being put right again, with myself and everything around me, changed my life forever. My mom put everything back into perspective. Just go upstairs, clean my bum, and change my pants. That was it.

But you see, it was my mother who put things right, not me. Yes, I had to clean my bum and change my pants, but that was just part of what needed to be done. It was my mother who made things right. Until she spoke those words, I was a shamed and demoralized little child. And I learned a lesson that day as well. When I'm in trouble, don't wait till it's too late! *Run for home!*

Christ's shed blood on the cross is what takes the shame and dismay of our own weakness away. He is the one who makes things right. He carried it all with him to the cross. He is the one who put us right with God, ourselves, and the world around us. "IT IS FINISHED!" He cried it out in triumph over sin and death itself! And the Father echoes in return, "Welcome, ransomed child! You are blood bought. Come close, for there is peace now between you and me!" The Father has declared us "not guilty!" All has been put right.

I am his child, and sometimes I make a mess of myself. Do you think for one moment that this surprises him? That he is shocked that I have sinned? Or that perhaps he thinks to himself, "How could he do such a thing as mess himself? Again?" The Psalms say, "he knows our frame; he remembers that we are dust. As for man, his days are like grass; he flourishes like a flower of the field; for the wind passes over it, and it is gone, ... but the steadfast love of the LORD is from everlasting to everlasting on those who fear him" (103:14–17).

I fell within four hours of leaving that treatment centre. It was only for a few hours, but it was defeat nonetheless. But I got up again. I also got up quickly, because I knew that I was loved and *accepted completely*. I had found that which sets us all free—the love of our God, expressed in Christ's blood on that tree—he who put me right with my God and myself.

There have been further struggles I've had to face, but I have changed, I have seen his love, and no one can ever be the same after seeing that! Nothing can take that away from me—ever.

The battle with our flesh remains a battle in spite of our growing ability to fight, but the real war is with the one who seeks to destroy our hearts and souls. "The Accuser of the Brethren." It is he who condemns us and would try to steal the truth and fruit of our real standing with God—*our hope*.

The first thing Adam and Eve did after discovering their own shame was to run and hide. I will run no further! His blood *is* enough! Nor will I hide in shame. My father once told me, "Come to him, Kevin, even with hands filthy with sin—come hold them up and ask *him* to cleanse them." God's conviction draws us back to him where we belong—to the warmth and gentle cleansing of our Father. It is the condemnation of the enemy that drives us away, slaves again to shame and fear. I have fallen so hard, so many times; I simply had no hope left in me anywhere. Then I saw him—and everything changed.

The battle is with the flesh, yes, but it is with the despiser of our souls that the true heart of the war rages. Thank God that he has given us the breastplate of *his* righteousness and his shield of faith to quench the flaming darts of our mortal enemy—all the lies crafted by the Father of Lies! And whose armour is it anyway? Put on the full armour of whom— Kevin? Our own? Of course not! Of God! It's *his* armour that we wear! Do you really think he would give us armour that doesn't work? I'm crazy now about learning swordplay. What a blast that's going to be!

What I have learned the *very* hard way is to stand up, spit on the face of the enemy, and trust that Christ's blood and sacrifice are sufficient. Harsh words, but that is all our enemy really deserves.

So get up, wipe your bum, and put some new pants on! They have been washed in his blood. Yes, defeat and disgrace are always hard to swallow, but we must constantly remember, *it's not us saving ourselves!* That's already been done by Christ's blood. Our task is to stand up as quickly as we can (even if it's the 999th time), clean up, and go play our hearts out on this battlefield called life, taking no prisoners—just setting them free! Amen?

23
AMEN

I did not have the slightest clue what I was doing when I began to write this thing. I originally thought it was to try to come to grips with and understand why my life had been an absolute catastrophe for as long as I could remember. Somehow, by an unusually complex set of small miracles spanning over four decades, there came a calm in the midst of this terrible whirlwind that had been my life up to that point. This "lull in the storm," so to speak, gave me a chance for the first time in many years to look back and examine in more detail what I knew were some particularly strange goings-on in my life. My plan was to categorize and examine in detail only one example from each grouping of what, over the years, I had grown to call "crazinesses." In order to make things simpler, I chose the least complicated in each category so I could make as accurate an analysis of it as possible. That decision to look back has proved to be life changing.

At some point, I'm not sure exactly when, as I was rereading some of these recollected events, I slowly began to see the one thing all of them had in common: for the first time in my life I saw just a glimpse of the incredible scope and depth of God's love for me. As my eyes were opened, I wept—again and again—and every time I did, I saw even more, and I wept even more. As I was writing down or meditating on some of these words, I would often be overwhelmed by the love that he had so faithfully shown me. On more than one occasion I would find myself scribbling through a haze of tears that would stain many of these pages, as I tried in vain to explain how kind and good he has been to me. Knowing that what I am writing is true, and knowing the kind of person I actually was (that I actually am), I couldn't help but weep at his love and gentleness.

You see, the things that he did were absolutely undeniable. They happened as they did, and there was no way possible I could argue with them. I just couldn't. I knew what happened. *I was there.* I have only put into this book those things that are at least coherent and somewhat believable. There are other stories I simply cannot share, because even I wonder at their content. But no matter how I view them, I am driven to the facts, and the facts are that he loves me and that this love is far beyond anything I have ever encountered before.

And another thing—he doesn't play by the rules. I'm positive he went to the manual, found the section entitled *"How to Love Kevin,"* took one look at it, and grunted, "Well, this sure ain't gonna work!" as he was firing it right out a heavenly window.

Every time he did something amazing, or wonderful, or both, he made absolutely certain there was no way in the world I could have any doubt about who did it, or why. There was no possible way that I could get around the fact that all fingers, elbows, and toes pointed right at him, and he'd always be smiling the way he does. "HA! *Gotcha!* Just like that! AGAIN!" (He loves it!)

That's bad, but it gets worse. To top everything off, almost every single time he did the most powerful and loving things was when I was at my weakest, most horrible, most vulnerable and sinful self. When according to all the rules he shouldn't have come within a billion light years and two dimensions of me, and time and again I would shake my head, utterly confounded, and ask, "God! Why in the world did you do that?!" More than once I would just stop dead in my tracks and weep right in the midst of my sin, amazed that he would be anywhere near me, never mind being kind to me. At times, in great fear of my sin and shame, my heart would cry out, "God, please …! Don't look at me—please, just don't look at me!" But despite my protestations, he would weep his tears of healing and love into my shame and say simply, "I love you, Kevin."

He loves me because he loves me, and he just doesn't stop. After a while I could almost hear him saying, "Kevin, after all you've gone through— what I've shown you … did you really expect anything less of me?"

I have reminded him many times that he's not supposed to do that, but he seems to take great delight in disobeying me. Yeah, I can just hear it. "Hey! Hey you up there! Big guy! You can't be doing that! Not around here! Go on now—nothing to see here. Move along ..." (HA!) You think it works? You try telling God not to love you—*I double dare you!*

No, his love came most powerfully when I was at my worst, most desperate self, and now, after seeing all this, after writing it down and looking at all the wonderful things he has done for me, all the love and the beauty, his kindness and forgiveness, it has just broken me in two. It has broken my heart, and I just don't want to hurt him anymore. I don't ever want to hurt him—ever again! I mean, didn't I hurt him enough at the cross? All he did, all he *ever* did, was to love me and bring me back to him where I belong—time and again.

Just look at what he did there. "For our sake he made him to be sin who knew no sin, *so that in him we might become the righteousness of God"* (2 Cor. 5:21, emphasis added). For my sake "who for the joy that was set before him endured the cross" (Heb. 12:2)! Guess what? *We are that joy!* He has a joy now that is far greater, far stronger, and far richer and deeper than all the sin, sorrow, and pain of this world combined. I have seen it! I have felt it! There are no words to describe its strength and power!

His greatest desire is to be with us! With you and me! With his church—his bride! *God has chosen a wife (see Rev. 21:9)! Get it?!* Even the angels stand overwhelmed in wonder.

Just as woman is the glory of man, so the glory of Christ is his church. He longs to be with us because we are his bride. That's why he's so concerned with everything about us. We are his glory—his crown! We make known to the rulers and principalities in the heavenly realms his manifold wisdom, his power, and his unending love. We show to all the authorities of heaven how perfectly beautiful he is. (And we're pretty damn cute too!) Everything was done to be united with us in this way. There was no other course he could take that could join us to him—for him to truly be one with us. Him! Reconciling us! Becoming one with us! *What wonder is this!* He has wed himself to his people—*and God hates divorce!* Can anyone possibly think for one moment he will not keep his vows to us?

Far from it. He dances and rejoices over us! He longs in anticipation for the feast to come—to dance with us on that day, with his own church.

I've seen him dance! I've seen how he looks at his bride! I have seen the joy he has as he gazes upon her! Such joy! So, so incredibly beautiful! I have wept uncontrollably as their lips touched and they became one in the heavens! His glorious bride, his church!

I long to share just some of this amazing love that I have found, the love I was never able to know before, if only a glimpse—even for a moment! That would be all it would take to touch you—to change you forever and heal you.

I long to share his love so much because I discovered it as I was writing these pages to you! *You* are the ones who helped me find the love that has changed me (changed everything) and set me free from a terrible nightmare—a bondage and a sorrow so deep that only his love could free me from it. So very rich, so very strong, so very, very real!

His love never ends! He remains forever faithful! You have helped me to see it and to know it—to know him. Finally, after so many terrible years, I can now at last surrender myself to him—to his love, every day for the rest of my life, and then beyond even death itself.

"The Spirit and the Bride say, 'Come.' And let the one who hears say, 'Come.' And let the one who is thirsty come; let the one who desires take the water of life without price" (Rev. 22:17).

"He who testifies to these things says, 'Surely I am coming soon.' Amen. Come, Lord Jesus! The grace of the Lord Jesus be with [you] all. Amen" (Rev. 22:20–21).

P.S. I wonder if we'll get pregnant? Now there's a thought for you, eh? (Just curious is all.)

The End?

But God chose what is foolish in the world to shame the wise;
God chose what is weak in the world to shame the strong; God
chose what is low and despised in the world, even things that are
not, to bring to nothing things that are, so that no human being
might boast in the presence of God. (1 Cor. 1:27–29)

AN UNEXPECTED MIRROR
BY DR. STEPHEN HILL

I first met Kevin as part of my routine work caring for inpatients who have no family doctor at our local hospital. I've met a lot of needy people as patients over the course of my many years in practice. Although some of them have had a particularly intriguing story, and with some there may have been interesting connections or acquaintances we shared, I have never felt the urge to take any of them home with me. That was not my initial reaction to Kevin either.

It was in the course of conversation during his first admission to the hospital that something began to work on me about him. He explained that he had moved to Huntsville from Western Canada some eight months before for two reasons. The first was in order to "reconnect with Jesus." The second was to reconnect with his children, who lived with their mom in a community nearby.

That Saturday morning in the hospital with Kevin, I set aside some extra time to talk. It was apparent to me that given his current course left unchecked, he was going to slowly (or not so slowly) literally drink himself to death. It was also apparent that he wanted otherwise but was completely unable to stay the course on his own. By this time, I had figured out who Kevin was. I also realized he had a very real personal faith, and it seemed to run deep, yet he had not been able to find victory over his addiction through his faith. This is where God started to challenge me in my own understanding of faith. I would normally have figured someone caught like Kevin could not to be a "true believer" or he would not keep going back to that lifestyle.

I was so wrong! And my eyes were being opened to see. I was also just starting to get a small glimpse of how blind I was to my own condition. How God sees *me!* I would say that I hadn't become consciously aware of this yet, but the door was soon going to be blown wide open for me in this regard.

I truly did want what was best for Kevin. I wanted to see for him ongoing success, and having safely dried him out, I looked to discharge him to a protected, alcohol-free place with a few people who could care for him. Then he would stay dry until we could set him up for a rehab program.

Well, Kevin lasted two hours or less despite the good intentions of his few sober friends. Had I known his history a little better, I would have found this to be of no surprise. Had I also ever been on the receiving end of the standard prescriptive treatment we hand out from our hospitals for "saving addicts" from themselves, I would have realized how grossly inadequate the "medical care" for treating them really is. We don't follow them home; we just pick up the same pieces again the next time they hit the hospital doors.

Nevertheless, we stayed in touch. A number of pivotal things happened with Kevin during this time. Some of these stories, amazing stories really, have already been described. However, it was the effect they had on me that helped pave the way for what would become a revelation of how God speaks and cares for those he knows and how he includes others he knows in the process.

I eventually convinced Kevin that he should join us again at church one Sunday morning with the intent of him quitting drinking. I would admit him again to the hospital to safely dry him out and this time find the safe place that kept eluding him, and now us, until such time as we could get him into a program. I can't say I knew exactly which program was best; nor did I have the assurance he would comply in the end. I was flying a bit by the seat of my pants, but I somehow knew this was the only course of action I could take and was feeling compelled to take it. (I might add that we live in a small rural community of northern Ontario with relatively little access to much-needed resources.) The first test of

Kevin's willingness to comply with the plan as it evolved was whether he would show up at the church in the first place.

Well, he did!

He arrived in all his splendour. Ragtag hat and hair. Dishevelled clothes. An awkward staggering gait and a cloud of thick vapour hovering over and around him that reminded me of Pigpen, the *Peanuts* character. His water bottle of brew (mouthwash and hand sanitizer with a dash of honey and lemon) was half empty but would be agreeably poured out before we left for the hospital. I must say that our church was not accustomed, nor was I, to dealing with this kind of thing as part of the usual fellowship time after the service.

I admitted Kevin to the hospital that Sunday afternoon. He had his work cut out for him to once again suffer withdrawal and all that it entails, and I had my own. I had about three days to figure out what I was going to do.

There was a part of me that wondered what I had got myself into. There was a part of me that questioned where this might be going and whether I would be stretching the "bounds" of the doctor-patient relationship. There was a sincere part of me that was asking God to make his ways clear, for both Kevin and me, and there was an equally hesitant part of me that resisted praying altogether, for fear of the answer I might get. (Yet at no time did I doubt God was in this, so I just kept moving ahead.)

A couple of mornings into this admission to the hospital I was sitting by myself at my place at our kitchen table. I had finished my breakfast, and the Scripture where John recounts the walk on the beach after *their* breakfast with Jesus following his resurrection was for no apparent reason brought to mind.

In John 21, verses 15 to 19, Jesus' conversation with Peter includes him asking, "Peter, do you love me?" and subsequently he gently follows Peter's affirmative answer with the instruction, "So, feed my sheep."

It was like I had been hit between the eyes. This time I heard Jesus speaking to *me*, saying, "Stephen, you know Kevin is one of my sheep."

I said, "Yes, I do."

Then I heard the inevitable follow-up in parallel with the Scripture: "So, feed my sheep."

Concurrent with that thought was a second one. I pictured Dr. John White, Kevin's father, somehow listening in on this same conversation, from somewhere in heaven I guess, and he asked me this question: "You know my son Kevin needs a safe place. Why then wouldn't *you* take him in?"

I was struck with the fact that sharing the same faith as Kevin meant that he was my brother, and I had a very real responsibility to care for him as such. Another thing that struck me, somewhat surprisingly, was that I was actually prepared to do this ... to take him in to our home.

You might think this whole discussion to be a bit off the wall, or maybe even a bit CRAZY! Well, in some ways it was. But I can't tell you how amazing was the peace that suddenly flooded my mind as I knew without a doubt what was the next step. I had no idea what that step was going to actually lead to—sacrifice, questions, doubts, emotional pain, stress, fear, anxiety, disappointment, inconvenience, and who knows what else—but it was without a doubt clear to me that that was the next step, and when it comes to steps, we take them one at a time.

But I couldn't take this one on my own.

I left the same verses on the kitchen table for Julie to read that day, to think about and pray about, and I went to work. We would talk about everything that evening when I got home. I needed time to digest it myself.

There are a couple of things I would like to make note of with respect to how these things I have shared have affected me personally.

The first is that I have been broadened in my understanding of how God communicates with us and even engages us in conversation with his Spirit. I am coming to see that as believers in Christ we not only have, or possess, a mind "for Christ" but in fact are developing the mind "of Christ" (1 Cor. 2:16). As the Spirit (the Spirit of Christ) indwells us, he reveals to us what is the good and perfect will of God for us (see Rom. 12:2) as he begins to think his thoughts with us in our minds. First and foremost, he does this through revelation of the Scripture to us. He has already laid it down perfectly for our instruction in life. But he can also take that same Scripture and reveal through it specifics for some of the everyday questions we might be facing, just as I believe he used John 21 to speak directly to me about Kevin.

So we live by revelation from the Spirit. It is significant to realize this process is at work in me as a believer even when I am "out of step" with the Spirit or may in fact be acting contrary to his leading altogether. This, I believe, is evidenced by Kevin's story itself. He was wandering for years, oftentimes shaking his fists at God for his relentless pursuit of him and his determination for making his rightful claim over his life, especially when he didn't want it or even ask for it. All the while, out of his unsearchable love for him, God was shaping, forming, and guiding Kevin in spite of himself. How much more freedom there is for all of us once we "give in"!

This leads to the second point I would like to emphasize, and that is how I have come to see myself through the lens of Kevin. It dovetails with the work of the Spirit revealing truth to us as well. You see, the other area of revelation, where the Spirit speaks to us, is not only truth about God and therefore what "godly living" looks like in Scripture, but he speaks truth to me about who I really am without him and why I so desperately need a Saviour … every day! I am incapable of coming up with the required "godly living" by my own efforts. I am not nearly as "good" a guy as I think I am. Not even close.

You don't have to read very far into Kevin's book without saying "Man … this guy is really messed up!" He kind of wears it on his sleeve. (Kudos to Kevin for being brave enough to put it out there for public perusal.)

What started to dawn on me after some time interacting in person with Kevin and with his story was a realization about me in my own story. When I am honest about things—I mean really honest—I am just as messed up as Kevin is. I may be a little more socially acceptable than Kevin. I may present well among friends and colleagues. I may even appear to have done more for my family, church, and community and have convinced myself of the same. I may not measure up as well in my own mind against some of the social activists that I know, but I do know this … I'm not on the same level as that homeless guy.

What began to stare me in the face as I looked into Kevin's eye (he's blind in the other one!) was me. I was staring at myself, right in the face. I was Kevin! I hadn't realized just how self-righteous I had become, and I'm not sure anyone else did either.

Just as God had been relentless in pursuing Kevin all those years, so he was pursuing me as well and was now using Kevin to help me see it. It suggests that I might have been an even tougher nut to crack than Kevin, stuck in my own self-appreciation.

The boundless love that God has had for Kevin has been there for me all along as well. It was not there for me because I earned it (or maybe in some way I felt that I might deserve it) but rather it was there, and is there, just because God loves me!

One final point I would make is probably the most important. Through all of this, my relationship with Kevin has taken a significant turn. What started out by first meeting him as a homeless alcoholic in a doctor-patient relationship has changed so that he has become not only a friend but also truly a brother. God has done this for both of us. It would never have happened otherwise. Together we are growing and sharing in many aspects of the depth and meaning of our faith. We have had completely different experiences in life, but we both realize how similar, in fact, we are in light of the gospel. Life with Kevin isn't always bliss, but it's real.

Praise God for bringing Kevin into our lives!

GRACE FINDS YOU
BY JULIE HILL

My husband and I are not in the habit of taking homeless people off the streets and bringing them into our home. We have our own busy lives, four kids, and not much time to give away. But in 2013, something happened to us. In fact, something happened to a whole group of us, and it literally changed our lives. It changed the way we see ourselves, the way we see people with addictions, and the way we see God.

For me, it all began when my husband came home from work at the hospital and told me about a patient he was looking after. This patient had been admitted for alcohol-related bleeding and seizures and had a long history of alcohol and drug abuse. Steve told me that after talking with the patient, he noticed the name on the chart said "John René White." He told me, "I think this is John White's son!"

I was a bit skeptical at first, but it turned out that he actually *was* John White's son. I happened to be a big fan of John White and had read many of his books over my lifetime. In fact, when I was 18, I had read his book *The Fight*, where he explained things I had heard all my life but hadn't made sense to me. He was the one who, through his books, formed my understanding of God and how to walk with him. That was a long time ago in South Carolina—we were now in a small town in Ontario, Canada. What is the likelihood?!

I kept hearing things about this patient of Steve's and was aware that Steve was deeply moved by his desperate condition. I never imagined that one day this man would become one of my dearest friends, whom God would use to teach me new things that I never knew about God and myself—not known to me as "John White's son" but as "Kevin."

Steve helped Kevin wean off of alcohol and dealt with his acute medical issues. He then discharged him to go home, but it wasn't long (15 minutes!) before Kevin was back to drinking any form of alcohol he could get a hold of—including hand sanitizer and rubbing alcohol.

Over the next few weeks, Steve kept in contact with Kevin and invited him to come to our church. Kevin decided to come, but he was very intoxicated when he arrived. The music group that Steve and I were part of were on stage waiting for the service to begin when we all saw Kevin walk in. (Steve had slipped out of the sanctuary, and we didn't know where he was.) Kevin walked all the way to the front of the church and approached our pastor, George Anderson, who was preparing to get on the stage. The two of them exchanged a few words, and then Kevin turned suddenly and headed toward the doors to leave. We couldn't believe our eyes—it looked like George was sending Kevin away! We had been so anxious to see Kevin come to church, and now he was leaving! If George only knew who he was sending away and that Steve had invited him!

After the service ended I went over to see my friend Lynda and her husband, Jim, and she mentioned that she had met a drunk man on the way into church. I excitedly blurted out, "Do you know who that was? It was John White's son!" She didn't know who John White was, but later that afternoon she was to find out.

We invited Jim and Lynda over for supper that night before they headed back from their cottage to go home to Toronto. It was during supper that they told us a strange story they'd heard that afternoon. Apparently after church, George Anderson, their former pastor—our present pastor—decided to pay Jim and Lynda a visit. While they were talking, they mentioned the drunk man who came into church that day, and Lynda said I had told her he was John White's son.

George's jaw dropped, and his eyes got big. He then told them of how he had met Kevin on the streets of Ottawa in 1990 when he and his wife were attending a conference where John White was speaking. Kevin had had no idea his father was in Ottawa that day—clear across the country from where his parents lived in Winnipeg. In fact, they hadn't seen each other in years.

Apparently, since that unusual meeting, George had referred to this story in his sermons on "the prodigal son." One of these times was at our church, and after the service that day, a woman came to George and told him she knew Kevin's mother and gave him her contact information. (His mother lived in Halifax, Nova Scotia, at the time.) It turned out that in speaking with Kevin's mother he discovered that Kevin was living about 45 minutes from Huntsville, *our town*! He tried to find him but was unsuccessful. Now God had plopped him right in the middle of our church. This story convinced me that God was doing something here, and it sparked a deep interest in me about this mysterious Christian alcoholic named Kevin White.

Now I must mention that prior to all this, as Steve had been contemplating how to help Kevin, the missing element for a successful recovery was having a safe place for Kevin to go to after getting weaned off of alcohol in the hospital. Steve kept wondering, "Who would take him?"

One morning I came to the table to eat breakfast, and Steve had left a scrap piece of paper with the reference scribbled on it, John 21:15–17. I looked it up, and it was the passage where Jesus and Peter were on the beach, and Jesus asked Peter three times if he loved him. Peter said each time, "Lord, you know that I love you." Jesus responded each time with "Feed my sheep." After reading it, I was at a loss as to why Steve had shared that particular passage with me.

That night Steve and I sat down in the living room and started talking about Kevin not having a safe place and something about picturing John White in heaven asking Steve if he would take Kevin in.

"You're not thinking about bringing him here, are you?!" I thought Steve was out of his mind! Sure, Kevin was from a solid Christian family, but that didn't mean he was safe.

Steve explained to me in his typical calm "Steve" manner what he strongly believed God was leading us to do. All I could think of was that this guy might hurt me and that I would not be able to leave our house. What if he stole things from us or snooped around in our stuff while I was gone?

Steve indicated that Kevin *could* hurt me! That didn't sit too well with me. Steve also said that this could be an opportunity for our church to step in and help us with Kevin.

We prayed about it over the next few weeks, and then another thing happened that convinced me that God was indeed directing us in this way. In fact, things started happening that convinced me more and more that God actually communicates with us and orchestrates events that only he could do, and it began to have a profound effect on my whole belief in the reality of God and his personal interest in *me*, involving me in his plans. This epiphany has ignited my faith in a whole new way, and the experience of these events has given me deep joy and exhilaration like I've never known before.

One day during this decision period I was fretting about my somewhat rebellious son who was in high school. I was searching for help with him when I recalled that I owned a book I had bought maybe eight years prior to that time. It was about how to deal with "problem children." I knew right where it was on a bookshelf in my kitchen.

Steve was on the phone by the sink when I ran down to find the book. He was calling Kevin to see how he was doing. I pulled the book off the shelf and to my amazement saw in bold print: *PARENTS IN PAIN* by JOHN WHITE. I couldn't believe it. I had no idea of the title or the author. I must have gotten it knowing I liked John White's books.

I interrupted Steve, who was still on the phone with Kevin, and showed him. "Look!" Kevin told him the book was dedicated to him and that three of the first four stories were about him, only the names were changed.

This was *not* a coincidence. I knew it was God. He was reassuring me that we were being led to get involved, as Steve had been sensing all along. What's incredible is that as I then read through the book, I was getting instruction from Kevin's own father about how to prepare my home to have Kevin live with us.

Part of the preparation involved removing all traces of alcohol and prescription medication from every drawer and medicine cabinet—and we had a lot that had accumulated over the years. I found out that rubbing alcohol, perfume, hairspray, and hand sanitizer can all be problems for someone like Kevin. Steve had to put a padlock on a closet door so we could protect medications, purses, wallets, and money from Kevin's curiosity and temptation. We put a padlock on the office door for the same reason. (By the way, never once in the time he stayed with us did Kevin steal anything from us.)

The First Step

There was one particular Sunday I distinctly remember when Kevin had come to visit the church again. After the service, during the crowded fellowship time, I noticed Steve and Kevin in the far corner of the fellowship hall in a deep conversation. After a while I glanced over to see them again, and they were gone. I rushed outside and discovered them getting into Steve's truck.

I ran to the truck to see what was happening.

Up to this point, I had not even met Kevin face to face. I had only seen him at a distance. He always had his black cowboy hat on so his face was hard to see because he was usually looking down. I approached the truck and met Kevin for the first time. He had a gentle smile on his face. He looked down at me from the truck and told me that I had a "wonderful husband." He was definitely under the influence, but I could see kindness in his eyes and gratitude in his countenance.

Steve drove Kevin by his home to pick up a few things (including his kitten), and then they stopped by our house so Steve could change his clothes and get some lunch before taking Kevin to the hospital. When I came to the door of our house (I had driven my own car), Kevin was playing the guitar just inside on one of our dining room chairs. His head was down, and his black hat covered his face.

Steve came downstairs to get lunch and invited Kevin to sit down at our kitchen table while he made a sandwich. I walked in and noticed that sitting right in front of Kevin was Steve's huge business chequebook, wide open with some bills right there! *Oh boy*, I thought. *We are going to have to be more aware of things!* I quickly cleared it away. Meanwhile the kitten was tearing through the house upstairs.

That day I heard Kevin say to Steve, "I'm ready to do whatever it takes to get out of this hole I'm in. But I need your help. Just tell me what to do, and I'll do it."

Now we had been members of our small Presbyterian church for over 20 years, but it wasn't until this situation that I experienced real church community as a living body of Christ. One of my concerned friends was aware of what we were planning to do—and probably thought we were crazy. She sensed some of my anxiety about the whole thing and asked if I wanted her to speak with our pastor to see if people in the church would help us somehow. I am so thankful for her intervention, because what resulted was a crew of about 18 people (mostly men) who agreed to take two-hour shifts at our house while Steve would be at work so I wouldn't have to be alone with this stranger.

And then there was George D. George was a big burly guy with a big dark beard and a big round belly. We didn't really know him well, but we were to learn so much from him over the next few years. He had a lot of experience with alcoholism, alcoholics, and AA. We had none. He once had his own struggle but had been sober for many years. One night while we were sitting around our kitchen table deciding how to deal with things, he offered to stay at our house at night so when Steve got called to the hospital, the kids and I wouldn't be alone with Kevin. He ended up becoming Kevin's tough friend. It was like all the people of the church were in the stands cheering Kevin on, but George D. was the coach. Our pastor, George Anderson, was key in all of this too, organizing people and regularly meeting with Kevin and Steve and me.

So that day after church, Steve took Kevin to the hospital to get weaned off of alcohol and hopefully begin a road to some sort of recovery. He came to our house after he was over the risk of having seizures. That was when our system of helpers began, and we all stepped out of our comfort zone.

This went on for two weeks. Kevin was extremely shaky at first. He slept a lot too. I guess a person doesn't feel too well after weaning off of hard drinking for years and years. Having the people come into our house every two hours was also a new experience. We began to know each other better through the shared efforts of working together to help someone. I watched God work through different individuals in their own way, showing kindness to their brother in need. I remember one person in particular who showed Kevin how to hold his vibrating hand still while he fed himself. Before that, everything just fell off of Kevin's fork because of his shaking.

It was touch and go whether Kevin would go to Hope Acres, the Salvation Army addiction treatment centre. First we had to convince him to be willing to go into a six-month program. He wasn't too keen on that. Then he had to be accepted. We didn't know what we would do if he wouldn't go into the program. Thankfully it all came together, but not without a lot of discussing, convincing, praying, and visiting the centre. He had to quit smoking to get in too!

He was accepted and began the program. I hadn't thought of the fact that there would be holidays and that he would need somewhere to go. So he joined us for Christmas, which was a huge change for our family, who had always spent Christmas alone together with lots of presents. We decided to do things differently that year and invited George D. to join us as well. It was a memorable Christmas.

Kevin did well at Hope Acres. He wrote his book there, and through the book he began to realize God's love for him all of these years. In a way, it was like he had been asleep for 40 years, and he was just waking up to begin life. He had not lived a sober life since the day he started drinking. He didn't know what to do with himself. He wasn't used to being with "normal" people. He was uncomfortable inside of buildings. He was afraid of the people in our church and what they might think of him … he was a very brave man to decide to walk this new path.

When he finished at Hope Acres I told him that he could stay with us for a few months until he could find a place to live. I didn't realize that it would turn into a yearlong stay!

A Rough Start

Kevin finally graduated after seven months (an extra month for good measure) and headed back to Huntsville. A friend drove him back and had to leave Kevin at his place while he checked on something at work before he could bring him to our house. This was the first test for Kevin being out of a protected environment. While he was alone there, he got afraid and was tempted to get some booze. He called a taxi a number of times and then hung up before they answered, but eventually he ended up connecting, went to the nearby liquor store and then to another friend's place, and got drunk.

This wasn't very encouraging to us, for sure. What do we do now? Somehow we convinced him to come back, pour out the liquor, and get back on the wagon. Kevin felt terrible when he saw the welcome home sign that said "Congratulations, Kevin! Seven months!" taped above the kitchen door.

The road ahead was not smooth. Over the next number of months Kevin experienced some falls back into drinking. It's called relapse. It happens! I don't know why I had it in my mind that all we had to do was get him into a treatment program and he would remain sober the rest of his life. How is that possible? He had lived for 40 years basically drunk all of the time. Have I ever been able to not have desert for the rest of my life? Have I ever been able to not criticize ever again? We all relapse. Whether it is a bad habit or sin or weakness. That is why we need a Saviour. None of us can live right all of the time. None of us *do!*

I mention this because this story isn't over yet. Kevin has lived most of the last five years as a growing, engaging, productive, and sober man, reaching out to others, helping others with their struggles, and encouraging the body of Christ in our church. But he still struggles. The ending of this story isn't too good to be true. Sometimes God delivers people completely from their struggles, and sometimes he allows them to continue in them. But all of us need to rely on God's mercy and unconditional love. Kevin believes in Christ. He loves Jesus. He relies on the gospel every day. He is blameless before God, not because of cleaning up his act but because of the blood of Jesus.

Our theology affected the way we dealt with Kevin. We believe that God is the "Hound of Heaven" who seeks out his lost sheep even when they don't want to have anything to do with him. He doesn't give up on them. He seeks them out, and he does whatever it takes to rescue them. So whenever Kevin took off and went on a binge, we searched for him. We found him. We loved him. We offered him a way out. We didn't give up on him. That's what God has done for us—he came and found us and rescued us. There is a place for letting a person go, subject to their own will, but if their will is to stop and they can't, they need someone who can help them stop. His reality was that, as much as he wanted to turn around again, he couldn't. He needed someone to help him. Jesus did more than help us—he rescued us. Jesus did what we couldn't do for ourselves. He used us to do for Kevin what he couldn't do for himself.

Also, this was not just *our* effort. Many others have become part of his support network. People in recovery need a group of individuals committed to them who will be there when they fall, who will pick them up and bring them back, who will forgive over and over and give them hope for living. There were men in our church who would sit with Kevin on his porch when he was drinking. They just loved him. They didn't even necessarily try to convince him to stop drinking. One time Kevin "fell off the wagon" when he was supposed to be at a church men's retreat. After it was over a group of 13 or 14 men from the retreat went to Kevin's place and found him sitting on his front porch drinking with a few friends. They then surrounded the porch and sang the song "Refiner's Fire" to him with the guitar and told him they would be there for him. He broke down in tears, he was so touched. He poured out his booze and came to our house to dry out and start over again.

I have learned a lot through all of this. First, that I am regularly guilty of being self-righteous. It is easy to feel good about yourself if your sins are socially acceptable and are easy to mask compared to someone whose sins are right out there, front and centre. Second, I have learned that serving God involves sacrifice. I think, before this, I have mostly served God out of convenience—as long as it didn't cost me too much or didn't get in the way of my or my family's plans. Third, I have learned that I am no different than Kevin. I am a sinner who deserves the wrath of a just God. And we each receive the same forgiveness because of the sacrifice of Jesus Christ for us. In Christ, we are both now *blameless* before God, able to be in his presence and have a relationship with him. That is what the gospel is all about.

We don't want people to think that what we did with Kevin is what should be done in every situation. We basically did what we strongly believed God was leading us to do. I think the fact that Kevin was not a member of our family made it easier for us to deal with him, and probably easier for him to follow our leading. We also sensed that he genuinely wanted to stop drinking but didn't have the ability or the resources to do it. I also pictured my own son being in the same situation as Kevin, which at the time seemed to be a real possibility, and I wanted to do for Kevin what I would want someone to do for my son in the future, if that were to be the case. Most of all we were responding to God's leading in helping our brother in Christ. I guess the take-home message is that we all need to learn to listen to God and respond to his leading, discerning when someone needs and will accept help and whether we are able to provide that help.

Epilogue: In the Shadow
of a Mountain
Attempt #27

That's right. This will be 27th time I have tried to write this. But this is something I absolutely had to put down on paper! I've been so close a couple of times. Once I actually got three whole paragraphs written—then I closed the computer without saving it … (sigh). I really did believe writing this part of the book would be one of the simplest things I could ever do. I figured, "Now how hard can it be to describe two people you have known for almost two years?" Then suddenly it was three years—even better, right? Oh sure! Until I turned around and realized I'd known Steve and Julie Hill now—for five years?! It all was really quite confusing for me—until finally it clicked. There was something in the equation that didn't quite equate. Some parameter just wasn't perambulating … exactly. An unforeseen variable had been messing with my ruthlessly cold calculations, and that's why it had been so hard to pinpoint these two people.

Then it finally dawned on me. *Love!* It was love! I actually loved them, and there is no way to factor in something like that—love doesn't play by the rules. It is a law unto itself—the perfect law that resolves every equation and levels every mathematician. That's why I'd had such a terribly hard time writing this piece. Everything was in a state of flux, so I couldn't focus in on anything. I mean, how do you calculate love?

I think what must have happened was that it snuck up on me while I wasn't looking. Because I didn't understand it, I wasn't able to recognize it for what it was. I honestly had no idea how potentially huge it could become—how vast and encompassing it was—so by the time I realized what had happened, it was far too late. The unthinkable had already occurred. Somehow love had bypassed, slowly filtered through, or snuck under or around or over that impenetrable force field I'd been wearing since I was seven years old and mercilessly nailed my heart to the wall. To my great dismay, I suddenly realized that I loved these two with a ferocity and a tenderness that were both startling and a bit frightening. I couldn't explain it. I was almost shocked at its power and intensity, and quite frankly, as it began to settle, I was flat-out baffled at what to do with it. I think I almost felt betrayed—by myself, and by them!

Now for someone like me, this predicament was terribly inconvenient and could quite possibly be dangerous for all parties involved. Someone had to be held responsible for this unforgivable intrusion, and it sure wasn't going to be me ... at least I was pretty sure. So, after much careful cogitation and many days of internalization, visualization, and brutally honest "reflectionization," I came to the one and only inescapably obvious conclusion that *this was all one certain Dr. Stephen Hill's fault!* He started it. He's the one who brought me home. Period. I had nothing to do with it! And then I had to meet Julie (which was completely unfair)! She was as vibrant, kind, and beautiful as Steve was quiet and, well ... let's just say Steve was quiet. So, having firmly fixed blame for this outrage (and thereby justifiably absolving myself of all responsibility), I was now free to calculate to my heart's content. This is what I discovered.

It was Julie who inspired me to go the distance. She was the one who convinced me to turn what was basically the ramblings of a still shaky and detoxifying wino into an actual book, but it was Steve who gently kept me on course and steady enough to do it. Yes, the Lord had drastically burst into my life; he had shown me his love in a most powerful way ... *but I was still savage!* I had been out of normal society for so long that ... well, to put it politely, I had very poor impulse control. (I'm not sure I'd ever actually lived in normal society.) This is something you must understand. For the longest time I had to *pretend* I was civil in order not to frighten these delicate souls away. For example, because I had decided to stay put and figure out how to live in one place, no matter how bad I wanted to there was to be *no hitting*—anyone—for any reason! It was a simple choice: stay and live in peace, or strike out and have to run. I chose to remain.

That one decision changed everything—like in practical, real "rubber hits the road" terms.

If I was to stay alive and succeed in stopping drinking, there were a number of things that had to happen. The first and most important was to break an extremely well-entrenched cycle of going through treatment, drinking, and then running away from every single positive thing in my life. My habit had been to get out of a treatment centre and then immediately go and bury myself so deep in a bottle that the only way you could get me to stop would be to pry it out of my cold dead hands.

The second thing was that I had to stop moving and stay in one place. I had not stopped moving since I was 13 years old. This was huge for me. I had every reason to run. But something real had happened to me. It was something substantial, and I felt it … I felt *him*—in my bones! I had to have more of the God I had met while writing this book, and I knew he was not out there.

But what didn't click was that Steve and Julie were telling me not only that I needed to stay but that I needed to stay with them. *They wanted me in their home!* At least they said they did. It didn't feel right to me—very confusing, actually. It went against every instinct I had ever nurtured or cultivated, never mind every kind of common sense known. I actually had to shake my head a few times to even get close to it. Yet deep down I knew in my heart that if I left that day I would die. But Huntsville? *Ontario?* I hated Ontario! And of all the ridiculous places I could have decided to stop in. I mean, really, Huntsville? Even the name sounded dorky! All I could think about when I heard it was that old TV show *Green Acres* and Zsa Zsa Gabor (and Mr. Tucker). Hooterville … Huntsville? Eh …

Home Sweet Home

For some indefinable reason that I can only attribute to God, in spite of getting drunk the day I got out of treatment I told my friend to take me to Steve and Julie's house instead of hitting the road. (That they still wanted me in their home is testament to their patience as well as their determination.) You see, despite my certainty that this would turn into a disastrous nightmare, these people (who had no idea that they had one of the world's worst, trickiest, manipulative, hard-core, full-on, flat-out, horrifyingly *hopeless* wino drunks who had ever existed on their hands) had somehow convinced me they actually wanted me in their beautiful home, on their beautiful property, with their beautiful horses and big barn and beautiful creek and their beautiful big back porch in the beautiful country (and *peace* everywhere), around their beautiful and intelligent children—*and were going to do this without the slightest clue as to what they were doing.* They'd never done anything like this before in their life! I mean, come on! *These were civilized people!*

I still reeked of a lifetime of living on the street. I know for a fact they had no idea what kind of danger they were in. They knew nothing of alcoholism or alcoholics. I firmly believe the only reason they had any success in helping me … *was because they did not have a clue that what they were doing was impossible.* I swear there were times when I thought them crazier than me, simply for being a friend to me. Oh, and how I did tax them! I was ill-mannered, self-centred, and moody as a camel. But instead of avoiding the changes I had to face, with their love and the kindness that they showed and with all the tremendous encouragement I got from them I continued to stand my ground and started looking at my life. This was the first time I had ever committed myself to doing that. (My heart is pounding now even as I now write these words!)

Actually, as I think on it, the Hills were to see a lot of firsts in my life. But I guarantee you that not one of them could have happened without the love and commitment I felt in Steve and Julie. When I sensed that, and when I actually saw them throw their balls in the ring, I determined in my heart that if these people were really willing to go the distance with me, then I would walk. If it got me more of what God showed me in that treatment program, if it got me more of *him*, then I would walk, and I would learn—and I would not quit either.

So I stayed put. I lived in their home, and for the first time in my life I really committed myself to getting and remaining sober. That's when the real fight began. I lived with them for at least a year and a half, and that first year Julie and Steve were always there. I must have repeatedly driven them insane. I was like a child learning how to walk. (Actually, it was more like a child learning how *not* to crawl.)

Sobriety did not come easy for me. For the first year I would stand for a month and go down for a day, stand for three months go down for two days, then up for another three months, then up for six months, and I was always expecting they'd say, "Enough!" and "This isn't working, so we think you'd better go somewhere else to get help," like I'd always heard before. But it never came. It seemed retreat was not an option for me—or for them. So, quite puzzled, but still determined, I would take up my mat and walk again.

No Hope Alone

Everything was new to me. I'd get frustrated and want to quit. I struggled with depression and terrible loneliness. I didn't know how to function in this new world. *I didn't even like this new world.* At least they had some information. There is no book entitled *Emily Post: The Alcoholic's Definitive Guide to Polite Society and Relative Normality.* They did read all the stuff I told them to read though. I explained my alcoholism as I then understood it. I explained what to look for in my behaviour that meant I was in trouble, and then I submitted myself to both their authority and their wisdom—and I kept walking.

I would often get terribly discouraged and ask myself why in the world I thought I could do this. I'd lose hope and swear I was done trying and "I'm not getting my heart or my hopes up again!" That's about when the rest of the church came in. They wouldn't leave me alone either. They wanted to know, to learn about alcoholism and alcoholics. They honestly wanted to know how to help but were either too afraid or simply had no clue how to go about doing it. My friend Doug, a member of St. Andrew's, deliberately spent time with me. He would ask many questions in a genuine effort to understand alcoholism. We sometimes spoke for hours. Now he no longer fears the addict or the alcoholic but identifies with us by examining his own weakness and sinfulness. Then there were others who would come to sit and talk with me and pray for me over and over again, sometimes two or three times a day. George Anderson, my pastor, was such an encouragement to me. He came and spoke with me often. That was the first time I got nine months. Then came a time when I really didn't want to talk to anybody, so the moment I heard my door open I'd yell real mean-like at whoever it was, "NOPE! OUT! AND DON'T EVEN THINK ABOUT WALKING UP THOSE DAMN STAIRS!"

But some were brave. One of my very best friends, John from church, was an unusually gifted cop. (HA! Me! *And one of my best friends is a cop?*) I guess he had lots of experience—*with rejection!* He just ignored my yelling completely and walked up anyway—because he knew. He knew I was ashamed. He knew what it was like. John was real, and he could make me laugh at myself. He knew my heart was aching and hurt. He knew that this was not what I wanted. He knew how frightened I was and how angry I was with myself. So he would call my bluff and just walk up those stairs—*like he didn't give a damn either*—and instead of preaching at me, he just sat with me, and we would begin to talk ... and slowly, somehow, my stupidity would lift, and I'd work up the courage to try again. John constantly reminded me that God's love doesn't depend on how good I am—that he doesn't love me because I'm good or because I try hard. He loves me because he is good and his name is Love. He shed blood for me! *Who does that?* And he is never ever not going to not love me—no matter what! *That's* the why and the when I would fall in love with my Lord again. That's when I knew his love—and it was understanding that love, sensing it, trusting in it, *trusting in him*, that gave me the freedom to stand and walk once more.

Listen to his words:

"No one can come to me unless the Father who sent me draws them ... Everyone who has heard the Father and learned from him comes to me ... All those the Father gives me will come to me, *and whoever comes to me I will never drive away* ... I am the bread of life. Whoever comes to me will never go hungry, and whoever believes in me will never be thirsty ... Let anyone who is thirsty come to me and drink. Whoever believes in me, as the Scripture has said, rivers of living water will flow from within them ... For I have come down from heaven not to do my will but to do the will of him who sent me. And this is the will of him who sent me, *that I shall lose none of all he has given me* ... *For my Father's will is that everyone who looks to the Son and believes in him shall have eternal life, and I will raise them up at the last day.*" (Jn. 6:44–45, 37, 35; 7:37–38; 6:38–40 NIV, emphasis added)

Those words that I'd heard and believed my entire life had finally become life—life to me and life in me. We don't have to be afraid to come to him anymore—*for any reason!* I mean, when we are bad, do we really think that God would leave our side? Does he say, "That's it! You are *definitely* on your own until you smarten up!"? Does he tell us to wait a couple of months before we come back to him, until he's sure we "really mean business this time"? Is that what he does—this God who died for our sakes?

The God I discovered while writing this book is the God who was and is always beside me—the one who showed himself most beautiful and faithful when I was at my most sinful! Isn't that when he came for us all? "While we were yet sinners ..." He has never tired of teaching me how much he loves me no matter how hard I tried to run. Nor has he ever stopped pursuing me, finding me, or loving me—he has never quit on me! Every time I stopped to listen, all I could hear him saying was "Did you really think I had abandoned you? ... *I shall not lose one of them! ... All who come to me I will never drive away! ... All the Father has given me!*" It says right in the Bible, "this is my Father's will"! Get it? Don't worry about "the condition of my heart"! Bring it along with you! He is the God who shows kindness and mercy when we absolutely do not deserve it! Approach him boldly, for he is the God of Grace. He's the one who invented it; he's the one who paid its cost.

This is the God who showed himself to me as I wrote. He reveals himself even now. And then, while I was still in the midst of writing this, Steve and Julie and what seemed to be an entire church came alongside me and demonstrated that God to me on a flesh-and-bone level. No matter where I turned, there was kindness. Somehow blessings were around every corner. Mercy seemed to jump out at me from the strangest places, and I still wonder when I will stop being so surprised at it. It surprises me to this very moment!

I spent almost all of the first three years after treatment sober, and one of those years I was clean a day shy of nine months. The following year it was 10 months. I'd never been sober that long in my life before. Yes, I stumbled. But never for long. Not like before ... for years dying slowly. Now it was only for days. I cannot explain to you how unlikely and amazing all this is for someone like me.

There were of course the many practical matters that needed to be dealt with. I was still a very frightened human being when I began this journey, and it took a lot of love and patience to get me where I am. I think it was at least two and a half months before I could even go into the sanctuary at church. I had to sit in the foyer behind the glass and listen to what was going on through the speakers. I couldn't sit still for more than 10 minutes (if that) and would have to go outside four or five times for a cigarette. I couldn't go into a restaurant (not even a Tim Horton's); a mall was unthinkable—even a 7-11 was tough for me. It was all the crashing and banging and flashing and talking and feeling and everything all at once. I had no protection from it anymore—no alcoholic shield to surround myself with. It was the emotions that were mingling and tinkling … everybody all feeling something at once, and sometimes it just got to be too much for me.

It was almost a year before I could settle down, even a bit. This was definitely not a magic wave of a wand and "Bingo! You're all better now!" I was a 54-year-old man who had spent 44 of them in hard-core alcoholism and drug addiction—not to mention being slaughtered physically, spiritually, and emotionally by everything from "gutter wars" to molestation to churches to manifested demons to death. I was one very, very sick puppy dog. Yes, D-Day had happened, but there were still a lot of furious battles to be fought. I was fighting an implacable and diabolical enemy who made *Nightmare on Elm Street* and Freddy Kruger look like playing pat-a-cake with a purple dinosaur.

That's where Steve and Julie came in most powerfully. *They broke every rule in the cotton-pickin' book!* Do not do what they did unless God himself speaks with an audible voice … and the ground shakes and a host of angels join in with the "Hallelujah Chorus" with a loud trumpet blast—and you have a soaking wet sheep skin (and your husband is inexplicably with child!). *There was no way they should have done what they did!* But they did it anyway. Every setback, they were there to counsel and encourage me. Every struggle or victory, they were there to plot the next step. Every failure, they would pick me up and set me on my feet, and together we'd start walking. Every time I fell it was back to the barn (my doghouse), sober up, figure what went wrong, adapt, create a new strategy, and give 'er again.

The Hills went contrary to everything I had ever learned about addiction and about how to handle someone who relapses. I can't tell how many times (not just when I was down, either) I'd asked myself, "What the hell is it with these people?" Anyone else would have quit on me long ago. As you can plainly see, this is not just my story. It is also a story of God's people. So many gave out of their hearts and love and time! If I mentioned everyone who blessed me, everyone who prayed for me or with me and over me, I would have a list as long as the entire church directory! I am the living result of God's love being expressed through God's people.

Steve and Julie were wonderfully perfect for me. They were like salt and pepper—peaches and pickles and cranberry ham. They didn't know that until later, though. They were like ... they were angels sent straight from heaven!

Julie

Julie was everything from a hand-to-hand combat instructor to a sister/friend/advisor/bodyguard/cook/health instructor/mother/mirror/mentor/etiquette adviser/counsellor/official worrier/editor *and my very, very best and most dearest and trusted friend*—and even after five years, she still worries as only a mother would and still loves as only a true friend could. I think she reached her highest pinnacle when, as I was packing and preparing to go to the Montreal "2017 Gathering," Julie actually worried, "Well ... what if you suddenly have a seizure while you're crossing some railway tracks—*and then you collapse on the tracks and you fall down ... and you get run over by a train? How will they know who you are?*" I think she was trying to get me to wear my ID around my neck in a plastic cover! (I am not epileptic ... sigh.) I was like a son and a brother, and I have no idea which one came first.

She was my big sister. Julie would always ask me how my AA meeting went and would listen patiently to all my ramblings, tirades, and latest theories—and even better, she was someone who would not only listen to them but could actually kind of understand and respond to *some* of what I said. (Goes to show she was a little odd as well, I think, eh?)

Julie accepted me as I was yet somehow made me want to do better—and be better. It was her drive and her vision that put this book into your hands. You see, I would have been dead were it not for her. Without all her work, her daily encouragement, her faith, and her enthusiasm, I would have long ago lost faith in both myself and what I had written. She spent countless hours trying to decipher the scribblings of someone who was almost literally half-crazy and whose comprehension of punctuation and grammar was limited to an exclamation point after a cuss word. Every page of this book has probably been changed 20 times. She was so patient with all my struggles and strange quirks, my being a hopelessly disorganized nightmare (never mind a total slob), but in spite of all my handicaps, slowly, Julie began to teach me how to live like a civilized human ... almost. And we would talk, and talk, and talk! We would argue the Scriptures and debate anything from animal training to predestination. (She really has no idea how much talking with her helped!) And I grew to love Julie, and I accepted her—as she was.

Dr. Steve

Steve was another matter entirely. He was in a class of his own—sophistication incarnate—the country doctor. A gentleman (and the real thing too), but he was also my secret weapon. He was like my long-range precision heavy-duty artillery attack that left nothing of whatever current problem I was struggling with but a smoking napalm crater and a three-legged cockroach running in circles screaming, "The horror!"

When I would encounter some serious problem, he was the first person I would seek out. He could understand my latest theological indigestions and, if I had the patience, would almost always have the appropriate remedy. Steve just had this way of seeing to the heart of an issue and knowing the appropriate course of action to take in any given situation. In other words, he could *gently* explain what needed to be done ... if I had the patience to sit still and listen. (Did I mention I was a little impatient?) He was *excruciatingly* precise but never clinical. I have seen him, time and again, while in the middle of discussing God's love or his glory or beauty, as his voice would crack and tremble, and I would watch as he would weep in wonder or in gratitude or in worship to this God that Steve loves so much. Steve was flat-out in love with his God. I know. I was there, and I saw it being poured out of Steve's soul. *It is this that makes him so precious to me!* He taught me—and I love him for it!

Then (poor guy), just when I thought I understood things, he had the patience to show me that I really didn't quite understand … exactly. However, getting me to slow down long enough to actually listen to *all* of what he was attempting to illuminate me with was the problem. He developed a perfect solution for that. He simply talked right over top of me until I realized he wasn't going to stop talking either! HA! He was good at it too (quite the steamroller actually). He was a father and a brother to me—and the one person whom I grew to trust with the most frightening parts of my life. There is almost nothing he does not know about me, and yet still he accepts me as the broken person I am. He is my mentor, and I love him very deeply. I think that other than my own father, he is quite possibly the wisest person I have ever known.

I have watched how carefully and how gently he treats those who are deeply wounded. Steve has a quick, wry sense of humour that encourages the shy and reassures the frightened, and all I ever see coming out of him is concern and wisdom and love—like a calm pool of clear water in the midst of a raging torrent. But I am not fooled. Nope, not for one second. Under all that coolness lies an unstoppable bulldozer. That's what he's like … and he wouldn't go away (although I'm pretty sure he must have secretly plotted ways to make me disappear—permanently—being a doctor and all).

You see, loving me and being my friend are always very risky, and a rather tiresome business at best. Taking me in and sharing your heart, never mind your home, was crazy! Yet this is what Steve and Julie both did. They didn't just open up their home; they let me in to their hearts. You know, I can tell the real thing from a mile away, and if their love had been anything less than genuine, I'd have booked it in a split second. Steve showed me love and mercy before he even really knew me. Who does that? I was no more than a ghost when I met these two, but the love of Christ that was shown to me through them brought me out from the realm of darkness and into the sunlight of God's love. You know, I have to laugh! I keep hearing this … ridiculousness that "Jesus is a gentleman, and he's not going to force himself on you!" Well, bull-pucky! *God does not believe in the "prime directive."* Like I said, Jesus booted my front door in, smiled at me through the splinters and dust, and said, *"Well, what do you think of me now?!"* That's when I turned into a puddle of mush at his feet. At least he didn't blind me like he did Paul! Doesn't force himself on you, eh? *Gentleman, my donkey!*

Love = Home

I guess what I started to say was that I have learned a little bit about what it means to love someone besides myself now ... and it hurts. That's why I never wanted to love anyone anymore. It hurts. It hurts when I can't see them. It hurts if I hurt them. But *this* hurt—this is the kind of hurt that, if I let it have its way in me and walk in it, seems to grow my soul. It's an odd ache that makes me want to give the very best of myself ... and more. It is a hurt that has been built on the joy of true fellowship—and of its absence. It is a joy to be always shared and always given away as fast as it comes. And then more.

The gift that Steve and Julie gave me wasn't sobriety; it was love. Not just them loving me, but me, for the first time, not being afraid to love back. You see, somehow they connected me to the author of love, and I now have available an endless, boundless, limitless source of love, and it's the kind of love that drives out fear—and I had been afraid all my life.

So there it is, a gaping hole punched right through my armour, and there is no fixing it. I could no more stop loving them than God could stop loving me. It's so strange how it works. Love just seems to produce love. First fearing it, then seeing it and feeling it—then being surrounded and encompassed in it, and for years expecting it to just evaporate, but yet it is there still, *right now*, solid as a rock, bigger than a mountain—a mountain in whose shadow I found refuge when I was dying. I found there, for the very first time, a place and a people whom I now call my own ... a place in the shadow of a mountain that I now call home ... at the Hills'.

RECOMMENDED READING

Gorski, Terence, and Merlene Miller. *Staying Sober: A Guide for Relapse Prevention*. Independence: Herald Publishing House/Independence Press, 1986.

The Life Recovery Bible NLT. Carol Stream: Tyndale House Publishers, 1998.

Twelve Steps and Twelve Traditions. New York: Alcoholics Anonymous World Services, 1989.

W., Bill. *Alcoholics Anonymous: The Story of How Many Thousands of Men and Women Have Recovered from Alcoholism*. New York: Alcoholics Anonymous World Services, 1976.

———. *As Bill Sees It: The A.A. Way of Life—Selected Writings of A.A.'s Co-Founder*. New York: Alcoholics Anonymous World Services, 1990.

White, John. *Parents in Pain: Overcoming the Hurt and Frustration of Problem Children*. Downers Grove: InterVarsity Press, 1979.

Bent Hope

a street journal

Tim Huff

Foreword by Michael Frost

Benediction by Steve Bell

BECAUSE GOD WAS THERE

A JOURNEY OF LOSS, HEALING AND OVERCOMING

BELMA VARDY

Lament
for Spilt Porter
LONGING FOR FAMILY AND HOME
Larry J. McCloskey

THE
TRUE STORY
OF CANADIAN HUMAN
TRAFFICKING

BY PAUL H. BOGE
FOREWORD BY PAUL BRANDT